NĀRADA-BHAKTI-SŪTRA

BOOKS by
His Divine Grace A. C. Bhaktivedanta
Swami Prabhupāda

Bhagavad-gītā As It Is
Śrīmad-Bhāgavatam, Cantos 1–10 (12 volumes)
Śrī Caitanya-caritāmṛta (17 volumes)
Teachings of Lord Caitanya
The Nectar of Devotion
The Nectar of Instruction
Śrī Īśopaniṣad
Easy Journey to Other Planets
Kṛṣṇa, the Supreme Personality of Godhead (3 vols.)
Perfect Questions, Perfect Answers
The Path of Perfection
Teachings of Queen Kuntī
Kṛṣṇa, the Reservoir of Pleasure
The Science of Self-Realization
Dialectical Spiritualism
The Journey of Self-Discovery
A Second Chance
Conversations with Śrīla Prabhupāda (30 volumes)
Letters from Śrīla Prabhupāda (5 volumes)
Kṛṣṇa Consciousness: The Topmost Yoga System
Teachings of Lord Kapila, the Son of Devahūti
Search for Liberation
Life Comes from Life
The Perfection of Yoga
Transcendental Teachings of Prahlāda Mahārāja
Beyond Birth and Death
On the Way to Kṛṣṇa
Message of Godhead
The Laws of Nature: An Infallible Justice
Civilization and Transcendence
Vairāgya-vidyā
Rāja-vidyā: The King of Knowledge
Elevation to Kṛṣṇa Consciousness
Kṛṣṇa Consciousness: The Matchless Gift
Back to Godhead magazine (founder)
Geetār-gān (Bengali)
Bhakti-ratna-boli (Bengali)

A complete catalog is available upon request.

In North America:
The Bhaktivedanta Book Trust
3764 Watseka Avenue
Los Angeles, California 90034

In Europe:
The Bhaktivedanta Book Trust
P.O. Box 324, Borehamwood,
Herts. WD6 1NB, U.K.

In Australasia:
The Bhaktivedanta Book Trust
P.O. Box 262
Botany, N.S.W., 2019 Australia

NĀRADA-BHAKTI-SŪTRA

THE SECRETS OF TRANSCENDENTAL LOVE

HIS DIVINE GRACE
A. C. BHAKTIVEDANTA SWAMI PRABHUPĀDA
Founder/*Ācārya* of the
International Society for Krishna Consciousness
And his Disciples

THE BHAKTIVEDANTA BOOK TRUST
Los Angeles • London • Stockholm • Bombay • Sydney • Hong Kong

THE COVER: Totally free of all mundane sex desire, the relationship between Kṛṣṇa, the Supreme Personality of Godhead, and Śrīmatī Rādhārāṇī, His eternal consort, is the pinnacle of transcendental love. We can begin to understand the profound mystery of Their loving relationship by sincerely taking up the process of *bhakti-yoga,* as outlined by Nārada Muni in his *Bhakti-sūtras.*

Readers interested in the subject matter of this book are invited by the International Society for Krishna Consciousness to correspond with its secretary at one of the following addresses:

International Society for Krishna Consciousness
3764 Watseka Avenue
Los Angeles, California 90034
USA
Telephone: (800) 927-4152

International Society for Krishna Consciousness
P.O. Box 324, Borehamwood
Herts. WD6 1NB
England
Telephone: 01-905 1244

International Society for Krishna Consciousness
P. O. Box 262
Botany
N.S.W. 2019
Australia

First printing, 1991: 2,000

Library of Congress Cataloging-in-Publication Data

Nārada.
[Bhakti-sūtra. English & Sanskrit]
Nārada-bhakti-sūtra: the secrets of transcendental love / A. C. Bhaktivedanta Swami Prabhupāda and his disciples.
p. cm.
English and Sanskrit; commentary in English.
Translation of: Bhaktisūtra.
Includes indexes.
ISBN 0-89213-273-6
1. Bhakti. 2. Nārada. Bhaktisūtra. I. A. C. Bhaktivedanta Swami Prabhupāda, 1896–1977. II. Title.
BL1214.32.B53N3713 1991
294.5'4—dc20 91-39764
CIP

Contents

Satsvarūpa dāsa Goswami
Commentator and Editor in Chief

Gopīparāṇadhana dāsa Adhikārī
Translator and Sanskrit Editor

Draviḍa dāsa Brahmacārī
English Editor

Introduction

In 1967, His Divine Grace A. C. Bhaktivedanta Swami Prabhupāda translated and wrote purports for thirteen of the eighty-four aphorisms (Śrīla Prabhupāda called them "codes") of the *Nārada-bhakti-sūtra.* In 1989, at their annual meeting, the Governing Body Commission of the International Society for Krishna Consciousness (ISKCON) suggested that I complete the book. I was pleased to accept the assignment, especially because of my involvement with Śrīla Prabhupāda's initial writing of the *Nārada-bhakti-sūtra.*

I was part of the small group of seekers who joined Śrīla Prabhupāda in the latter part of 1966 at his storefront temple at 26 Second Avenue, in New York City. At one point we began passing around a Gita Press edition of Nārada's *Philosophy of Love—Nārada-bhakti-sūtra.* Some of us were attracted to the nectar and simplicity of the aphorisms. In those days it wasn't unusual for us naive followers to pick up all sorts of translations of Sanskrit Indian books. We tended to think that anything Hindu was salutary and within Kṛṣṇa consciousness. It wasn't long before Śrīla Prabhupāda made it clear to us that we had to discriminate. Many books, we learned, were the works of Māyāvādīs, a brand of atheists in the guise of *svāmīs, gurus,* and scholars. It was hard to break our attachments to some of these books, but we always did so once Śrīla Prabhupāda explained that a particular book or *guru* was not bona fide.

But when I showed Śrīla Prabhupāda the *Nārada-bhakti-sūtra* and told him I liked it, he encouraged me and said he might translate it.

In our edition of the *Nārada-bhakti-sūtra* was a beautiful color illustration of Śrī Śrī Rādhā and Kṛṣṇa. They looked young, about eight years old, and stood gracefully by the edge of the Yamunā River with a cow behind Them. I took the illustration to a photography shop and had a dozen color copies made. With Śrīla Prabhupāda's approval, I gave a photo to each of his initiated disciples. It became like an ISKCON membership photo and was used by devotees on their personal altars.

When Śrīla Prabhupāda left our New York home early in 1967 and went to San Francisco, I wrote him to ask if he would translate the *Nārada-bhakti-sūtra.* Here is Śrīla Prabhupāda's reply, dated February 10, 1967:

> Yes, please send me immediately one copy of *Bhakti Sutra* (with original Sanskrit text). I shall immediately begin the commentary.

At first Śrīla Prabhupāda's translation of the *Nārada-bhakti-sūtra* went quickly. He sent tapes of his dictation in the mail, and I transcribed them along with the tapes he sent for his major work, *Teachings of Lord Caitanya.* From the beginning it was understood that *Nārada-bhakti-sūtra* was a kind of "extra" for Śrīla Prabhupāda. But it had its own charm, and Prabhupāda approached it in his own inimitable way. I was surprised, on receiving the translation for the first aphorism, to see how Śrīla Prabhupāda translated the word *bhakti.* The edition he was using translated *bhakti* as "devotion" or "Divine Love." But Śrīla Prabhupāda translated *bhakti* as "devotional service." Even by this one phrase he indicated that *bhakti* was active and personal. He would not tolerate any hint that *bhakti* was a state of impersonal "Love."

It was significant that Śrīla Prabhupāda began his first purport with a reference to *Bhagavad-gītā,* the foremost scripture for teaching *bhakti-yoga.* The *Nārada-bhakti-sūtra,* or any other treatise on devotion to God, should be supported by Lord Kṛṣṇa's direct teachings in *Bhagavad-gītā.* By their nature, *sūtras* require explanation. As Lord Caitanya explained while discussing the *Vedānta-sūtra,* the aphorisms have a direct meaning, but their brevity allows devious commentators to distort the meaning through misinterpretation. How safe we were when reading the Bhaktivedanta purports to the *Nārada-bhakti-sūtra,* and how dangerous it is to read these aphorisms when interpreted by those who lack pure devotion to the Supreme Person!

As with his other works, Śrīla Prabhupāda's purports to the *Nārada-bhakti-sūtra* were completely in line with the teachings of the *paramparā,* or disciplic succession, and at the same time full of his own realizations.

One particular statement that attracted me was his reference to enthusiasm in *bhakti.* Commenting on Sūtra 5, Śrīla Prabhupāda compared enthusiasm to a powerful engine that has to be used properly. He wrote, "If one, however, becomes disappointed in his enthusiasm for serving the Supreme Lord, that disappointment must also be rejected." As a neophyte devotee, I was well aware of the danger of depression, which we sometimes refer to in ISKCON as being "fried." But just as a serious practitioner restrains his tongue and other senses, so one should not indulge in too much depression or disappointment.

It was comforting to hear this from Śrīla Prabhupāda and to gain conviction that it *is* within our control—we are not helpless before unlimited waves of depression.

One simply has to follow the rules and regulations patiently "so that the day will come when he will achieve, all of a sudden, all the perfection of devotional service."

I have to admit that I acquired a personal attachment for Śrīla Prabhupāda's *Nārada-bhakti-sūtra* as I happily watched its progress. I noticed that some of the same material Śrīla Prabhupāda was putting into *Teachings of Lord Caitanya* also appeared in the *Nārada-bhakti-sūtra,* but I didn't think anything was wrong in that. Yet at some point Śrīla Prabhupāda began to think that perhaps *Nārada-bhakti-sūtra* was a bit redundant, at least while he was also working on *Teachings of Lord Caitanya.* I might have suspected this when he wrote in his purport to Sūtra 12, "There are many authoritative books of spiritual knowledge, but all of them are more or less supplements to the *Bhagavad-gītā* and *Śrīmad-Bhāgavatam.* Even the *Nārada-bhakti-sūtra* is a summary of the *Bhagavad-gītā* and the *Śrīmad-Bhāgavatam.* Therefore the beginning of devotional service is to hear these two important transcendental books of knowledge."

Then, in March of 1967, while Śrīla Prabhupāda was still residing in San Francisco, he wrote me this letter:

> Please accept my blessings. I have seen the typed copies of *Narada Bhakti Sutras* as well as *Teachings of Lord Caitanya.* Both of them are nicely made. I think let us finish first *Teachings of Lord Caitanya* and then we may take again *Narada Bhakti Sutras.* The subject matter discussed with *Narada Sutras* is already there in the *Teachings of Lord Caitanya.*
>
> I have sent you matter for the second part of the *Teachings* and please go on sending me a copy of your typewritten matter. I shall be glad to hear from you.

And so Śrīla Prabhupāda's work on the *Nārada-bhakti-sūtra* stopped, and it was never resumed. It was a personal choice by the author, who wanted to concentrate on *Teachings of Lord Caitanya.* But we should not see it as a rejection of the *Nārada-bhakti-sūtra.* Śrīla Prabhupāda intended to "take again *Narada Bhakti Sutras.*" And so more than twenty years later we are taking up the work again, on the authority of Śrīla Prabhupāda. Whatever we have written to complete the work we have done as Śrīla Prabhupāda's student, using his commentated translations of the *Śrīmad-Bhāgavatam,* the *Bhagavad-gītā,* and the *Caitanya-caritāmṛta,* and his summary studies of the *Bhakti-rasāmṛta-sindhu* (*The Nectar of Devotion*) and the *Bhāgavatam's* Tenth Canto (*Kṛṣṇa, the Supreme Personality of Godhead*).

There is a particular charm to the *Nārada-bhakti-sūtra* in its brevity, universality, and emphasis on total surrender to Lord Kṛṣṇa. The aphorisms are strong and can be easily remembered and confidently quoted in devotional discussions and preaching. Śrīla Prabhupāda refers to the *Nārada-bhakti-sūtra* several times in his writings, as in this statement from *Teachings of Lord Caitanya* (p. 53–4): "In the *Nārada-bhakti-sūtra* it is said that one who is very serious about developing Kṛṣṇa consciousness has his desire to understand Kṛṣṇa fulfilled very soon by the grace of the Lord."

The major importance of the present publication is that another of Śrīla Prabhupāda's literary works is now available in book form for his growing reading audience. The GBC's request to Gopiparāṇadhana Prabhu and me to complete the *Nārada-bhakti-sūtra* is their mercy upon us. We pray that we have not deviated from Śrīla Prabhupāda's intentions and that this edition of the *Nārada-bhakti-sūtra* will bring pleasure and enlightenment to the hearts of everyone who reads it.

Satsvarūpa dāsa Goswami

Editor's note: Citations from *Kṛṣṇa, the Supreme Personality of Godhead* and *Teachings of Lord Caitanya* are from "The Great Classics of India" editions (1985). Citations from *The Nectar of Devotion* are from the 1982 edition.

CHAPTER 1

The Value of Devotion

SŪTRA 1*

अथातो भक्तिं व्याख्यास्यामः ॥१॥

athāto bhaktiṁ vyākhyāsyāmaḥ

atha—now; *ataḥ*—therefore; *bhaktim*—devotional service; *vyākhyāsyāmaḥ*—we shall try to explain.

TRANSLATION

Now, therefore, I will try to explain the process of devotional service.

PURPORT

Devotional service to the Supreme Personality of Godhead is explained in the *Bhagavad-gītā,* where the Lord says that a self-realized person is always in the transcendental state known as *brahma-bhūta,* which is characterized by joyfulness. When one is self-realized he becomes joyful. In other words, he is free from the material contamination of lamentation and hankering. As long as we are in material existence, we lament for the losses in our life and hanker for that which we do not have. A self-realized person is joyful because he is free from material lamentation and hankering.

A self-realized person also sees all living entities equally. For him, there is no distinction between the higher and lower species of life. It is also stated that a learned man does not distinguish between a wise *brāhmaṇa* and a dog because he sees the soul within the body, not the external bodily features. Such a perfected, self-realized person becomes eligible to understand *bhakti,* or devotional service to the Lord.

Bhakti is so sublime that only through *bhakti* can one understand

---

*Translations and purports of the *sūtras* marked with an asterisk are by His Divine Grace A. C. Bhaktivedanta Swami Prabhupāda.

the constitutional position of the Lord. That is clearly stated in the *Bhagavad-gītā* (18.55): *bhaktyā mām abhijānāti.* "One can understand the Supreme Lord through devotional service, and by no other process." There are different processes of understanding the Absolute Truth, but if a person wants to understand the Supreme Lord as He is, he has to take to the process of *bhakti-yoga.* There are other mystic processes, such as *karma-yoga, jñāna-yoga,* and *dhyāna-yoga,* but it is not possible to understand the Supreme Lord, the Personality of Godhead, except through His devotional service. This is confirmed in the Fourth Chapter of the *Bhagavad-gītā* (4.3), where we learn that Kṛṣṇa spoke the *Bhagavad-gītā* to Arjuna simply because he was the Lord's devotee and friend. The *Bhagavad-gītā* teaches the process of *bhakti-yoga,* and therefore Lord Kṛṣṇa explained it to Arjuna because he was a great devotee. As far as spiritual life is concerned, becoming a devotee of the Lord is the high-est perfection.

People are generally misled by the spell of the illusory energy of material nature. There are innumerable living entities within the material nature, and only some of them are human beings. According to the Vedic literature, there are 8,400,000 species of life. In the *Padma Purāṇa* it is said that there are 900,000 species of life in the water, 2,000,000 species of plants, 1,100,000 species of insects and reptiles, 1,000,000 species of birds, 3,000,000 species of beasts, and only 400,000 species of human beings. So the humans are the least numerous species of all.

All living entities can be divided into two divisions: those that can move and those that are stationary, such as trees. But there are also many further divisions. Some species fly in the air, some live in the water, and some live on the ground. Among the living entities who live on the ground, only 400,000 are human species, and out of these 400,000 human species, many are uncivilized or unclean; they are not up to the standard of proper civilization. From the historical point of view, the Āryans are the most civilized section of human beings, and among the Āryans, the Indians are especially highly cultured. And among the Indians, the *brāhmaṇas* are the most expert in knowledge of the *Vedas.*

The Vedic culture is respected all over the world, and there are people everywhere eager to understand it. The highest perfectional stage of understanding Vedic culture is explained in the *Bhagavad-gītā*, in the Fifteenth Chapter (15.15), where the Lord says that the purpose of all the *Vedas* is to understand Him (Lord Kṛṣṇa). Fortunate are those who are attracted to the Vedic cultural life.

The Hindus call themselves followers of the *Vedas*. Some say they follow the *Sāma Veda*, and some say they follow the *Ṛg Veda*. Different people claim to follow different sections of the *Vedas*, but in fact for the most part they are not followers of the *Vedas* because they do not follow the rules and regulations of the *Vedas*. Therefore Lord Caitanya says that since the so-called followers of the *Vedas* perform all kinds of sinful activities, the number of actual followers of the *Vedas* is very small; and even among this small, exclusive number, most are addicted to the processes described in the *Vedas' karma-kāṇḍa* section, by which one can elevate oneself to the perfectional stage of economic development.

The strict followers of the *karma-kāṇḍa* portions of the *Vedas* perform various sacrifices for worship of different demigods in order to achieve particular material results. Out of many millions of such worshipers, some may actually engage in the process of understanding the Supreme, the Absolute Truth. They are called *jñānīs*. Perfection for a *jñānī* lies in attaining the stage of *brahma-bhūta*, or self-realization. Only after self-realization is attained does the stage of understanding devotional service begin. The conclusion is that one can begin the process of devotional service, or *bhakti*, when one is actually self-realized. One who is in the bodily concept of existence cannot understand the process of devotional service.

It is for this reason that the *Nārada-bhakti-sūtra* begins, "Now, therefore, I shall try to explain the process of devotional service." The word "therefore" indicates that this process of devotional service is for the self-realized soul, one who is already liberated. Similarly, the *Vedānta-sūtra* begins *athāto brahma-jijñāsā*. The word *brahma-jijñāsā* refers to inquiry into the Supreme Absolute Truth, and it is recommended for those who have been elevated from the lower stage of addiction to the *karma-kāṇḍa* portion of the *Vedas* to the position of interest in the *jñāna-kāṇḍa* portion. Only when a person is perfectly situated in the realization that he is not the body but a spirit soul can he begin the process of *bhakti*, or devotional service.

SŪTRA 2*

सा त्वस्मिन् परमप्रेमरूपा ॥२॥

sā tv asmin parama-prema-rūpā

sā—it; *tu*—and; *asmin*—for Him (the Supreme Lord); *parama*—highest; *prema*—pure love; *rūpā*—having as its form.

TRANSLATION

Devotional service manifests as the most elevated, pure love for God.

PURPORT

As stated before, after attaining the highest stage of self-realization, one becomes situated in devotional service to the Lord. The perfection of devotional service is to attain love of God. Love of God involves the Supreme Personality of Godhead, the devotee, and the process of devotional service. Self-realization, the *brahma-bhūta* stage, is the beginning of spiritual life; it is not the perfectional stage. If a person understands that he is not his body and that he has nothing to do with this material world, he becomes free from material entanglement. But that realization is not the perfectional stage. The perfectional stage begins with activity in the self-realized position, and that activity is based on the understanding that a living entity is eternally the subordinate servitor of the Supreme Lord. Otherwise, there is no meaning to self-realization. If one is puffed up with the idea that he is the Supreme Brahman, or that he has become one with Nārāyaṇa, or that he has merged into the *brahmajyoti* effulgence, then he has not grasped the perfection of life. As the *Śrīmad-Bhāgavatam* (10.2.32) states,

ye 'nye 'ravindākṣa vimukta-māninas
tvayy asta-bhāvād aviśuddha-buddhayaḥ
āruhya kṛcchreṇa paraṁ padaṁ tataḥ
patanty adho 'nādṛta-yuṣmad-aṅghrayaḥ

Persons who are falsely puffed up, thinking they have become liberated simply by understanding their constitutional position as Brahman, or spirit soul, are factually still contaminated. Their intelligence is impure because they have no understanding of the Personality of Godhead, and ultimately they fall down from their puffed-up position.

According to the *Bhāgavatam* (1.2.11) there are three levels of transcendentalists: the self-realized knowers of the impersonal Brahman feature of the Absolute Truth; the knowers of the Paramātmā, the localized aspect of the Supreme, which is understood by the process of mystic *yoga;* and the *bhaktas,* who are in knowledge of the Supreme Personality of Godhead and engage in His devotional service. Those who understand simply that the living being is not matter but spirit soul and who desire to merge into the Supreme Spirit Soul are in the lowest transcendental position. Above them are the mystic *yogīs,* who by meditation see within their hearts the four-handed Viṣṇu form of the Paramātmā, or Supersoul. But persons who actually associate with the Supreme Lord, Kṛṣṇa, are the highest among all transcendentalists. In the Sixth Chapter of the *Bhagavad-gītā* (6.47) the Lord confirms this:

yoginām api sarveṣāṁ mad-gatenāntar-ātmanā
śraddhāvān bhajate yo māṁ sa me yukta-tamo mataḥ

"And of all *yogīs,* the one with great faith who always abides in Me, thinks of Me within himself, and renders transcendental loving service to Me—he is the most intimately united with Me in *yoga* and is the highest of all. That is My opinion." This is the highest perfectional stage, known as *prema,* or love of God.

In the *Bhakti-rasāmṛta-sindhu* (1.4.15–16), Śrīla Rūpa Gosvāmī, a great authority in the devotional line, describes the different stages in coming to the point of love of Godhead:

ādau śraddhā tataḥ sādhu-saṅgo 'tha bhajana-kriyā
tato 'nārtha-nivṛttiḥ syāt tato niṣṭhā rucis tataḥ

athāsaktis tato bhāvas tataḥ premābhyudañcati
sādhakānām ayaṁ premṇaḥ prādurbhāve bhavet kramaḥ

The first requirement is that one should have sufficient faith that the only process for attaining love of Godhead is *bhakti,* devotional service to the Lord. Throughout the *Bhagavad-gītā* Lord Kṛṣṇa teaches that one should give up all other processes of self-realization and fully surrender unto Him. That is faith. One who has full faith in Kṛṣṇa (*śraddhā*) and surrenders unto Him is eligible for being raised to the level of *prema,* which Lord Caitanya taught as the highest perfectional stage of human life.

Some persons are addicted to materially motivated religion, while others are addicted to economic development, sense gratification, or the idea of salvation from material existence. But *prema,* love of God, is above all these. This highest stage of love is above mundane religiosity, above economic development, above sense gratification, and above even liberation, or salvation. Thus love of God begins with the firm faith that one who engages in full devotional service has attained perfection in all these processes.

The next stage in the process of elevation to love of God is *sādhu-saṅga,* association with persons already in the highest stage of love of God. One who avoids such association and simply engages in mental speculation or so-called meditation cannot be raised to the perfectional platform. But one who associates with pure devotees or an elevated devotional society goes to the next stage—*bhajana-kriyā,* or acceptance of the regulative principles of worshiping the Supreme Lord. One who associates with a pure devotee of the Lord naturally accepts that person as his spiritual master, and when the neophyte devotee accepts a pure devotee as his spiritual master, the duty of the spiritual master is to train the neophyte in the principles of regulated devotional service, or *vaidhi-bhakti.* At this stage the devotee's service is based on his capacity to serve the Lord. The expert spiritual master engages his followers in work that will gradually develop their consciousness of service to the Lord. Therefore the preliminary stage of understanding *prema,* love of God, is to approach a proper pure devotee, accept him as one's spiritual master, and execute regulated devotional service under his guidance.

The next stage is called *anartha-nivṛtti,* in which all the misgivings of material life are vanquished. A person gradually reaches this stage by regularly performing the primary principles of devotional service under the guidance of the spiritual master. There are many bad habits we acquire in the association of material contamination, chief of which are illicit sexual relationships, eating animal food, indulging in intoxication, and gambling. The first thing the expert spiritual master does when he engages his disciple in regulated devotional service is to instruct him to abstain from these four principles of sinful life.

Since God is supremely pure, one cannot rise to the highest perfectional stage of love of God without being purified. In the *Bhagavad-gītā* (10.12), when Arjuna accepted Kṛṣṇa as the Supreme Lord, he said, *pavitraṁ paramaṁ bhavān:* "You are the purest of the pure." The Lord is the purest, and thus anyone who wants to serve the Supreme Lord must also be pure. Unless a person is pure, he can neither understand what the Personality of Godhead is nor engage in His service in love, for devotional service, as stated before, begins from the point of self-realization, when all misgivings of materialistic life are vanquished.

After following the regulative principles and purifying the material senses, one attains the stage of *niṣṭhā,* firm faith in the Lord. When a person has attained this stage, no one can deviate him from the conception of the Supreme Personality of Godhead. No one can persuade him that God is impersonal, without a form, or that any form created by imagination can be accepted as God. Those who espouse these more or less nonsensical conceptions of the Supreme Lord cannot dissuade him from firm faith in the Supreme Personality of Godhead, Kṛṣṇa.

In the *Bhagavad-gītā* Lord Kṛṣṇa stresses in many verses that He is the Supreme Personality of Godhead. But despite Lord Kṛṣṇa's stressing this point, many so-called scholars and commentators still deny the personal conception of the Lord. One famous scholar wrote in his commentary on the *Bhagavad-gītā* that one does not have to surrender to Lord Kṛṣṇa or even accept Him as the Supreme Personality of Godhead, but that one should rather surrender to "the Supreme within Kṛṣṇa." Such fools do not know what is within and what is without. They comment on the *Bhagavad-gītā* according to their own whims. Such persons cannot be elevated to the highest stage of love of Godhead. The may be scholarly, and they may be elevated in other departments of knowledge, but they are not even neophytes in the process of attaining the highest stage of perfection, love of Godhead. *Niṣṭhā* implies that one should accept the words of *Bhagavad-gītā,* the words of the Supreme Personality of Godhead, as they are, without any deviation or nonsensical commentary.

If a person is fortunate enough to vanquish all misgivings caused by material existence and rise up to the stage of *niṣṭhā,* he can then rise to the stages of *ruci* (taste) and *āsakti* (attachment for the Lord). *Āsakti* is the beginning of love of Godhead. By progressing, one then advances to the stage of relishing a reciprocal exchange with the Lord in ecstasy (*bhāva*). Every living entity is eternally related to the Supreme Lord, and this relationship may be in any one of many transcendental humors. At the stage called *āsakti,* attachment, a person can understand his relationship with the Supreme Lord. When he understands his position, he begins reciprocating with the Lord. By constant reciprocation with the Lord, the devotee is elevated to the highest stage of love of Godhead, *prema.*

SŪTRA 3*

अमृतस्वरूपा च ॥३॥

amṛta-svarūpā ca

amṛta—immortality; *svarūpā*—having as its essence; *ca*—and.

TRANSLATION

This pure love for God is eternal.

PURPORT

When a person attains to the perfectional stage of love of Godhead, he becomes liberated even in his present body and realizes his constitutional position of immortality. In the *Bhagavad-gītā* (4.9), the Lord says,

janma karma ca me divyam evaṁ yo vetti tattvataḥ
tyaktvā dehaṁ punar janma naiti mām eti so 'rjuna

Here the Lord says that any person who simply understands His transcendental activities and His appearance and disappearance in this material world becomes liberated, and that after quitting his present body he at once reaches His abode. Therefore it is to be understood that one who has attained the stage of love of God has perfect knowledge, and even if he may fall short of perfect knowledge, he has the preliminary perfection of life that a living entity can attain.

To conceive of oneself as being one with the Supreme is the greatest misconception of self-realization, and this misconception prevents one from rising to the highest stage of love of God. But a person who understands his subordinate position can attain the highest stage of loving service to the Lord. Although the Lord and the living entities are qualitatively one, the living entities are limited, while the Lord is unlimited. This understanding, called *amṛta-svarūpa,* makes one eligible for being eternally situated.

In the *Śrīmad-Bhāgavatam* (10.87.30) the personified *Vedas* pray to the Lord, "O supreme eternal, if the living entities were equal with You and thus all-pervading and all-powerful like You, there would be no possibility of their being controlled by Your external energy, *māyā.*" Therefore, the living entities should be accepted as fragmental portions of the Supreme. This is confirmed in *Bhagavad-gītā* (15.7) when the Lord says, *mamaivāṁśo jīva-loke jīva-bhūtaḥ sanātanaḥ:* "The living entities are My fragmental portions, eternally." As fragmental portions, they are qualitatively one with the Supreme, but they are not unlimited.

One who is convinced that he is eternally a servitor of the Supreme Lord is called immortal because he has realized his constitutional position of immortality. Unless one can understand his position as a living entity and an eternal servitor of the Lord, there is no question of immortality. But one who accepts these facts becomes immortal. In other words, those who are under the misconception that the living entity and the Supreme Lord are equal in all respects, both qualitatively and quantitatively, are mistaken, and they are still bound to remain in the material world. They cannot rise to the position of immortality.

Upon attaining love of God, a person immediately becomes immortal and no longer has to change his material body. But even if a devotee of the Lord has not yet reached the perfectional stage of love of Godhead, his devotional service is considered immortal. Any action in the stage of *karma* or *jñāna* will be finished with the change of body, but devotional service, even if not executed perfectly, will continue into the next life, and the living entity will be allowed to make further progress.

The constitutional position of the living entity as a fragment of the Supreme Lord is confirmed in the *Śrīmad-Bhāgavatam* and the *Upaniṣads*. The *Śvetāśvatara Upaniṣad* (5.9) states,

bālāgra-śata-bhāgasya śatadhā kalpitasya ca
bhāgo jīvaḥ sa vijñeyaḥ sa cānantyāya kalpate

"If the tip of a hair were divided into one hundred parts, and if one of those parts were again divided into a hundred parts, that one ten-thousandth part of the tip of the hair would be the dimension of the living entity." As already mentioned, this position of the living entity as a fragment of the Supreme Lord is declared in the *Bhagavad-gītā* (15.7) to be eternal; it cannot be changed. A person who understands his constitutional position as a fragment of the Supreme Lord and engages himself in devotional service with all seriousness at once becomes immortal.

SŪTRA 4*

यल्लब्ध्वा पुमान् सिद्धो भवत्यमृतो भवति तृप्तो भवति ॥४॥

yal labdhvā pumān siddho bhavaty amṛto bhavati tṛpto bhavati

yat—which; *labdhvā*—having gained; *pumān*—a person; *siddhaḥ*—perfect; *bhavati*—becomes; *amṛtaḥ*—immortal; *bhavati*—becomes; *tṛptaḥ*—peaceful; *bhavati*—becomes.

TRANSLATION

Upon achieving that stage of transcendental devotional service in pure love of God, a person becomes perfect, immortal, and peaceful.

PURPORT

The part-and-parcel living entities are entangled in the conditioned life of material existence. Because of their diverse activities they are wandering all over the universe, transmigrating from one body to another and undergoing various miseries. But when a fortunate living entity somehow comes in contact with a pure devotee of the Lord and engages in devotional service, he enters upon the path of perfection. If someone engages in devotional service in all seriousness, the Lord instructs him in two ways—through the pure devotee and from within—so that he can advance in devotional service. By cultivating such devotional service, he becomes perfect.

Lord Kṛṣṇa describes this form of complete perfection in the *Bhagavad-gītā* (8.15):

mām upetya punar janma duḥkhālayam aśāśvatam
nāpnuvanti mahātmānaḥ saṁsiddhiṁ paramāṁ gatāḥ

"The great souls who engage in My devotional service attain Me, the Supreme Lord, and do not come back to this miserable material life, for they have attained the highest perfection." Both while in the material body and after giving it up, a devotee attains the highest perfection in service to the Lord. As long as a devotee is in his material body, his probational activities in devotional service prepare him for being transferred to the Lord's supreme abode. Only those who are one hundred percent engaged in devotional service can achieve this perfection.

In material, conditioned life a person always feels the full miseries caused by the transmigration of the soul from body to body. Before taking birth, he undergoes the miseries of living in the womb of his mother, and when he comes out he lives for a certain period and then again has to die and enter a mother's womb. But one who attains the highest perfection goes back to Godhead after leaving his present body. Once there, he doesn't have to come back to this material world and transmigrate from one body to another. That transfer to the spiritual world is the highest perfection of life. In other words, the devotee achieves his constitutional position of immortality and thus becomes completely peaceful.

Until a person achieves this perfection, he cannot be peaceful. He may artificially think he is one with the Supreme, but actually he is not; therefore, he has no peace. Similarly, someone may aspire for one of the eight yogic perfections in the mystic *yoga* process, such as to become the smallest, to become the heaviest, or to acquire anything he desires, but these achievements are material; they are not perfection. Perfection means to regain one's original spiritual form and engage in the loving service of the Lord. The living entity is part and parcel of the Supreme Lord, and if he performs the duties of the part and parcel, without proudly thinking he is one in all respects with the Supreme Lord, he attains real perfection and becomes peaceful.

SŪTRA 5*

यत् प्राप्य न किञ्चिद्वाञ्छति न शोचति न द्वेष्टि
न रमते नोत्साही भवति ॥५॥

yat prāpya na kiñcid vāñchati na śocati na dveṣṭi na ramate notsāhī bhavati

yat—which; *prāpya*—having attained; *na kiñcit*—nothing; *vāñchati*—hankers for; *na śocati*—does not lament; *na dveṣṭi*—does not hate; *na ramate*—does not rejoice; *na*—not; *utsāhī*—materially enthusiastic; *bhavati*—becomes.

TRANSLATION

A person engaged in such pure devotional service neither desires anything for sense gratification, nor laments for any loss, nor hates anything, nor enjoys anything on his personal account, nor becomes very enthusiastic in material activity.

PURPORT

According to Śrīla Rūpa Gosvāmī, there are six impediments to the discharge of devotional service, and also six activities favorable to progress in devotional service.

The first impediment is *atyāhāra,* overeating or accumulating more wealth than we need. When we give free rein to the senses in an effort to enjoy to the highest degree, we become degraded. A devotee should therefore eat only enough to maintain his body and soul together; he should not allow his tongue unrestricted license to eat anything and everything it likes. The *Bhagavad-gītā* and the great *ācāryas,* or spiritual masters, have prescribed certain foods for human beings, and one who eats these foods eats in the mode of goodness. These foods include grains, fruits, vegetables, milk products, and sugar—and nothing more. A devotee does not eat extravagantly; he simply eats what he offers to the Supreme Lord, Kṛṣṇa. He is interested in *kṛṣṇa-prasādam* (food offered to the Lord) and not in satisfying his tongue. Therefore he does not desire anything extraordinary to eat.

Similarly, a devotee does not wish to accumulate a large bank balance: he simply earns as much as he requires. This is called *yāvad-artha* or *yuktāhāra*. In the material world everyone is very active in earning more and more money and in increasing eating and sleeping and gratifying the senses; such is the mission of most people's lives. But these activities should be absent from the life of a devotee.

The next impediment Śrīla Rūpa Gosvāmī mentions is *prayāsa,* endeavoring very hard for material things. A devotee should not be very enthusiastic about attaining any material goal. He should not be like persons who engage in fruitive activities, who work very hard day and night to attain material rewards. All such persons have some ambition—to become a very big businessman, to become a great industrialist, to become a great poet or philosopher. But they do not know that even if their ambition is fulfilled, the result is temporary. As soon as the body is finished, all material achievements are also finished. No one takes with him anything he has achieved materially in this world. The only thing he can carry with him is his asset of devotional service; that alone is never vanquished.

The next impediment to devotional service is *prajalpa,* talking of mundane subject matter. Many people unnecessarily talk of the daily happenings in the newspapers and pass the time without any profit. A devotee, however, does not indulge in unnecessary talks of politics or economics. Nor is a devotee very strict in following ritualistic rules and regulations mentioned in the *Vedas*. Becoming enamored of these rituals is the next impediment, called *niyamāgraha*. Because a devotee fully engages in the supreme service of the Lord, he automatically fulfills all other obligations and doesn't have to execute all the details of Vedic rituals. As the *Śrīmad-Bhāgavatam* (11.5.41) says,

devarṣi-bhūtāpta-nṛṇāṁ pitṝṇāṁ
na kiṅkaro nāyam ṛṇī ca rājan
sarvātmanā yaḥ śaraṇaṁ śaraṇyaṁ
gato mukundaṁ parihṛtya kartam

"Every human being born in this world is immediately indebted to the demigods, the great sages, ordinary living entities, the family, society, and so on. But a person who surrenders unto the lotus feet of the Lord and engages fully in His service is no longer indebted to anyone. In other words, he has no obligations to fulfill except executing devotional service."

Finally, a devotee should not be greedy (*laulyam*), nor should he mix with ordinary materialistic men (*jana-saṅga*).

These are six negatives, or "do-nots," for the devotee; therefore one who wants to attain the perfectional stage of love of Godhead refrains from these things.

Similarly, there are six positive items for advancing in devotional service. First, while one should not be enthusiastic to attain material achievements, one should be very enthusiastic to attain the perfectional stage of devotional service. This enthusiasm is called *utsāha.* A living entity cannot stop acting. So when he is forbidden to become enthusiastic about material achievements, he should at once be encouraged to be enthusiastic about spiritual achievements. Enthusiasm is a symptom of the living entity; it cannot be stopped. It is just like a powerful engine: if you utilize it properly, it will give immense production. Therefore enthusiasm should be purified. Instead of employing enthusiasm for attaining material goals, one should be enthusiastic about achieving the perfectional stage of devotional service. Indeed, enthusing His devotees in devotional service is the purpose for which Kṛṣṇa descends to this material world.

The next item favorable for devotional service is *niścaya,* confidence. When one becomes disappointed in his service to the Supreme Lord, that disappointment must be rejected and replaced with confidence in attaining the ultimate goal, love of Godhead. The devotee should patiently follow the rules and regulations of devotional service so that the day will come when he will achieve, all of a sudden, all the perfection of devotional service. He should not lament for any loss or any reverse in his advancement in spiritual life. This patience (*dhairya*) is the third positive item for advancing in devotional service.

Furthermore, a pure devotee is not envious, hateful, or lazy in the discharge of devotional service. Confident of his advancement, he continually performs his prescribed devotional duties. This is called *tat-tat-karma-pravartana.*

The last two items are *saṅga-tyāga,* giving up the association of nondevotees, and *sato-vṛtti,* following in the footsteps of the previous *ācāryas.* These practices greatly help the devotee remain fixed on the path of devotional service and avoid the tendency to enjoy temporary, material things. Thus the activities of a devotee remain always pure and without any contamination of the material world.

SŪTRA 6*

यज्ज्ञात्वा मत्तो भवति स्तब्धो भवत्यात्मारामो भवति ॥६॥

yaj jñātvā matto bhavati stabdho bhavaty ātmārāmo bhavati

yat—which; *jñātvā*—having known; *mattaḥ*—intoxicated; *bhavati*—becomes; *stabdhaḥ*—stunned (in ecstasy); *bhavati*—becomes; *ātma-ārāmaḥ*—self-content (because of being engaged in the service of the Lord); *bhavati*—becomes.

TRANSLATION

One who understands perfectly the process of devotional service in love of Godhead becomes intoxicated in its discharge. Sometimes he becomes stunned in ecstasy and thus enjoys his whole self, being engaged in the service of the Supreme Self.

PURPORT

The *Śrīmad-Bhāgavatam* (1.7.10) states,

ātmārāmāś ca munayo nirgranthā apy urukrame
kurvanty ahaitukīṁ bhaktim itthaṁ-bhūta-guṇo hariḥ

"Although those who are *ātmārāma,* self-satisfied, are liberated from all material contamination, they are still attracted by the pastimes of the Supreme Lord, and thus they engage themselves in His transcendental service." When Lord Caitanya explained this *ātmārāma* verse to Śrīla Sanātana Gosvāmī, He described sixty-one meanings, and all of them point toward the devotional service of the Lord.

How one becomes intoxicated in devotional service is very nicely described in the *Śrīmad-Bhāgavatam* (11.2.40):

evaṁ-vrataḥ sva-priya-nāma-kīrtyā
jātānurāgo druta-citta uccaiḥ

hasaty atho roditi rauti gāyaty
unmāda-van nṛtyati loka-bāhyaḥ

"A person engaged in the devotional service of the Lord in full Kṛṣṇa consciousness automatically becomes carried away by ecstasy when he chants and hears the holy name of Kṛṣṇa. His heart becomes slackened while chanting the holy name, he becomes almost like a madman, and he does not care for any outward social conventions. Thus sometimes he laughs, sometimes he weeps, sometimes he cries out very loudly, sometimes he sings, and sometimes he dances and forgets himself." These are the signs of becoming intoxicated in devotional service. This stage, called the *ātmārāma* stage, is possible when the Lord bestows His mercy upon a devotee for his advanced devotional activity. It is the highest perfectional stage because one cannot reach it unless one has attained pure love of God.

Neither formal religious rituals, economic development, sense gratification, nor liberation can compare with this sweet stage of perfection of love of Kṛṣṇa, love of the Supreme Lord. The *Caitanya-caritāmṛta* (*Ādi-līlā* 7.97) describes this stage of ecstasy and intoxication as being far above the ecstasy of realizing oneself as Brahman, or the supreme spirit. Lord Caitanya says that the ecstasy of *bhakti* (love of Godhead) is so vast that it is like an ocean compared to the drop of pleasure derived from understanding oneself as one with Brahman. In all Vedic literature, the highest perfectional stage is said to be the state of intoxication of devotional service. It is not achieved by ordinary persons, the nondevotees.

In the stage of perfection, one's heart becomes slackened and one becomes more and more attached to attaining the lotus feet of the Lord. Śrīla Rūpa Gosvāmī, a great *ācārya* in the line of devotional service, has described this stage as follows: "Although appearing just like a madman, a person in the ecstasy of devotional service is not mad in the material conception of the term; this ecstasy is the manifestation of the pleasure potency of the Supreme Lord." The Lord has various potencies, one of which is called *āhlādinī-śakti,* His internal pleasure potency. Only one who becomes a little conversant with this potency can taste such ecstasy. The *Vedānta-sūtra* (1.1.12) states, *ānanda-mayo 'bhyāsāt:* "By nature the Lord is always joyful." This joyfulness of the

Lord is due to His pleasure potency.

One who becomes affected by the pleasure potency of the Supreme Lord manifests various symptoms of ecstasy, such as slackening of the heart, laughing, crying, shivering, and dancing. These symptoms are not material. However, exhibiting such ecstatic symptoms just to get credit from the public is not approved by pure devotees. Śrīla Bhaktisiddhānta Sarasvatī Prabhupāda says, "Persons without attainment of the highest perfectional stage of loving service cannot achieve any auspiciousness simply by artificially laughing, crying, or dancing without any spiritual understanding. Artificial movement of the body . . . must always be rejected. One should wait for the natural sequence within devotional service, and at that time, when one cries or dances or sings, it is approved. A person artificially showing symptoms of the pleasure potency creates many disturbances in the ordinary way of life."

A person who attains the perfectional stage of devotional service under the guidance of a bona fide spiritual master may preach the science of devotion as Lord Caitanya did. When Lord Caitanya preached, He danced and showed other symptoms of ecstasy. Once, in Benares, a Māyāvādī *sannyāsī* named Prakāśānanda Sarasvatī objected to these activities. He said that since Lord Caitanya had taken *sannyāsa,* the renounced order of life, He should not act in such an intoxicated way.

The Lord explained that these symptoms of intoxication had automatically arisen when He had chanted the Hare Kṛṣṇa *mantra,* and that upon seeing this His spiritual master had ordered Him to preach devotional service all over the world. While speaking with Prakāśānanda, Lord Caitanya quoted an important verse from the *Hari-bhakti-sudhodaya* (14.36):

tvat-sākṣāt-karaṇāhlāda-viśuddhābdhi-sthitasya me
sukhāni goṣpadāyante brāhmāṇy api jagad-guro

"My dear Lord, O master of the universe, since I have directly seen You, my transcendental bliss has taken the shape of a great ocean. Thus I now regard the happiness derived from understanding impersonal Brahman to be like the water contained in a calf's hoofprint."

In this way, one who reaches the perfectional stage of devotional service becomes so satisfied that he does not want anything more, and thus he always engages in pure devotional service.

SŪTRA 7*

सा न कामयमाना निरोधरूपत्वात् ॥७॥

sā na kāmayamānā nirodha-rūpatvāt

sā—that devotional service in pure love of God; *na*—not; *kāmayamānā*—like ordinary lust; *nirodha*—renunciation; *rūpatvāt*—because of having as its form.

TRANSLATION

There is no question of lust in the execution of pure devotional service, because in it all material activities are renounced.

PURPORT

In pure devotional service there is no question of sense gratification. Some people mistake the loving affairs between Kṛṣṇa and the *gopīs* (cowherd girls) for activities of ordinary sense gratification, but these affairs are not lustful because there is no material contamination. As Rūpa Gosvāmī states in his *Bhakti-rasāmṛta-sindhu* (1.2.285),

premaiva gopa-rāmāṇāṁ kāma ity agamat prathām
ity uddhavādayo 'py etaṁ vāñchanti bhagavat-priyāḥ

"Although the dealings of the *gopīs* with Kṛṣṇa are wrongly celebrated by many as lust, great sages and saintly persons like Uddhava hanker for such loving affairs with Kṛṣṇa." Śrīla Kṛṣṇadāsa Kavirāja, the author of *Caitanya-caritāmṛta,* has therefore said,

kāma, prema,— doṅhākāra vibhinna lakṣaṇa
lauha āra hema yaiche svarūpe vilakṣaṇa

"As there is a difference between iron and gold, so there is a difference between material lust and Kṛṣṇa's loving affairs with the *gopīs*" (Cc. *Ādi*

4.164). Although such loving affairs may sometimes resemble material lust, the difference is as follows:

ātmendriya-prīti-vāñchā — tāre bali 'kāma'
kṛṣṇendriya-prīti-icchā dhare 'prema' nāma

"The desire to satisfy one's own senses is called lust, while the desire to satisfy the senses of Kṛṣṇa is called *prema,* love of God" (Cc. *Ādi* 4.165).

The impersonalists cannot understand the principle of satisfying Kṛṣṇa's senses because they reject the personality of Godhead. Thus they think God has no senses and therefore no sense satisfaction. But the devotees simply want to satisfy the senses of the Supreme Lord, and so they take part in the pure activities of love of Godhead. There is no question of lust in that category of pure transcendental love.

Lust leads to fruitive activity for sense gratification. There are different kinds of duties for the human being, such as political obligations, performance of Vedic rituals, obligations for maintaining the body, and social formalities and conventions, but all such activities are directed toward satisfying one's own senses. The *gopīs,* however, simply wanted to satisfy Kṛṣṇa's senses, and thus they completely gave up the conventional path of social restriction, not caring for their relatives or the chastisement of their husbands. They gave up everything for the satisfaction of Kṛṣṇa, showing their strong attachment to Kṛṣṇa to be as spotless as washed white cloth.

It is said that when conjugal affection between a lover and beloved comes to the point of being destroyed and yet is not destroyed, such a relationship is pure love, or *prema.* In the material world it is not possible to find this kind of love, for it exists only between Kṛṣṇa and His intimate devotees, such as the *gopīs.* The sentiment between the *gopīs* and Kṛṣṇa was so strong that it could not be destroyed under any circumstances. Kṛṣṇa praises the *gopīs'* pure love in the *Śrīmad-Bhāgavatam* (10.32.22):

na pāraye 'haṁ niravadya-saṁyujāṁ
sva-sādhu-kṛtyaṁ vibudhāyuṣāpi vaḥ
yā mābhajan durjaya-geha-śṛṅkhalāḥ
saṁvṛścya tad vaḥ pratiyātu sādhunā

"My dear *gopīs,* I am not able to repay My debt for your spotless service, even within a lifetime of Brahmā. Your connection with Me is beyond reproach. You have worshiped Me, cutting off all domestic ties, which are difficult to break. Therefore please let your own glorious deeds be your compensation."

SŪTRA 8*

निरोधस्तु लोकवेदव्यापारन्यासः ॥८॥

nirodhas tu loka-veda-vyāpāra-nyāsaḥ

nirodhaḥ—renunciation; *tu*—moreover; *loka*—of social custom; *veda*—and of the revealed scripture; *vyāpāra*—of the engagements; *nyāsa*—renunciation.

TRANSLATION

Such renunciation in devotional service means to give up all kinds of social customs and religious rituals governed by Vedic injunction.

PURPORT

In a verse in the *Lalita-mādhava* (5.2), Śrīla Rūpa Gosvāmī describes renunciation in devotional service:

ṛddhā siddhi-vraja-vijayitā satya-dharmā samādhir
brahmānando gurur api camatkārayaty eva tāvat
yāvat premṇāṁ madhu-ripu-vaśīkāra-siddhauṣadhīnāṁ
gandho 'py antaḥ-karaṇa-saraṇī-pānthatāṁ na prayāti

"Activities such as mystic trance, becoming one with the Supreme, and the religious principles of brahminism, such as speaking the truth and tolerance, have their own respective attractions, but when one becomes captivated by love of Kṛṣṇa, the Supreme Personality of Godhead, all attraction for mystic power, monistic pleasure, and mundane religious principles becomes insignificant."

In other words, by discharging pure devotional service one attains the highest stage of love of Godhead and is freed from all other obligations, such as those mentioned in the *karma-kāṇḍa, jñāna-kāṇḍa,* and *yoga-kāṇḍa* sections of the *Vedas.* One who engages in pure devotional service has no desire to improve himself—except in the service of the Lord. In such devotional service there cannot be any worship of the impersonal or localized features of the Supreme Lord. The devotee simply performs activities that satisfy the Supreme Personality of Godhead and thus attains pure love for the Lord.

Only by the combined mercy of the pure devotee—the bona fide spiritual master—and the Supreme Lord Himself can one attain pure devotional service to the Lord. If someone is fortunate enough to find a pure devotee and accept him as his spiritual master, then this spiritual master, out of his causeless mercy, will impart the knowledge of pure devotional service. And it is the Lord, out of *His* causeless mercy, who sends His most confidential servitor to this world to instruct pure devotional service.

By the divine grace of the spiritual master, the seed of pure devotional service, which is completely different from the seed of fruitive activities and speculative knowledge, is sown in the heart of the devotee. Then, when the devotee satisfies the spiritual master and Kṛṣṇa, this seed of devotional service grows into a plant that gradually reaches up to the spiritual world. An ordinary plant requires shelter for growing. Similarly, the devotional plant grows and grows until it takes shelter in the spiritual world, without taking shelter on any planet in the material world. In other words, those who are captivated by pure devotional service have no desire to elevate themselves to any material planet. The highest planet in the spiritual world is Kṛṣṇa-loka, or Goloka Vṛndāvana, and there the devotional plant takes shelter.

The *Nārada Pañcarātra* defines pure devotional service as follows:

sarvopādhi-vinirmuktaṁ tat-paratvena nirmalam
hṛṣīkena hṛṣīkeśa-sevanaṁ bhaktir ucyate

"Devotional service to the Supreme Lord means engagement of all the senses in His service. In such service there are two important features: first, one must be purified of all designations, and second, the senses should be engaged only in the service of the Supreme Lord, the master of the senses. That is pure devotional service."

Everyone is now contaminated by various designations in relation to the body. Everyone is thinking, "I belong to such-and-such country;

I belong to a certain society; I belong to a certain family." But when a person comes to the stage of pure devotional service, he knows that he does not belong to anything except the service of the Lord.

The symptom of unflinching faith in pure devotional service is that one has overcome the many disruptive desires that impede pure devotional service, such as (1) the desire to worship the demigods, (2) the desire to serve someone other than Kṛṣṇa, (3) the desire to work for sense gratification, without understanding one's relationship with Kṛṣṇa, (4) the desire to cultivate impersonal knowledge and thereby forget the Supreme Lord, and (5) the desire to establish oneself as the Supreme, in which endeavor there is no trace of the bliss of devotional service. One should give up all these desires and engage exclusively in the loving devotional service of the Lord. Except for the service of the Lord, anything done is in the service of illusion, or *māyā*.

One should try to get out of illusion and be engaged in the factual service of Kṛṣṇa. Service to Kṛṣṇa utilizes all the senses, and when the senses are engaged in the service of Kṛṣṇa, they become purified. There are ten senses—five active senses and five knowledge-acquiring senses. The active senses are the power of talking, the hands, the legs, the evacuating outlet, and the generating organ. The knowledge-acquiring senses are the eyes, the ears, the nose, the tongue, and the sense of touch. The mind, the center of all the senses, is sometimes considered the eleventh sense.

One cannot engage in the transcendental loving service of the Lord with these senses in their present materially covered state. Therefore one should take up the process of devotional service to purify them. There are sixty-four items of regulative devotional service for purifying the senses, and one should strenuously undergo such regulative service. Then one can enter into the transcendental loving service of the Lord. (See Sūtra 12 for a full discussion of these sixty-four items of devotional service.)

SŪTRA 9

तस्मिन्ननन्यता तद्विरोधिषूदासीनता च ॥९॥

tasminn ananyatā tad-virodhiṣūdāsīnatā ca

tasmin—for Him; *ananyatā*—exclusive dedication; *tat*—to Him;

virodhiṣu—for those things which are opposed; *udāsīnatā*—indifference; *ca*—and.

TRANSLATION

Renunciation also means being exclusively dedicated to the Lord and indifferent to what stands in the way of His service.

PURPORT

The exclusive nature of devotional service has also been described by Śrīla Rūpa Gosvāmī in the *Bhakti-rasāmṛta-sindhu* (1.1.11):

anyābhilāṣitā-śūnyaṁ jñāna-karmādy-anāvṛtam
ānukūlyena kṛṣṇānu-śīlanaṁ bhaktir uttamā

"When first-class devotional service develops, one must be devoid of all material desires, knowledge obtained by monistic philosophy, and fruitive action. The devotee must constantly serve Kṛṣṇa favorably, as Kṛṣṇa desires."

Pure devotees are so exclusive in their intent to serve the Supreme Lord without any reward that they do not accept any kind of liberation, even though it may be offered by the Supreme Lord. This is confirmed in the *Śrīmad-Bhāgavatam* (3.29.13).

There is also something called "mixed *bhakti,*" which occurs before the stage of pure devotional service. It is sometimes called *prākṛta-bhakti,* or devotional service mixed with material desires. Śrīla Prabhupāda writes, "When one has even a tinge of personal interest, his devotion is mixed with the three modes of material nature" (*Bhāg.* 3.29.9, purport). Thus mixed devotion can occur in various combinations within the modes of ignorance, passion, and goodness. Śrīla Prabhupāda elaborately explains mixed devotion as follows:

> Devotional service in the modes of ignorance, passion, and goodness can be divided into eighty-one categories. There are different devotional activities, such as hearing, chanting, remembering, worshiping, offering prayers, rendering service, and surrendering everything, and each of them can be divided into three categories. There is hearing in the mode of passion, in the mode of ignorance, and in

> the mode of goodness. Similarly, there is chanting in the mode of ignorance, passion, and goodness, etc. . . . One has to transcend all such mixed materialistic devotional service in order to reach the standard of pure devotional service. [*Bhāg.* 3.29.10, purport]

One kind of mixed devotional service is known as *jñāna-miśra-bhakti,* or devotional service mixed with empiric knowledge. Śrīla Prabhupāda writes, "People in general, who are under the influence of *avidyā-śakti,* or *māyā,* have neither knowledge nor devotion. But when a person who is a little advanced and is therefore called a *jñānī* advances even more, he is in the category of a *jñāna-miśra-bhakta,* or a devotee whose love is mixed with empiric knowledge" (*Bhāg.* 4.9.16, purport).

Nārada's definition of *bhakti,* being "exclusively dedicated to the Lord," refers to pure devotional service in the liberated stage. This has also been noted by Śrīla Prabhupāda in his commentary on the first *sūtra* of the *Nārada-bhakti-sūtra,* wherein he says that pure devotional service begins after the *brahma-bhūta,* or liberated, stage.

A pure devotee is *akāma,* free of material desire. He is conscious of his actual position and derives satisfaction only from serving the Supreme Lord. Śrīla Prabhupāda writes, "Śrīla Jīva Gosvāmī has explained this desirelessness as *bhajanīya-parama-puruṣa-sukha-mātra-sva-sukhatvam* in his *Sandarbhas.* This means that one should feel happy only by experiencing the happiness of the Supreme Lord" (*Bhāg.* 2.3.10, purport).

In the present *sūtra* Nārada Muni states that a pure devotee is "indifferent toward what stands in the way of [the Lord's] service." If a devotee encounters some hindrance in his service to the Lord, he prays to the Lord to please remove it. A good example is Queen Kuntī:

atha viśveśa viśvātman viśva-mūrte svakeṣu me
sneha-pāśam imaṁ chindhi dṛḍhaṁ pāṇḍuṣu vṛṣṇiṣu

tvayi me 'nanya-viṣayā matir madhu-pate 'sakṛt
ratim udvahatād addhā gaṅgevaugham udanvati

"O Lord of the universe, soul of the universe, O personality of the form of the universe, please, therefore, sever my tie of affection for my kinsmen, the Pāṇḍavas and the Vṛṣṇis. O Lord of Madhu, as the

Ganges forever flows to the sea without hindrance, let my attraction be constantly drawn unto You without being diverted to anyone else" (*Bhāg.* 1.2.40–41).

The supreme examples of devotees who let nothing stand in the way of their service to Kṛṣṇa are the *gopīs* of Vṛndāvana. And among all the *gopīs,* the best is Śrīmatī Rādhārāṇī. Her determination to serve Kṛṣṇa is beautifully described in this verse from Śrīla Rūpa Gosvāmī's *Vidagdha-mādhava* (3.9):

hitvā dūre pathi dhava-taror antikaṁ dharma-setor
bhaṅgodagrā guru-śikhariṇaṁ raṁhasā laṅghayantī
lebhe kṛṣṇārnava-nava-rasā rādhikā-vāhinī tvāṁ
vāg-vīcībhiḥ kim iva vimukhī-bhāvam asyās tanoṣi

"O Lord Kṛṣṇa, You are just like an ocean. The river of Śrīmatī Rādhārāṇī has reached You from a long distance—leaving far behind the tree of Her husband, breaking through the bridge of social convention, and forcibly crossing the hills of elder relatives."

Although pure devotion to Lord Kṛṣṇa is exclusive, it is not a narrow-minded, sectarian devotion. Lord Kṛṣṇa is the Supreme Personality of Godhead, the source of all emanations; therefore love for Kṛṣṇa includes within it love for all living entities. Śrīla Prabhupāda explained this by the homely example of a girl who marries and joins with her husband's family. Just by the act of marrying one man, she automatically becomes intimately related with his family members, who now become her brothers-in-law, father-in-law, mother-in-law, and so on. Similarly, when we join with Kṛṣṇa by rendering Him loving service, we enter into His family, which includes *all living beings.* Śrīla Prabhupāda describes this in the preface to *The Nectar of Devotion:*

> The basic principle of the living condition is that we have a general propensity to love someone. No one can live without loving someone else. . . . The missing point, however, is where to repose our love so that everyone can become happy. . . . *The Nectar of Devotion* teaches us the science of loving every one of the living entities perfectly by the easy method of loving Kṛṣṇa. We have failed to create peace and harmony in human society, even by such great attempts as the United Nations, because we do not know the right method.

At the conclusion of the *Bhagavad-gītā* (18.66), Lord Kṛṣṇa states,

sarva-dharmān parityajya mām ekaṁ śaraṇaṁ vraja
ahaṁ tvāṁ sarva-pāpebhyo mokṣayiṣyāmi mā śucaḥ

"Abandon all varieties of religion and just surrender unto Me. I shall deliver you from all sinful reactions. Do not fear." If one hesitates to take up exclusive devotion to the Lord because of obstacles or fear of being lax in other obligations, Kṛṣṇa assures us that there is nothing to fear. Śrīla Prabhupāda writes, "The particular words used here, *mā śucaḥ*, 'Don't fear, don't hesitate, don't worry,' are very significant. One may be perplexed as to how one can give up all kinds of religious forms and simply surrender unto Kṛṣṇa, but such worry is useless."

SŪTRA 10

अन्याश्रयाणां त्यागोऽनन्यता ॥१०॥

anyāśrayāṇāṁ tyāgo 'nanyatā

anya—other; *āśrayāṇām*—of shelters; *tyāgaḥ*—the giving up; *an-anyatā*—exclusiveness.

TRANSLATION

Exclusive dedication to the Lord means giving up all shelters other than Him.

PURPORT

As mentioned above, in the *Bhagavad-gītā* (18.66) Lord Kṛṣṇa advises Arjuna to give up all processes of self-realization and surrender unto Him only. Knowledge of the self, knowledge of the localized Supersoul, knowledge of executing the work prescribed for the four divisions of human society, knowledge of renunciation, knowledge of detachment, knowledge of controlling the senses and the mind, knowledge of meditation, and knowledge of how to acquire material power by mystic perfection—all these are different kinds of "shelters" leading to various degrees of spiritual perfection. But the Lord's last instruction in the *Bhagavad-gītā* is that one should give up all these different shelters and simply take to His loving devotional service, and this surrender to the Lord will save one from all kinds of sinful reaction. In other words, direct attachment for the Supreme Personality of Godhead, Kṛṣṇa, and engagement in His transcendental service are the topmost perfections of spiritual life.

SŪTRA 11*

लोकवेदेषु तदनुकूलाचरणं तद्विरोधिषूदासीनता ॥११॥

loka-vedeṣu tad-anukūlācaraṇaṁ tad-virodhiṣūdāsīnatā

loka—in society and politics; *vedeṣu*—and in the Vedic rituals; *tat*—for that; *anukūla*—of what is favorable; *ācaraṇam*—performance; *tat*—for that; *virodhiṣu*—for what is opposed; *udāsīnatā*—indifference.

TRANSLATION

Indifference toward what stands in the way of devotional service means to accept only those activities of social custom and Vedic injunction that are favorable to devotional service.

PURPORT

Material existence is a life of revolt against the Supreme Personality of Godhead. There are many ways in which the living entities can manifest this spirit of revolt, such as engaging in fruitive activities, mental speculation, or mystic *yoga* to achieve material perfections. Generally, all conditioned souls desire to lord it over the material nature. Everyone wants to become a demilord, either by social or political activities or by Vedic rituals. Everyone wants to elevate himself to a higher status of existence or, out of frustration, become one with the Supreme. All these desires are different types of materialism; they are not favorable for devotional service.

A pure devotee rejects demigod worship and worships only Lord Kṛṣṇa or His Viṣṇu expansions. Until a person is completely free of material contamination, he might want to worship God in hope of fulfilling material desires. But even if a person has material desires, if he scrupulously worships the Supreme Lord he will very soon become purified of all such desires. On the other hand, persons whose activities are dictated by material desires and who are also addicted to worshiping the demigods cannot become pure devotees at any stage of their lives. The Lord, situated within everyone's heart, fulfills the desires of the demigod-worshipers—but in the *Bhagavad-gītā* the Lord says that such demigod-worshipers are of small intelligence (*alpa-medhasaḥ*). In other words, as long as one is controlled by the modes of nature, one will be prone to worship the demigods for material purposes, but one who curbs this tendency and worships Kṛṣṇa exclusively can rise above the modes and attain pure devotional service.

One cannot be situated on the platform of pure devotional service, however, unless one is freed from all kinds of sinful reactions. To counteract various sinful reactions, there are prescribed duties in the ritualistic section of the *Vedas,* and those in the lower stage of life can become freed from all sinful reactions by strictly following the Vedic ritualistic processes. Then they can become situated in pure devotional service. Thus it should be understood that a person who is situated in pure devotional service must have in his past life already executed all the Vedic rituals with great determination. In other words, after reaching the stage of devotional service, a person does not have to execute any process of atonement mentioned in the ritualistic section of the *Vedas.* He is already sinless.

SŪTRA 12*

भवतु निश्चयदाढर्याद्रूर्ध्वं शास्त्ररक्षणम् ॥१२॥

bhavatu niścaya-dārḍhyād ūrdhvaṁ śāstra-rakṣaṇam

bhavatu—let there be; *niścaya*—of certainty; *dārḍhyāt*—the firm fixing; *ūrdhvam*—after; *śāstra*—of scripture; *rakṣaṇam*—the observance.

TRANSLATION

One must continue to follow scriptural injunctions even after one is fixed up in determined certainty that devotional service is the only means for reaching the perfection of life.

PURPORT

When a person becomes firmly convinced about the importance of devotional service, he surrenders unto the Supreme Lord. There are six symptoms of surrender: (1) One should perform only those actions favorable for devotional service to Kṛṣṇa. (2) One should give up everything unfavorable for discharging devotional service. (3) One should firmly believe that Kṛṣṇa will protect one in all circumstances and that no one is a better protector than Kṛṣṇa. This conviction should be distinct from the monistic philosophy that one is as good as Kṛṣṇa. Rather, one should always think that Kṛṣṇa, or God, is great and that one is always protected by Him. (4) One should have the conviction that Kṛṣṇa is one's maintainer, and one should not take shelter of any demigod for maintenance. (5) One should always remember that one's activities and desires are not independent. In other words, the devotee should feel completely dependent on Kṛṣṇa, and thus he should act and think as Kṛṣṇa desires. (6) One should always think himself the poorest of the poor and feel totally dependent on the mercy of Kṛṣṇa.

A devotee who follows these six principles of surrender always thinks, "O Lord, I am Yours in every respect; I am Your eternal servant." In this way a pure devotee becomes cleansed. There is a nice verse in this connection in the *Śrīmad-Bhāgavatam* (11.29.34):

martyo yadā tyakta-samasta-karmā
niveditātmā vicikīrṣito me
tadāmṛtatvaṁ pratipadyamāno
mayātma-bhūyāya ca kalpate vai

"A person who gives up all fruitive activities and offers himself entirely unto Me, eagerly desiring to render service unto Me, achieves liberation from birth and death and is promoted to the status of sharing My own opulences." To be elevated to such a point of devotional life, one has to execute the directions of the scriptures. But even after becoming elevated in devotional life, one should not think, "Oh, I am already elevated to the highest stage; therefore I may violate the scriptural regulations for executing devotional service."

Devotional service is dormant in every living being, for by nature every living being is part and parcel of the Supreme Lord and it is the healthy condition of the part to serve the whole. It is just like the situation of the parts of the body. The hand and the leg serve the body; similarly, as part and parcel of the Supreme Lord, every living entity is bound to serve the Supreme Lord in his healthy condition. When he is not thus engaged, he is in a diseased condition, but as soon as he engages all his senses in the transcendental loving service of the Lord, he is in his normal, healthy condition.

The devotee should engage his senses in the Lord's service according to the directions of the authoritative scriptures and under the guidance of a bona fide spiritual master. The beginning of one's devotional training is to engage the ear in aural reception of the teachings of the *Bhagavad-gītā* and the *Śrīmad-Bhāgavatam.* There are many authoritative books of spiritual knowledge, but all of them are more or less supplements to the *Bhagavad-gītā* and *Śrīmad-Bhāgavatam.* Even the *Nārada-bhakti-sūtra* is a summary of the *Bhagavad-gītā* and the *Śrīmad-Bhāgavatam.* Therefore the beginning of devotional service is to hear these two important transcendental books of knowledge. Simply by aural reception of these two books from the bona fide spiritual master, one becomes enlightened about devotional service, which is dormant within the heart.

Devotional service executed under the guidance of the spiritual master and according to scriptural injunctions is called *vaidhi-bhakti,* a part of *sādhana-bhakti,* or devotional service in practice. The other division of *sādhana-bhakti* is *rāgānuga-bhakti,* spontaneous devotional service.

One who wishes to advance to the platform of *rāgānuga-bhakti* must follow the injunctions of the authoritative scriptures under the direction of the spiritual master. According to Sūtra 12, even a person on a highly elevated platform of devotional service must execute the rules and regulations of the scripture, what to speak of persons who are not elevated. In other words, neophytes in devotional service must strictly and scrupulously follow the rules and regulations of the scriptures to rise to the platform of unalloyed devotional service.

As mentioned above, a devotee who strictly practices regulative devotional service, or *vaidhi-bhakti.* The prime principle of *vaidhi-bhakti* is stated in the *Śrīmad-Bhāgavatam* (2.1.5):

tasmād bhārata sarvātmā bhagavān īśvaro hariḥ
śrotavyaḥ kīrtitavyaś ca smartavyaś cecchatābhayam

"A person serious about making progress in devotional service must always think of the Supreme Personality of Godhead, must always chant

His glories, and must always hear about His activities." These are the preliminary principles of following the scriptural rules and regulations.

The *Śrīmad-Bhāgavatam* (11.5.2) states,

mukha-bāhūru-pādebhyaḥ puruṣasyāśramaiḥ saha
catvāro jajñire varṇā guṇair viprādayaḥ pṛthak

Every person, whatever he may be, emanates from some part of the universal form of the Supreme Lord, the *virāṭ-puruṣa.* The *brāhmaṇas* (intelligentsia) emanate from the face, the *kṣatriyas* (warriors and administrators) emanate from the arms, the *vaiśyas* (farmers and merchants) emanate from the thighs, and the *śūdras* (laborers) emanate from the feet. But wherever we may be situated, we have some particular function to execute in the service of the Supreme Whole, the Personality of Godhead. If we do not, therefore, engage our particular propensities in the service of the Lord, then we are fallen, just like a useless limb amputated from the body.

According to the *Padma Purāṇa,* the sum and substance of all the regulative principles of the scripture is that Lord Viṣṇu, or Kṛṣṇa, should always be remembered and should never be forgotten. We should therefore mold our lives in such a way that in every activity we shall be able to remember the Supreme Lord. Any activity that reminds one of the Supreme Lord is a regulative principle in devotional service, and any activity that makes one forget the Supreme Lord is a forbidden activity for a devotee.

In the *Caitanya-caritāmṛta* (*Madhya* 22.115–28), Lord Caitanya lists sixty-four regulative principles one must follow to be elevated to the highest platform of devotional service. And, as stressed here in Sūtra 12, even after being elevated to the highest platform of devotional service, one must continue following the scriptural injunctions for devotional life. The sixty-four regulative principles are as follows:

(1) To accept a bona fide spiritual master. (2) To become initiated by the spiritual master. (3) To engage oneself in the service of the spiritual master. (4) To receive instructions from the spiritual master and inquire about advancing on the path of devotional service. (5) To follow in the footsteps of previous *ācāryas* and follow the directions given by the spiritual master. (6) To give up anything for the satisfaction of Kṛṣṇa, and to accept anything for the satisfaction

of Kṛṣṇa. (7) To live in a place where Kṛṣṇa is present—a city like Vṛndāvana or Mathurā, or a Kṛṣṇa temple. (8) To minimize one's means of living as much as one can, while living comfortably to execute devotional service. (9) To observe fasting days, such as Ekādaśī. (10) To worship cows, *brāhmaṇas,* Vaiṣṇavas, and sacred trees like the banyan.

These ten principles of devotional service are the beginning. Additional principles are as follows: (11) One should avoid committing offenses against the holy name, the Deity, etc. (12) One should avoid associating with nondevotees. (13) One should not aspire to have many disciples. (14) One should not unnecessarily divert his attention by partially studying many books so as to appear very learned. For devotional service, it is sufficient to scrutinizingly study books like the *Bhagavad-gītā,* the *Śrīmad-Bhāgavatam,* and the *Caitanya-caritāmṛta.* (15) One should not be disturbed in either loss or gain. (16) One should not allow oneself to be overwhelmed by lamentation for any reason. (17) One should not blaspheme the demigods, although one should not worship them. Similarly, one should not criticize other scriptures, although one should not follow the principles therein. (18) One should not tolerate blasphemy of the Supreme Lord or His devotees. (19) One should not indulge in idle talks, such as those about relationships between men and women. (20) One should not unnecessarily disturb any living being, whatever he may be.

The above-mentioned twenty items are the doorway to devotional service. And among them, the first three—namely, acceptance of the spiritual master, initiation by the spiritual master, and service to the spiritual master—are the most important. Then come the following items: (21) To hear about the Lord. (22) To chant His glories. (23) To remember Him. (24) To serve and meditate upon the lotus feet of the Lord and His devotees. (25) To worship Him. (26) To pray to Him. (27) To think of oneself as the Lord's eternal servant. (28) To become the Lord's friend. (29) To offer everything to the Lord. (30) To dance before the Deity. (31) To sing before the Deity. (32) To inform the Lord of everything about one's life. (33) To bow down to the Lord. (34) To offer respect to the spiritual master and the Supreme Lord by standing up at the appropriate time. (35) To follow the spiritual master or the Supreme Lord in procession. (36) To visit places of pilgrimage and temples of the Supreme Lord. (37)

To circumambulate the temple. (38) To recite prayers. (39) To chant the Lord's name softly to oneself. (40) To chant the Lord's name loudly in congregation. (41) To smell incense and flowers offered to the Deity. (42) To eat the remnants of food offered to the Deity. (43) To regularly attend the *ārati* offered to the Deity, as well as special festivals. (44) To regularly look upon the Deity. (45) To offer one's dearmost possessions to the Supreme Lord. (46) To meditate on the Lord's name, form, pastimes, etc. (47) To water the *tulasī* plant. (48) To serve the Lord's devotees. (49) To try to live in Vṛndāvana or Mathurā. (50) To relish the topics of the *Śrīmad-Bhāgavatam.* (51) To take all kinds of risks for Kṛṣṇa. (52) To always expect the mercy of Kṛṣṇa. (53) To observe ceremonies like Janmāṣṭamī (the appearance day of Lord Kṛṣṇa) and Rāma-navamī (the appearance day of Lord Rāmacandra) with devotees. (54) To fully surrender to Kṛṣṇa. (55) To observe special regulations like those followed during the month of Kārtika (Oct.-Nov.). (56) To mark the body with Vaiṣṇava *tilaka* (clay markings). (57) To mark the body with the holy names of God. (58) To accept the remnants of garlands that have been offered to the Supreme Lord. (59) To drink *caraṇāmṛta,* the water that has washed the lotus feet of the Deity.

Among these fifty-nine items, five are considered so important that they are mentioned again separately, thus completing the sixty-four items of devotional service. These five are (60) associating with devotees, (61) chanting the holy name of the Lord, (62) hearing the *Śrīmad-Bhāgavatam,* (63) residing at a place of pilgrimage like Mathurā, and (64) worshiping the Deity with faith and veneration.

SŪTRA 13*

अन्यथा पातित्यशङ्कया ॥१३॥

anyathā pātitya-śaṅkayā

anyathā—otherwise; *pātitya*—of falling down; *śaṅkayā*—because of anticipating the possibility.

TRANSLATION

Otherwise there is every possibility of falling down.

PURPORT

If a diseased person is being cured of the symptoms of his disease but does not care for the principles of healthy living, there is every possibility of a relapse. Similarly, the neophyte devotee serious about advancing in devotional service must carefully follow the principles of regulative devotional service; otherwise there is every possibility of his falling down. Strictly speaking, if a devotee ignores the regulative principles and acts according to his whims—if, for example, he does not eat *kṛṣṇa-prasādam* but eats anywhere and everywhere, such as in restaurants—there is every possibility of his falling down. If he accumulates money without spending it for devotional service, there is every possibility of his falling down. If he applies his energy not in the service of the Lord but in some material activity, there is every possibility of his falling down. If the devotee does not engage himself always in hearing and chanting the topics of Kṛṣṇa and His activities but instead indulges in idle talk, there is every chance of his falling down. If a neophyte devotee does not follow the orders of the spiritual master and simply officially sticks to the principles, or if he does not strictly follow the principles, there is every possibility of his falling down. To become greedy is another cause of falldown. And to associate with persons who are not in devotional service is the last word in *māyā's* allurements for causing a devotee to fall down.

In the *Bhagavad-gītā* (18.5), Kṛṣṇa clearly states that sacrifice, charity, and penance are never to be given up by a transcendentalist. If he is at all intelligent he must continue these three activities, even if he is highly elevated. A devotee is naturally very humble, and even if he is highly elevated he does not consider himself to be so. A practical example is found in the life of the author of the *Caitanya-caritāmṛta,* Kṛṣṇadāsa Kavirāja Gosvāmī. He was a vastly learned scholar and a first-class devotee, yet he still referred to himself as the lowest of mankind, lower than the bacteria in the stool. He wrote that he was so sinful that no one should even utter his name, lest that person fall down! Of course, when a great devotee speaks this way, we should not believe that he is actually in the lower status of life; we should rather take it as evidence that out of humility a pure devotee never thinks he is elevated. He always thinks he is in the lowest status of spiritual life.

As stated above, in the *Bhagavad-gītā* Kṛṣṇa states that no one should give up the sacrificial portion of spiritual life. And the scriptures recommend that the best sacrifice in this Age of Kali is to chant Hare Kṛṣṇa, Hare Kṛṣṇa, Kṛṣṇa Kṛṣṇa, Hare Hare/ Hare Rāma, Hare Rāma, Rāma Rāma, Hare Hare. Therefore, a devotee's prime duty is to continue chanting this *mahā-mantra,* even if he is highly elevated. Otherwise, at any stage one can fall down.

SŪTRA 14*

लोकऽपि तावदेव भोजनादिव्यापारस्त्वाशरीरधारणावधि ॥१४॥

loke 'pi tāvad eva bhojanādi-vyāpāras tv ā-śarīra-dhāraṇāvadhi

loke—in social behavior; *api*—also; *tāvat*—for that long; *eva*—indeed; *bhojana*—eating; *ādi*—and so on; *vyāpāraḥ*—the activity; *tu*—and; *ā-śarīra-dhāraṇā-avadhi*—for as long as one still has this body.

TRANSLATION

For as long as the body lasts, one should engage minimally in social and political activities and in such matters as eating.

PURPORT

Spiritual life begins when a person understands that he is not the body. In the material world, all our connections—whether social or political or in the field of eating, sleeping, defending, and mating—are due only to the material body. Unless one is completely conversant with the fact that one is not the body, it is not possible to become self-realized.

In the *Bhagavad-gītā* (18.54), Lord Kṛṣṇa describes self-realization as follows:

brahma-bhūtaḥ prasannātmā na śocati na kāṅkṣati
samaḥ sarveṣu bhūteṣu mad-bhaktiṁ labhate parām

"Self-realization [the *brahma-bhūta* stage] is symptomized by joyfulness. One never laments for any loss, nor is one very enthusiastic when there is some gain. One sees everyone on an equal level through spiritual understanding. These qualities are preliminary to entering into pure devotional service."

Pure devotional service is so powerful, however, that one may at once take to it without acquiring the previous qualification of *brahma-bhūta* life. A sincere devotee who engages in the service of the Lord automatically becomes situated in the *brahma-bhūta* stage. The devotee's duty is only to strictly follow the principles of regulated devotional service, as previously mentioned. Therefore a devotee should not be too concerned about social and political obligations, since all such activities belong to the body. He should similarly restrict his eating; this is essential to the execution of devotional service. A devotee cannot eat anything and everything he likes; he must eat only foods that have been offered to the Lord. The Lord clearly says (*Bhagavad-gītā* 9.26) that He will accept a flower, a fruit, a leaf, or a little water if they are offered to Him with devotional love. (One should note that the Supreme Lord accepts only foods from the vegetable kingdom, as well as milk products. "Water" includes milk and its products.) The Lord is not hungry or poor, in need of our offering. Actually, it is to our advantage to offer Him something to eat. If the Supreme Lord kindly accepts our offering, then we are benefited. The Lord is full, but to establish the universal principle that everyone can offer something to the Lord, He accepts even the most meager offering—when it is presented with love. Even the poorest of the poor can collect a flower, a leaf, and a little water and offer them to the Supreme Lord.

It is incumbent upon all devotees of Kṛṣṇa to avoid eating anything that has not been offered to the Supreme Lord. A devotee who does not strictly follow this principle is sure to fall down. Similarly, one who refuses to accept *prasādam,* the remnants of food offered to Kṛṣṇa, cannot become a devotee.

In the *Śrīmad-Bhāgavatam* (5.5.3) Lord Ṛṣabhadeva states that one who is determined to become a pure devotee avoids associating with the general mass of people, who are simply engaged in the animal propensities of eating, sleeping, defending, and mating. The general mass of people mistake the body for the self, and therefore they are always busy trying to maintain the body very nicely. A devotee should not associate with such people. Nor should he be overly attached to his family members, knowing that he has been accidentally thrown together with his wife, children, and so on. Spiritually, no one is a wife, child, husband, or father of anyone else. Everyone comes into this world according to his past deeds and takes shelter of a father and a mother, but actually no one is anyone's father or mother. While a devotee must know this, that does not mean he should neglect his family. As a matter of duty he should maintain his family members without attachment and instruct them in Kṛṣṇa consciousness.

So, whether in social life or political life, or in the matter of eating, sleeping, mating, and defending, a devotee should avoid performing any action tainted by material attachment. The word used here is *bhojanādi,* which indicates the four propensities of eating, sleeping, defending, and mating. As the devotee does not eat anything that has not been offered to Kṛṣṇa, so he does not sleep more than is absolutely necessary. In the lives of the great devotees Sanātana Gosvāmī and Rūpa Gosvāmī, we see that they did not sleep more than one and a half hours a day, and they were reluctant even to accept that. So sleeping is also restricted. Naturally one who is always engaged in devotional service of the Lord has very little time to sleep. Sleep is a necessity of the body, not the spirit soul, and therefore as one advances in devotional service one's propensity to sleep decreases.

Similarly, a devotee minimizes his defending propensity. A pure devotee knows he is under the shelter of the all-powerful Supreme Lord, and so he is not very anxious about defending himself. Although he should use his common sense in the matter of defending, he is sure that without being protected by Lord Kṛṣṇa no one can defend himself, however expert he may be in the art of defense.

In the same way, a devotee minimizes or eliminates sex. He does not indulge indiscriminately in sex, begetting offspring as the cats and dogs do. If he begets any children at all, he takes charge of them to elevate them to Kṛṣṇa consciousness so that they may not have to suffer in material life again, in future lives. That is the duty of a devotee.

In this material world, people in general engage in sense-gratificatory activities, which keep them bound up by the laws of the material modes of nature. Indeed, the more a person engages in such activities, the more he expands his life in material existence. A devotee acts differently: he knows he is not the body and that as long as he is in his body he will have to suffer the threefold material miseries. Therefore to decrease his material entanglement and help his advancement in spiritual life, he always minimizes his social and political activities and his eating, sleeping, defending, and mating.

CHAPTER 2

Defining Bhakti

SŪTRA 15*

तल्लक्षणानि वाच्यन्ते नानामतभेदात् ॥१५॥

tal-lakṣaṇāni vācyante nānā-mata-bhedāt

tat—of it (devotional service); *lakṣaṇāni*—the characteristics; *vācyante*—are enunciated; *nānā*—various; *mata*—of theories; *bhedāt*—according to the differences.

TRANSLATION

Now the characteristics of devotional service will be described according to various authoritative opinions.

PURPORT

In the *Śrīmad-Bhāgavatam* (7.5.23), Prahlāda Mahārāja very clearly states what the essential activities of devotional service are:

śravaṇaṁ kīrtanaṁ viṣṇoḥ smaraṇaṁ pāda-sevanam
arcanaṁ vandanaṁ dāsyaṁ sakhyam ātma-nivedanam

"Devotional service consists of (1) hearing about the Lord, (2) chanting His glories, (3) remembering Him, (4) serving and meditating upon His lotus feet, (5) worshiping Him, (6) praying to Him, (7) thinking oneself His eternal servant, (8) becoming His friend, and (9) surrendering everything to Him."

One should surrender to the Lord as much as an animal purchased from the market surrenders to its master. Such an animal never thinks of his maintenance because he knows that his master will look after him. A soul totally surrendered to the Supreme Lord is similarly never anxious for his maintenance. Śrīla Sanātana Gosvāmī gives further symptoms of full surrender in his *Hari-bhakti-vilāsa* (11.417):

ānukūlyasya saṅkalpaḥ prātikūlyasya varjanam
rakṣiṣyatīti viśvāso goptṛtve varaṇaṁ tathā
ātma-nikṣepa-kārpaṇye ṣaḍ-vidhā śaraṇāgatiḥ

"The six divisions of surrender are: accepting those things favorable to devotional service, rejecting unfavorable things, the conviction that Kṛṣṇa will give protection, accepting the Lord as one's guardian or master, full self-surrender, and humility." Nārada will gradually explain these principles of devotion in the remaining *sūtras.*

SŪTRA 16

पूजादिष्वनुराग इति पाराशर्यः ॥१६॥

pūjādiṣv anurāga iti pārāśaryaḥ

pūjā-ādiṣu—for worship and so on; *anurāgaḥ*—fondness; *iti*—so thinks; *pārāśaryaḥ*—Vyāsadeva, the son of Parāśara.

TRANSLATION

Śrīla Vyāsadeva, the son of Parāśara Muni, says that *bhakti* is fond attachment for worshiping the Lord in various ways.

PURPORT

In the previous *sūtra,* Nārada Muni promised that he would tell us some of the symptoms of devotional service according to various authoritative opinions. The *Śrīmad-Bhāgavatam* (6.3.20) mentions twelve *mahā-janas,* or Kṛṣṇa conscious authorities, and among them, one *mahā-jana* may emphasize a different aspect of *bhakti* than another. The Supreme Lord possesses an unlimited variety of qualities and pastimes, and it is natural that devotees favor particular modes of service. All devotees, however, agree on the *siddhānta,* or accepted conclusion. *Bhakti* is not open to continual speculation, such as the kind Western philosophers indulge in.

The first opinion Nārada offers is that of Śrīla Vyāsadeva, one of Nārada's many exalted disciples. Besides being a faithful disciple of Nārada's, Vyāsadeva is the compiler of the *Vedas,* and so his opinions are not contrary to Nārada's.

The words Vyāsa uses to describe *bhakti* are *pūjā* and *anurāga*. These refer to worship of the Lord performed with sincere love and great attachment. Nondevotees may perform *pūjā,* but they think of it as an external ritual. The Māyāvādī, for example, has an offensive concept of worship. He sees it as "a great aid in fixing one's mind on the Supreme." But what the Māyāvādī really has in mind is that his *pūjā* will lead him to see God and Brahman and the Ātman, or self, as one. In other words, he thinks that by worshiping God he will become God. The Māyāvādīs plainly advocate that while a person worships the Deity his first and foremost meditation should be on his unity with Brahman. This is a faithless and duplicitous form of "worship." The Māyāvādī may even offer a fruit or flower to the Deity, but his motivation is not to develop love for God but to attain absolute oneness with the Supreme, which he thinks he can do by imitating the activities of a devotee. Kṛṣṇa declares in the *Bhagavad-gītā* (4.11), *ye yathā māṁ prapadyante tāṁs tathaiva bhajāmy aham:* "As they approach Me, I reward them." And so those who desire to merge into the effulgence of the Supreme Person are awarded that impersonal status.

Some say that mental worship of the Lord is superior to external worship. But Śrīla Prabhupāda did not make such distinctions. In *The Nectar of Devotion* we read of a *brāhmaṇa* in South India who worshiped the Deity within his mind. The *brāhmaṇa* was poor and could not afford paraphernalia for *pūjā,* but in his mental worship he imagined that he was fetching golden and silver pots, filling them with water, and performing very opulent Deity worship. An intimate devotee of Lord Caitanya's, Nṛsiṁhānanda Brahmacārī, also performed mental worship. Once he mentally decorated a road with flowers and gems in anticipation that Lord Caitanya would walk there. So mental worship of the Lord is certainly bona fide. But while devotees may perform mental worship according to time and circumstances, when the opportunity arises they do not avoid offering flaming lamps, incense, and so on, as prescribed for temple worship. Moreover, whether mentally or externally, they always worship the spiritual *form* of the Personality of Godhead.

A sincere devotee's *pūjā* is never merely mechanical but is offered with *anurāga,* strong feelings of attachment for the Lord. True worship is performed with the mind, the senses, and all the bodily limbs. Therefore the meaning of worship is not limited; it includes the engagement of all one's sensory and mental functions in service to the Supreme. As Lord Kṛṣṇa says,

ahaṁ sarvasya prabhavo mattaḥ sarvaṁ pravartate
iti matvā bhajante māṁ budhā bhāva-samanvitāḥ

"I am the source of all spiritual and material worlds. Everything emanates from Me. The wise who perfectly know this engage in My devotional service and worship Me with all their hearts" (Bg. 10.8). Lord Kṛṣṇa also describes the *mahātmās* as "great souls [who] perpetually worship Me with devotion" (Bg. 9.14).

Worship may include many activities, but the word *pūjā* particularly refers to the worship of the *arcā-vigraha,* the form of the Deity in the temple. Although Lord Caitanya was Śrī Kṛṣṇa Himself, He worshiped Lord Jagannātha at the temple in Purī. Lord Caitanya went to see the Deity every day and experienced great transcendental bliss. When Lord Jagannātha was absent from the temple during His renovation before Ratha-yātrā, Lord Caitanya acutely felt the pain of His absence and went into solitude at Ālālanātha.

Thus Deity worship is not just for beginners, nor is it merely an aid to impersonal meditation. It is a necessary part of devotional service. Although in this age the chanting of the holy names is the foremost method of devotional service, the *bhakta* should also worship the *arcā-vigraha* to counteract his tendencies for contamination, which are so strong in the Kali-yuga. This is the opinion of Śrīla Jīva Gosvāmī.

We know from reading Vyāsadeva's *Śrīmad-Bhāgavatam* that his understanding of what constitutes worship of the Lord is not confined to temple worship of the *arcā-vigraha.* In the Seventh Canto of the *Śrīmad-Bhāgavatam,* Prahlāda Mahārāja mentions nine processes of devotional service. Śrīla Vyāsadeva—and Śrīla Prabhupāda—often stressed the first two items, hearing and chanting the glories of the Lord, as the most important, especially in the present age. But by faithfully executing any of the nine processes of *bhakti,* one can achieve fond attachment to worshiping the Lord.

SŪTRA 17

कथादिष्विति गर्गः ॥१७॥

kathādiṣv iti gargaḥ

kathā-ādiṣu—for narrations and so on; *iti*—so; *garga*—Garga Muni.

TRANSLATION

Garga Muni says that *bhakti* is fondness for narrations about the Lord, by the Lord, and so on.

PURPORT

As Garga Muni taught the importance of attachment for hearing *kṛṣṇa-kathā,* so Śrīla Prabhupāda also stressed *kṛṣṇa-kathā.* One type of *kṛṣṇa-kathā* consists of words directly spoken from the mouth of the Lord, such as the *Bhagavad-gītā.* Lord Caitanya advocated that we repeat the words spoken by Kṛṣṇa (*kṛṣṇa-upadeśa*) to whomever we meet. Another kind of *kṛṣṇa-kathā* consists of words spoken about Kṛṣṇa, such as those spoken by Śukadeva Gosvāmī to Mahārāja Parīkṣit in *Śrīmad-Bhāgavatam.* Śukadeva speaks throughout all twelve cantos about the wonderful pastimes of the Lord in His various incarnations. In the Tenth Canto he describes the original form of the Personality of Godhead, Lord Kṛṣṇa in Vṛndāvana, Mathurā, and Dvārakā. All of this is *kṛṣṇa-kathā.*

It is a characteristic of pure devotees that they speak only on transcendental subjects. A devotee practices *mauna,* or silence, by refraining from all mundane talk, but he is always pleased to speak *kṛṣṇa-kathā.* As Kṛṣṇa states in the *Bhagavad-gītā* (10.9),

mac-cittā mad-gata-prāṇā bodhayantaḥ parasparam
kathayantaś ca māṁ nityaṁ tuṣyanti ca ramanti ca

"The thoughts of My pure devotees dwell in Me, their lives are fully devoted to My service, and they derive great satisfaction and bliss from always enlightening one another and conversing about Me." Before beginning his Tenth Canto descriptions of Lord Kṛṣṇa, Śukadeva tells Mahārāja Parīkṣit,

nivṛtta-tarṣair upagīyamānād
bhavauṣadhāc chrotra-mano-'bhirāmāt

ka uttamaśloka-guṇānuvādāt
pumān virajyeta vinā paśu-ghnāt

"Descriptions of the Lord spoken by those who are free of material desires are the right medicine for the conditioned soul undergoing repeated birth and death, and they delight the ear and the mind. Therefore who will cease hearing such glorification of the Lord except a butcher or one who is killing his own self?" (*Bhāg.* 10.1.4).

Nārada Muni attributed his own Kṛṣṇa consciousness to the pure devotees (*bhakti-vedāntas*) whom he had served and heard speaking *kṛṣṇa-kathā* when he was only a five-year-old boy: "O Vyāsadeva, in that association and by the mercy of those great Vedāntists, I could hear them describe the attractive activities of Lord Kṛṣṇa. And thus listening attentively, my taste for hearing of the Personality of Godhead increased at every step" (*Bhāg.* 1.5.26). And so the opinion of Garga Muni—that *bhakti* consists of attraction for *kṛṣṇa-kathā*—is approved and practiced by the *mahā-janas.*

SŪTRA 18

अत्मरत्यविरोधेनेति शाण्डिल्यः ॥१८॥

ātma-raty-avirodheneti śāṇḍilyaḥ

ātma—in relation with the Supreme Soul; *rati*—of pleasure; *avirodhena*—by freedom from obstruction; *iti*—so; *śāṇḍilyaḥ*—Śāṇḍilya.

TRANSLATION

Śāṇḍilya says that *bhakti* results from one's removing all obstructions to taking pleasure in the Supreme Self.

PURPORT

Śāṇḍilya speaks of *ātma-rati,* "taking delight in the self." But what does "taking delight in the self" mean? According to the science of *bhakti,* that which delights the individual self (*jīvātmā*) is devotional service unto the Supreme Self, the Personality of Godhead. Śrīla Prabhupāda comments in *The Nectar of Devotion* (p. 288), "The devotees and self-realized persons who are engaged in preaching the glories of the Lord always maintain an ecstatic love for the Lord within their hearts. Thus they are benefited by the rays of the ecstatic moon, and they are called saintly persons." The state of *brahma-bhūta,* or the joy of discovering one's eternal nature, is only the beginning of spiritual life. *Mukti,* or liberation, when conceived of as impersonal liberation from birth and death, is also not the ultimate goal. As stated in the *Ādi Purāṇa,* "A person who is constantly engaged in chanting the holy name and who feels transcendental pleasure, being engaged in devotional service, is certainly awarded the facilities of devotional service, and never given just *mukti*" (*The Nectar of Devotion*, p. 104). There are many other statements in the Vedic scriptures that prove devotional service surpasses all other forms of liberation. In the *Dāmodarāṣṭaka,* part of the *Padma Purāṇa,* a devotee prays,

varaṁ deva mokṣaṁ na mokṣāvadhiṁ vā
na cānyaṁ vṛṇe 'haṁ vareśād apīha
idaṁ te vapur nātha gopāla-bālaṁ
sadā me manasy āvirāstāṁ kim anyaiḥ

"O Lord Dāmodara, although You are able to give all kinds of benedictions, I do not pray to You for the boon of impersonal liberation, nor for the highest liberation of eternal life in Vaikuṇṭha, nor for any other, similar boon. O Lord, I simply wish that this form of Yours as baby Gopāla in Vṛndāvana may ever be manifest in my heart, for what is the use to me of any other boon besides this?" (*Dāmodarāṣṭaka* 4).

A transcendentalist may seek *ātma-rati* in impersonal realization before he hears the glories of devotional service from pure devotees. For example, the four Kumāras and Śukadeva Gosvāmī were all Brahman-realized—but they were never offensive to the Supreme Personality of Godhead. As soon as the Kumāras and Śukadeva were introduced to pure Kṛṣṇa consciousness, they at once gave up their impersonal conceptions and became eager to render devotional service to the Lord. But stubborn Māyāvādīs who deride devotional service are in a different category. Lord Caitanya declared that the Māyāvādīs are great offenders to the Lord and that one should avoid their association.

A typical example of Māyāvādī poison is their interpretation of the word *ātma-rati* in this *sūtra.* The Māyāvādī claims that the worship (*pūjā*) and talking of the Lord (*kṛṣṇa-kathā*) mentioned in the two previous *sūtras* are meant to lead one beyond the Personality of Godhead to the *ātmā*. This is the impersonalist's timeserving attitude toward *bhakti*. He will worship the Lord and hear His *līlā,* but with the aim of finally denying the Personality of Godhead. He mistakenly thinks his meditation will lead him to realize that he is the all-pervading Brahman: "I am everything."

But if, as the Māyāvādīs claim, the ultimate bliss is to know that "I am God," then why has that bliss been missing up until now? If my identity is actually one in all respects with the all-pervading Godhead, then how did that identity become covered? What force has overcome the supreme *ātmā*? The fact is that the individual *ātmās,* being tiny, are prone to be covered by *māyā,* while the supreme *ātmā,* the Personality of Godhead, is never covered by *māyā* or separated from His *sac-cid-ānanda-vigraha,* His spiritual form of eternity, bliss, and knowledge. So while the individual soul can never become God—because he never *was* God—he can strive for his constitutional perfection as the eternal loving servant of God.

The Māyāvādīs are consistently defeated by the direct statements of Vedic scriptures. In the beginning of the *Bhagavad-gītā* (2.12), Lord Kṛṣṇa makes it clear that both He and the individual *ātmās* eternally exist as distinct entities. On the Battlefield of Kurukṣetra, where two huge armies had massed for war, Kṛṣṇa said to Arjuna,

na tv evāhaṁ jātu nāsaṁ na tvaṁ neme janādhipāḥ
na caiva na bhaviṣyāmaḥ sarve vayam ataḥ param

"Never was there a time when I did not exist, nor you, nor all these kings, nor in the future shall any of us cease to be." Kṛṣṇa reiterates this idea later in the *Bhagavad-gītā* (15.7): *mamaivāṁśo jīva-loke jīva-bhūtaḥ sanātanaḥ.* "The living entities in this conditioned world are My eternal fragmental parts." Also, the *Ṛg Veda* and the *Upaniṣads* state that the individual *ātmā* and the Paramātmā both reside in the heart of the living being, just as two birds sit in a tree. By the mercy of the Paramātmā, or "God in the heart," the individual *ātmā* may come to realize his eternal, blissful state of loving service to the Supreme Personality of Godhead. Attempts at concocting a *bhakti* devoid of eternal service to the Supreme Personality of Godhead are the works of demoniac minds. For genuine *bhakti* to exist, there must always be three factors: Bhagavān (the Supreme Lord), the *bhakta* (the eternal, subordinate servitor), and *bhakti* (loving exchanges between Bhagavān and the *bhakta*).

The Māyāvādīs ignore or distort the direct statements of the scriptures, as well as the words of the *mahā-janas*. We need not discuss their interpretations here, except to note that the Māyāvādīs are often attracted to the *bhakti-śāstras* because they find their own meditations too dry. Thus they approach books like the *Bhagavad-gītā*, the *Śrīmad-Bhāgavatam*, and the *Nārada-bhakti-sūtra*, but with an intention opposed to the aims of *bhakti*. By preaching that the forms of Lord Viṣṇu and His incarnations are material, the Māyāvādī commits a severe offense against the Lord. As Lord Kṛṣṇa says in the *Bhagavad-gītā* (9.11–12),

avajānanti māṁ mūḍhā mānuṣīṁ tanum āśritam
paraṁ bhāvam ajānanto mama bhūta-maheśvaram

moghāśā mogha-karmāṇo mogha-jñānā vicetasaḥ
rākṣasīṁ āsurīṁ caiva prakṛtiṁ mohinīṁ śritāḥ

"Fools deride Me when I descend in the human form. They do not know My transcendental nature as the Supreme Lord of all that be. Those who are thus bewildered are attracted by demoniac and atheistic views. In that deluded condition, their hopes for liberation, their fruitive activities, and their culture of knowledge are all defeated."

We can experience true *ātma-rati* only in the context of our eternal loving relationship with Kṛṣṇa, the reservoir of all pleasure. Even when we seek happiness with our material senses, we are indirectly seeking *ātma-rati*. We derive pleasure with the eyes or tongue or ears only because the *ātmā* is present within the living body. Therefore bodily pleasure depends on the existence of the *ātmā*. Furthermore, the *ātmā's* pleasure is dependent on the Paramātmā. And the Paramātmā is an expansion of Śrī Kṛṣṇa, the original form of the Personality of Godhead. So in all circumstances we are looking for our blissful relationship with Kṛṣṇa. Self-satisfaction actually means the satisfaction of serving and loving Kṛṣṇa, the Supreme Self.

SŪTRA 19

नारदस्तु तदर्पिताखिलाचारता तद्विस्मरणे परमव्याकुलतेति ॥१९॥

nāradas tu tad-arpitākhilācāratā tad-vismaraṇe parama-vyākulateti

nāradaḥ—Nārada; *tu*—but; *tat*—to Him; *arpita*—offered; *akhila*—all; *ācāratā*—having one's activities; *tat*—Him; *vismaraṇe*—in forgetting; *parama*—supreme; *vyākulatā*—distress; *iti*—so.

TRANSLATION

Nārada, however, says that *bhakti* consists of offering one's every act to the Supreme Lord and feeling extreme distress in forgetting Him.

PURPORT

Nārada previously gave three definitions of *bhakti,* according to three sages: (1) fondness for worshiping the Lord in various ways, (2) fondness for hearing narrations by or about the Lord, and (3) removing all obstacles to enjoying pleasure in the Self. Now Nārada gives his own opinion, which does not contradict these views but is their culmination.

Among all forms of the Supreme Lord, Śrī Kṛṣṇa is the original and most attractive. Similarly, among all Vaiṣṇavas, the pure devotees of Kṛṣṇa in Vṛndāvana are the best. Lord Caitanya declared that there is no better method of worshiping Kṛṣṇa than that practiced by the *gopīs* of Vṛndāvana. Here Nārada says that a pure devotee feels great distress upon forgetting the Lord even for a moment—but in the case of the *gopīs* there was never any question of forgetting Kṛṣṇa. They were so absorbed in thinking of Him that they could not even perform their household duties. In their intense loving dealings, the *gopīs* sometimes accused Kṛṣṇa of unfaithfulness, and they expressed a wish that they *could* forget Him. But they could not. As stated by Śrīmatī Rādhārāṇī, the chief of all the *gopīs:*

> We know all about Kṛṣṇa and how ungrateful He is. But here is the difficulty: In spite of His being so cruel and hardhearted, it is very difficult for us to give up talking about Him. Not only are we unable

to give up this talk, but great sages and saintly persons also engage in talking about Him. We *gopīs* of Vṛndāvana do not want to make any more friendships with this blackish boy, but we do not know how we shall be able to give up remembering and talking about His activities. [*Kṛṣṇa,* p. 377]

Out of intense humility Lord Caitanya once said that He did not have even a drop of love for Kṛṣṇa. He claimed that if He actually loved Kṛṣṇa, then how could He live in His absence? Far from proving a lack of love, of course, this kind of sentiment proves just the opposite—that Lord Caitanya was filled with the most exalted pure love for Kṛṣṇa. Although it was not possible for Lord Caitanya or the *gopīs* to forget Kṛṣṇa at any time, they still experienced the pain of separation from Him. In His *Śikṣāṣṭaka* (7), Lord Caitanya prays,

yugāyitaṁ nimeṣeṇa cakṣuṣā prāvṛṣāyitam
śūnyāyitaṁ jagat sarvaṁ govinda-viraheṇa me

"O Govinda! Because of separation from You, I consider even a moment a great millennium. Tears flow from my eyes like torrents of rain, and I see the entire world as void."

Here Nārada says that an essential ingredient of *bhakti* is dedicating one's every act to the service of the Lord. Unlike what passes for commitment to a cause in the material world, such dedication to Kṛṣṇa is all-encompassing. Because Lord Kṛṣṇa is the *summum bonum* of existence, the pure devotee can be with Him in every circumstance. And because the Lord is all-attractive, the devotee becomes increasingly attached to his beloved. As Kṛṣṇa declares in the *Bhagavad-gītā* (6.30),

yo māṁ paśyati sarvatra sarvaṁ ca mayi paśyati
tasyāhaṁ na praṇaśyāmi sa ca me na praṇaśyati

"For one who sees Me everywhere and sees everything in Me, I am never lost, nor is he ever lost to Me." To the materialists, with their splayed interests in sense gratification, the devotee's love may appear to be obsessive madness. But love for Kṛṣṇa actually brings one in touch with the truth, that *Kṛṣṇa is everything.*

One may ask whether the devotees' intense anguish experienced in separation from Kṛṣṇa contradicts Sūtra 18, wherein Śāṇḍilya defined *bhakti* as the bliss of self-realization. There is no contradiction, because the pain of separation felt by Lord Caitanya and other pure devotees is a variety of transcendental bliss. In the realm of spiritual emotions experienced by those at the stage of *prema,* love of God, both sadness and happiness are absolute and blissful. Speculative philosophers and less advanced devotees cannot know this, but we may hear about it from the scriptures and see it in the lives of self-realized saints.

A devotee's self-surrender means that he wants nothing in return for his loving service. He only wants Kṛṣṇa to be pleased. Selflessness does not mean a complete loss of ego. Total self-annihilation is impossible (despite the wishes of the voidists), but *ahaṅkāra,* or false ego, is dissolved by devotional service and replaced by true ego, the understanding that "I am an eternal servant of the Lord." The true self-interest of the living being lies in freedom from selfishness and, as Nārada says here, "the offering of one's every act to the Supreme Lord." We are all eternally part and parcel of the Supreme Being, Kṛṣṇa; as such, we can experience full satisfaction only through giving Him pleasure. *Kṛṣṇe tuṣṭe jagat tuṣṭam:* "When Kṛṣṇa is satisfied, everyone is satisfied."

The beginner in devotional service can practice selflessness by surrendering to the bona fide spiritual master. The devotee is advised to give all he has to the service of his *guru* and to always consider his *guru* his well-wisher. Devotees who practice such selfless service of the *guru* and the Supreme Lord never want anything in return, yet they eventually receive the greatest reward—the Lord's intimate association. As Kṛṣṇa says,

man-manā bhava mad-bhakto mad-yājī māṁ namas-kuru
mām evaiṣyasi satyaṁ te pratijāne priyo 'si me

"Always think of Me, become My devotee, worship Me, and offer your homage unto Me. Thus you will come to Me without fail. I promise you this because you are My very dear friend" (Bg. 18.65).

SŪTRA 20

अस्त्येवमेवम् ॥२०॥

asty evam evam

asti—it is; *evam evam*—like each of these.

TRANSLATION

***Bhakti* is, in fact, correctly described in each of these ways.**

PURPORT

The definitions of *bhakti* given above—by Śrīla Vyāsadeva, Garga Muni, Śāṇḍilya, and Nārada Muni—are not in conflict. While Nārada has given us his own definition, here he says that the others are also valid. *Bhakti* is in fact a universal principle present at least partially in all theistic religions. Indeed, within many religions one could find a definition of love of God that would not contradict the conclusions of Nārada Muni and the principles of Kṛṣṇa consciousness taught by the followers of Lord Caitanya.

Nārada has defined the highest form of *bhakti*. But is such a perfect state possible? The answer is yes. Unless devotees from time to time manifest pure *bhakti*, aspirants on the spiritual path would have nothing to emulate and strive for, and they might conclude that *parama-bhakti* is only an imaginary ideal. As Lord Caitanya says, *dharma-sthāpana-hetu sādhura vyavahāra:* "A devotee's behavior establishes the true purpose of religious principles" (Cc. *Madhya* 17.185).

Once Sanātana Gosvāmī pretended to be devoted to a *sannyāsī* named Mukunda Sarasvatī, rather than to Lord Caitanya. When Lord Caitanya's intimate servant Jagadānanda Paṇḍita saw Sanātana's behavior, he became very angry and threatened to beat Sanātana. Sanātana then revealed his purpose: "My dear Jagadānanda Paṇḍita, you are a greatly learned saint. No one is dearer to Śrī Caitanya Mahāprabhu than you. This faith in Lord Caitanya befits you quite well. Unless you demonstrate it, how could I learn such faith?" (Cc. *Antya* 13.59).

We have seen the example of complete self-surrender and dedication of one's activities to Kṛṣṇa in the life of His Divine Grace

A. C. Bhaktivedanta Swami Prabhupāda. Śrīla Prabhupāda's sanctity was not a private affair: he gave of himself profusely and was empowered to bring thousands of people to Kṛṣṇa consciousness. Thus he perfectly fulfilled the criterion given by Śrīla Bhaktivinoda Ṭhākura—that one can tell the quality of a Vaiṣṇava by how many persons he convinces to become Vaiṣṇavas. By his personal preaching, by his books, and by the Kṛṣṇa consciousness movement he created and nurtured, Śrīla Prabhupāda showed the example of a life dedicated purely to pleasing Kṛṣṇa. The potency of his acts continues as an ongoing legacy, accessible to anyone interested in taking up the path of *bhakti-yoga.* We are assured, therefore, of finding examples of perfect *bhakti* in the past, at present, and in the future.

Here Nārada states that each authority he has quoted has described *bhakti* in his own authentic way. But in the next *sūtra* Nārada will say that the *gopīs* of Vraja are exemplars of *bhakti.* Of the brief definitions of *bhakti* given in Sūtras 16 through 19, we find that Nārada's own definition best fits the *gopīs:* "*Bhakti* consists of offering one's every act to the Supreme Lord and feeling extreme distress in forgetting Him."

SŪTRA 21

यथा व्रजगोपिकानाम् ॥२१॥

yathā vraja-gopikānām

yathā—as; *vraja*—of Vraja; *gopikānām*—of the cowherd women.

TRANSLATION

The cowherd women of Vraja are an example of pure *bhakti.*

PURPORT

In Sūtra 19, Nārada gave the ultimate definition of *bhakti.* This has led him inevitably to mention the topmost of all devotees, the *gopīs* of Vraja. Nārada might have mentioned other renowned *bhaktas,* such as Uddhava, Arjuna, Prahlāda Mahārāja, or mother Yaśodā, but he has chosen to give the singular example of the *gopīs.* Nārada's opinion is shared by all realized Vaiṣṇavas, because the *gopīs* are renowned as the best lovers of Lord Kṛṣṇa. The *gopīs* are most exalted because they gave everything, and sacrificed everything, for their beloved. As Śrīla Kṛṣṇadāsa Kavirāja writes in the *Caitanya-caritāmṛta* (*Ādi* 4.167–69),

> Social customs, scriptural injunctions, bodily demands, fruitive action, shyness, patience, bodily pleasures, self-gratification on the path of *varṇāśrama-dharma,* which is difficult to give up—the *gopīs* have forsaken all these, along with their families, and suffered their relatives' punishment and scolding, all for the sake of serving Lord Kṛṣṇa. They render loving service to Him for the sake of His enjoyment.

The *gopīs' rasa* with Kṛṣṇa is *mādhurya,* or conjugal love. But even *bhaktas* who worship the Lord in other *rasas* acknowledge the supermost place of the *gopīs* in the kingdom of *bhakti.* Nārada Muni, for example, usually associates with Lord Kṛṣṇa in His opulent features in Vaikuṇṭha or Dvārakā. In his exchanges with Lord Kṛṣṇa, Nārada often praises the Lord's inconceivable opulence. For example, once when Nārada visited Kṛṣṇa in many of His sixteen thousand palaces, he was astonished to see how the Lord had expanded Himself so He could be alone with each of His queens. "Your transcendental position is always inconceivable to everyone," said Nārada. "As far as I am concerned, I can simply offer my respectful obeisances to You again and again" (*Kṛṣṇa,* p. 603). Since Nārada is one of the Lord's learned and intimate devotees, he is aware that the *gopīs* exemplify the topmost expression of love for Kṛṣṇa. Similarly, devotees such as Śukadeva Gosvāmī, Bhīṣmadeva, and Vyāsadeva appreciate the *gopīs'* exalted position.

Even the impersonalists are attracted to Kṛṣṇa's loving affairs with the *gopīs,* although they cannot understand them. Attempting to praise the *gopīs* of Vṛndāvana, one impersonalist "Swami" said, "*Gopī-līlā* is the acme of the religion of love, in which individuality vanishes and there is communion." But it's not a fact that "individuality vanishes," either for the *gopīs* or for any other living entity. As we have pointed out above, Lord Kṛṣṇa clearly and repeatedly states that both His individuality and the living entities' are eternal. The *gopīs* did, however, completely lose their selfish interest—their interest became entirely one with Lord Kṛṣṇa's. To consider the *gopīs' rāsa* dance with Kṛṣṇa merely a stage leading to merging into the impersonal Brahman is a great insult to the *gopīs* and to *gopī-līlā,* even though one's intent is to praise. When they appeared before Kṛṣṇa in the moonlit forest of Vṛndāvana, the *gopīs* certainly did not want Him to instruct them about "merging" with Him through *jñāna-yoga,* nor did they see the *rāsa* dance in that way. Speaking in the mood of Śrīmatī Rādhārāṇī as She met with Kṛṣṇa at Kurukṣetra, Lord Caitanya once complained to Him about His attempt to teach *yoga* and meditation to the *gopīs:*

> My dear Kṛṣṇa, formerly, when You were staying at Mathurā, You sent Uddhava to teach Me speculative knowledge and mystic *yoga.* Now You Yourself are speaking the same thing, but My mind does not accept it. There is no place in My mind for *jñāna-yoga* or *dhyāna-yoga.* Although You know Me very well, You are still instructing Me in *dhyāna-yoga* and *jñāna-yoga.* It is not right for You to do so. I would like to withdraw My consciousness from You and engage it in material activities, but even though I try, I cannot do so. I am naturally inclined to You only. Therefore Your instructions for Me to meditate on You are simply ludicrous. . . . . It is not very good for You to think of Me as a candidate for Your instructions. [Cc. *Madhya* 13.139–40]

SŪTRA 22

तत्रापि न माहात्म्यज्ञानविस्मृत्यपवादः ॥२२॥

tatrāpi na māhātmya-jñāna-vismṛty-apavādaḥ

tatra—in that case; *api*—even; *na*—there is not; *māhātmya*—of greatness; *jñāna*—of awareness; *vismṛti*—of forgetting; *apavādaḥ*—criticism.

TRANSLATION

Even in the case of the *gopīs,* one cannot criticize them for forgetting the Lord's greatness.

PURPORT

Nārada is replying to a possible criticism: Although all Vaiṣṇavas praise the *gopīs,* and though even the impersonalists join in the chorus, some philosophers think the *gopīs'* love is uninformed. Because the *gopīs* were attracted to Kṛṣṇa as a beautiful young boy, and because they ran from their homes in the dead of night to dance with Him in the moonlit Vṛndāvana forest, foolish critics think the *gopīs* did not know that Kṛṣṇa is the Supreme Personality of Godhead.

The accusation against the *gopīs* is false, says Nārada. The *gopīs* knew that Śrī Kṛṣṇa is the Supreme Person, but in their intimate *rasa* with Him they put aside the awe and reverence usually offered to the Supreme Lord. The Lord's internal potency, Yogamāyā, allows loving intimacy to overshadow God's majesty. But this does not mean that pure devotees like the *gopīs* lack spiritual advancement. Except for the *gopīs* Kṛṣṇa brought with Him from the spiritual world, all the *gopīs* came to their position of *mādhurya-rasa* only after many lifetimes of austerity and spiritual cultivation. Regarding the cowherd boys (*gopas*) who play with Kṛṣṇa, the *Śrīmad-Bhāgavatam* states that they attained their position "only after accumulating heaps of pious activities" in many lives. So although it may sometimes appear that the liberated devotees have forgotten that Lord Kṛṣṇa is God, this is actually an arrangement by Yogamāyā for increasing the pleasure of the Lord and His devotees.

For example, as Vasudeva carried his baby son Kṛṣṇa across the Yamunā River, the baby fell into the river. Śrīla Prabhupāda writes, "Just to test the intense love of Vasudeva, Lord Kṛṣṇa fell down into the waters of the Yamunā while His father was crossing the river. Vasudeva became mad after his child as he tried to recover Him in the midst of the rising river" (*Bhāg.* 3.2.17, purport). Lord Kṛṣṇa did not want Vasudeva to think, "Oh, Kṛṣṇa will save Himself; He's God," but He wanted to evoke the paternal *rasa* in full intensity. In a similar way, mother Yaśodā sometimes expressed her maternal love for baby Kṛṣṇa by punishing Him. And when His mother came to punish Him, Kṛṣṇa reciprocated by running away in fear. Śrīla Prabhupāda describes this apparent contradiction as follows:

> The Lord's pure devotee renders service unto the Lord out of unalloyed love only, and while discharging such devotional service the pure devotee forgets the position of the Supreme Lord. The Supreme Lord also accepts the loving service of His devotees more relishably when the service is rendered spontaneously out of pure affection, without any reverential admiration. . . . If mother Yaśodā had been conscious of the exalted position of the Lord, she would

> certainly have hesitated to punish the Lord. But she was made to forget this situation because the Lord wanted to make a complete gesture of childishness before the affectionate Yaśodā. . . . Mother Yaśodā is praised for her unique position of love, for she could control even the all-powerful Lord as her beloved child. [*Bhāg.* 1.8.31, purport]

Another prominent example is Arjuna, Kṛṣṇa's friend, who accepted the infallible Lord as his chariot driver.

As for the *gopīs* of Vraja, they often manifested deep knowledge of Kṛṣṇa's divinity. But they never diminished their conjugal mood in order to become scholars or meditators. Kṛṣṇa wanted to dance with the most beautiful girls in the universe, and so the *gopīs,* His completely surrendered servants, happily complied. When Kṛṣṇa called the *gopīs* to Him in the dead of night, He first began to lecture them on morality. The *gopīs* complained to Him about this attitude, and yet their statements indicate that they knew very well who He was. The *gopīs* said to Kṛṣṇa,

> Within these three worlds there is no distinction between men and women in relation to You because both men and women belong to the marginal potency, or *prakṛti.* No one is actually the enjoyer, or male; everyone is meant to be enjoyed by You. There is no woman within these three worlds who cannot but deviate from her path of chastity when she is attracted to You because Your beauty is so sublime that not only men and women, but cows, birds, beasts, and even trees, fruits, and flowers—everyone and everything—become enchanted, and what to speak of ourselves? [*Kṛṣṇa,* p. 252]

After Lord Kṛṣṇa left Vṛndāvana, He sent Uddhava to deliver a message to the *gopīs*. When Uddhava saw the *gopīs'* undying devotion for Śrī Kṛṣṇa, he praised their transcendental perfection:

> My dear *gopīs,* the mentality you have developed in relationship to Kṛṣṇa is very, very difficult to attain, even for great sages and saintly persons. You have attained the highest perfectional stage of life. It is a great boon for you that you have fixed your minds upon Kṛṣṇa and have decided to have Kṛṣṇa only, giving up your family, homes, relatives, husbands, and children for the sake of the Supreme Personality. Because your minds are now fully absorbed in Kṛṣṇa, the

> Supreme Soul, universal love has automatically developed in you. I think myself very fortunate that I have been favored, by your grace, to see you in this situation. [*Kṛṣṇa*, p. 380]

The *gopīs* were always impatient when either Uddhava or Kṛṣṇa spoke philosophy to them, because all they wanted was to be alone with Kṛṣṇa in the Vṛndāvana mood. So when Uddhava praised them, they did not find it very pleasing. Sometimes they even denounced Kṛṣṇa's behavior, and yet they remained aware of His supreme and independent position. As one *gopī* said, "Kṛṣṇa is the Supreme Personality of Godhead, the husband of the goddess of fortune, and He is self-sufficient. He has no business either with us—the girls of Vṛndāvana forest—or with the city girls in Mathurā. He is the great Supersoul; He has nothing to do with any of us, either here or there" (*Kṛṣṇa*, p. 386).

It is offensive to judge the *gopīs* according to ordinary standards of human behavior. The intimacy Kṛṣṇa allowed them is inconceivable, and no one can understand it except those who are completely free of material desires. The *gopīs'* love is certainly beyond awe and reverence, and yet it is never mundane.

The impersonalist sometimes tries to jump on the bandwagon of praise for the *gopīs*. He says that the *gopīs* cannot be understood by people infected with worldly lust, but then he himself commits an even worse offense: he thinks Kṛṣṇa's affairs with the *gopīs* are "allegories that contain profound spiritual truths." Behind the Māyāvādī's admiration of *gopī-bhāva* is the desire to commit spiritual annihilation, to become one with God. In other words, the impersonalist thinks that at the last stage of perfection, a *gopī* will realize that her beloved Kṛṣṇa is her very self. We have already pointed out the foolishness of these claims, but we do so again just to expose the impersonalist's so-called praise of *kṛṣṇa-līlā*.

By contrast, Nārada Muni's praise of the *gopīs'* devotion to Lord Kṛṣṇa is upheld by all *śāstras* and sages.

SŪTRA 23

तद्विहीनं जाराणामिव ॥२३॥

tad-vihīnaṁ jārāṇām iva

tat—of it (awareness of the Lord's greatness); *vihīnam*—devoid; *jārāṇām*—of illicit lovers; *iva*—like.

TRANSLATION

On the other hand, displays of devotion without knowledge of God's greatness are no better than the affairs of illicit lovers.

PURPORT

The *gopīs'* loving exchanges with Kṛṣṇa have nothing to do with mundane passion, but because they resemble lusty activities in the material world, those with impure minds mistake them for such. Śrīla Prabhupāda was therefore always very cautious in presenting Lord Kṛṣṇa's *rāsa-līlā.* Lord Caitanya was also very cautious in discussing such topics. Although He was always merged in *gopī-bhāva,* He discussed Kṛṣṇa's loving affairs with the *gopīs* only with a few intimate disciples. For the mass of people, Lord Caitanya distributed love of God by propagating the congregational chanting of the holy name.

Śrīla Prabhupāda would sometimes tell a story to show how most people mistake the transcendental loving affairs of Rādhā and Kṛṣṇa as mundane dealings between an ordinary boy and girl. Once there was a fire in a barn, and one of the cows almost died of fright. Afterward, whenever that cow saw the color red, she would think a fire was burning and become panic-stricken. Similarly, as soon as an ordinary man or woman sees a picture of Rādhā and Kṛṣṇa, he or she immediately thinks Their relationship is just like that between an ordinary boyfriend and girlfriend or husband and wife. Unfortunately, professional reciters of the *Bhāgavatam* promote this misconception by jumping into Lord Kṛṣṇa's conjugal pastimes in the Tenth Canto, although neither they nor their audience are fit to hear them. The authorized approach to the *Bhāgavatam* is to first carefully read the first nine cantos, which establish the greatness of the Supreme Lord, His universal form, His material and spiritual energies, His creation of the cosmos, His incarnations, and so on. Reading the first two cantos is like contemplating the lotus feet of the Lord, and as one gradually progresses, one looks upon the Lord's various bodily limbs, until finally one sees His smiling face in the Tenth Canto's account of His pastimes with the *gopīs.*

If Kṛṣṇa's pastimes with the *gopīs'* were lusty affairs, neither pure *brahmacārīs* like Nārada and Śukadeva nor liberated sages like Uddhava and Vyāsadeva would have praised them so highly. Such great devotees are free from all mundane passion; so how could they be interested in Rādhā and Kṛṣṇa if Their love were a worldly sex affair?

From the *Śrīmad-Bhāgavatam* we learn that all the *gopīs* had spiritual bodies. This is another proof that Kṛṣṇa's pastimes with the *gopīs* are supramundane. When Kṛṣṇa played His flute in Vṛndāvana on the full-moon night of the autumn season, the *gopīs* went to Him in their spiritual bodies. Many of these *gopīs* are eternal companions of Kṛṣṇa, and when He exhibits His transcendental pastimes within the material world, they come with Him. But some of the *gopīs* who joined Kṛṣṇa's pastimes within this material world came from the status of ordinary human beings. By always thinking of Kṛṣṇa as their beloved, they became purified of all material contamination and elevated to the same status as the eternally liberated *gopīs*. Śrīla Prabhupāda writes, "All the *gopīs* who concentrated their minds on Kṛṣṇa in the spirit of paramour love became fully uncontaminated from all the fruitive reactions of material nature, and some of them immediately gave up their material bodies developed under the three modes of material nature" (*Kṛṣṇa,* p. 242). Śrīla Viśvanātha Cakravartī Ṭhākura explains in his commentary on the *Śrīmad-Bhāgavatam* that here "giving up the material body" does not mean dying but rather purification of all material contamination and attainment of a purely spiritual body.

When Śukadeva Gosvāmī began reciting Kṛṣṇa's *rāsa-līlā* pastimes, Mahārāja Parīkṣit raised a doubt similar to that addressed in this *sūtra.* He asked, "How could the *gopīs* attain liberation by thinking of a paramour?" Śukadeva replied that even if one thinks that the *gopīs* were motivated by lust, *any* association with Kṛṣṇa will purify one of all material desires. Because He is the Supreme Personality of Godhead, even someone like Śiśupāla, who was absorbed in thinking of Kṛṣṇa out of envy, gained salvation. As Śrīla Prabhupāda explains in *Kṛṣṇa* (p. 245):

> The conclusion is that if one somehow or other becomes attached to Kṛṣṇa or attracted to Him, either because of His beauty, quality, opulence, fame, strength, renunciation, or knowledge, or even through lust, anger, or fear, or through affection or friendship, then one's salvation and freedom from material contamination are assured.

The society girl Kubjā is an example of how even lusty attraction to Kṛṣṇa frees one from material contamination. She approached Kṛṣṇa with lusty desire, but her lust was relieved just by smelling the fragrance of Kṛṣṇa's lotus feet.

While the word *kāma* (lust) is used to describe the *gopīs'* feelings toward Kṛṣṇa, in their case it is actually a transcendental emotion. The *gopīs* wanted Kṛṣṇa to be their husband, but there was no possibility of His marrying all of them in the usual sense. So they married regular husbands (though some were unmarried at the time of the *rāsa* dance) but retained their love for Kṛṣṇa. Therefore Kṛṣṇa's loving relationship with the *gopīs* is known as *pārakīya-rasa* (paramour love). But whereas in the material world the relationship of a married woman with a paramour is abominable, in the spiritual world it is the most exalted relationship one can have with Kṛṣṇa. Just as a tree reflected in the water appears upside down, so that which is topmost in the spiritual world—Kṛṣṇa's loving dealings with the *gopīs*—becomes abominable when reflected in the material world as illicit sexual affairs. When people imitate Kṛṣṇa's *rāsa* dance with the *gopīs,* they enjoy only the perverted reflection of the transcendental *pārakīya-rasa.* Śrīla Prabhupāda writes in *Kṛṣṇa* (p. 240), "It is stated in the *Śrīmad-Bhāgavatam* that one should not imitate this *pārakīya-rasa* even in dream or imagination. Those who do so drink the most deadly poison."

Another characteristic of mundane paramour love is that it is unsteady. As soon as one's sex pleasure is disrupted, one seeks out a new partner. The *Śrīmad-Bhāgavatam* predicts that in the Age of Kali marriage will become degraded to a mere convenience for sex pleasure and will break apart as soon as that pleasure abates. But once one revives one's loving relationship with Kṛṣṇa, that relationship will remain steady and ever fresh.

The *gopīs'* love for Kṛṣṇa is within Śrī Kṛṣṇa's *hlādinī-śakti,* or internal pleasure potency. When Śrī Kṛṣṇa wants to enjoy, He associates with the *gopīs,* not with women of the material world. This is another indication of the *gopīs'* superexcellent spiritual position. In Kṛṣṇa's exchanges with the *gopīs* through the *hlādinī-śakti,* there is unlimited and unending ecstasy; this pleasure is far different from the quickly satiated lusts of sexual affairs, which are soon followed by painful entanglements and karmic reactions.

Even after Śukadeva Gosvāmī had explained the spiritual nature of the love that Kṛṣṇa and the *gopīs* exchanged during the *rāsa* dance, Mahārāja Parīkṣit questioned Śukadeva as to why Kṛṣṇa would act in a way that would make ordinary people see Him as immoral. Śukadeva replied that because Lord Kṛṣṇa is the supreme *īśvara,* or controller, He is independent of all social and religious principles. This is simply more evidence of His greatness. As the supreme *īśvara,* Lord Kṛṣṇa may sometimes violate His own instructions with impunity, but that is possible only for the supreme controller, not for us. Since no one can imitate such astounding activities of Lord Kṛṣṇa's as creating the universe or lifting Govardhana Hill, no one should try to imitate His *rāsa* dance, either. To further clear up all doubts about Kṛṣṇa and the *gopīs,* one may read Chapter Thirty-two of *Kṛṣṇa, the Supreme Personality of Godhead.*

SŪTRA 24

नास्त्येव तस्मिंस्तत्सुखसुखित्वम् ॥२४॥

nāsty eva tasmiṁs tat-sukha-sukhitvam

na—there is not; *eva*—indeed; *tasmin*—in it; *tat*—His; *sukha*—in the happiness; *sukhitvam*—finding happiness.

TRANSLATION

In such false devotion one does not find pleasure exclusively in the Lord's pleasure.

PURPORT

As already explained, lust is as different from love as iron is from gold. Śrīla Kṛṣṇadāsa Kavirāja states,

ātmendriya-prīti-vāñchā—tāre bali 'kāma'
kṛṣṇendriya-prīti-icchā dhare 'prema' nāma

"The desire to gratify one's own senses is *kāma* [lust], but the desire to please the senses of Lord Kṛṣṇa is *prema* [love]" (Cc. *Ādi* 4.165). Śrīmatī Rādhārāṇī expresses Her pure love for Kṛṣṇa in this way:

"I do not mind My personal distress. I only wish for the happiness of Kṛṣṇa, for His happiness is the goal of My life. However, if He feels great happiness in giving Me distress, that distress is the best of My happiness" (Cc. *Antya* 20.52).

Kṛṣṇadāsa Kavirāja informs us, "The *gopīs* have no inclination for their own enjoyment, and yet their joy increases. That is indeed a contradiction." The solution to this contradiction is that "the joy of the *gopīs* lies in the joy of their beloved Kṛṣṇa" (Cc. *Ādi* 4.188–89). Although the *gopīs* are the leaders in this selfless love for the Lord, all Vaiṣṇavas share in this sentiment. When Lord Nṛsiṁhadeva wanted to offer a benediction to Prahlāda Mahārāja, who had undergone so much suffering on the Lord's account, Prahlāda declined. He said he had not performed his devotional service in the mood of a merchant seeking profit in exchange for service: "O my Lord, I am Your unmotivated servant, and You are my eternal master. There is no need for our being anything other than master and servant. You are naturally my master, and I am naturally Your servant. We have no other relationship" (*Bhāg.* 7.10.6).

In a similar mood, Mādhavendra Purī underwent difficult austerities in order to carry a load of sandalwood for the sake of his beloved Gopāla Deity. Mādhavendra walked thousands of miles through territory governed by Muhammadans and filled with thieves and watchmen. Describing Mādhavendra's service, Lord Caitanya said, "This is the natural result of intense love of Godhead. The devotee does not consider personal inconveniences or impediments. In all circumstances he wants to serve the Supreme Personality of Godhead" (Cc. *Madhya* 4.186).

Like the *gopīs,* all pure devotees feel great happiness when serving Kṛṣṇa, even when that service entails severe austerity. Śrīla Prabhupāda writes, "It is said that when one sees apparent unhappiness or distress in a perfect Vaiṣṇava, it is not at all unhappiness for him; rather it is transcendental bliss" (Cc. *Madhya* 4.186, purport).

We may ask, Why does a devotee approach Lord Kṛṣṇa with pure selfless love, seeking only to please Him? To understand the answer to this question, one has to personally experience such love. There are glimmers of such love even in the material world, as in the love a mother feels for her child. Even within the animal kingdom a mother sometimes risks her life to protect her offspring. But *pure* selfless love exists only in relation to the all-attractive Personality of Godhead. One cannot precisely analyze this love in intellectual terms, but one can experience it with a purified heart.

The secret driving force for the devotees is the all-attractive nature of Kṛṣṇa and the fact that He is the Self of all selves. Śukadeva Gosvāmī explains this in the *Śrīmad-Bhāgavatam* (10.14.50–57), after he relates how Kṛṣṇa expanded Himself into all the calves and cowherd boys of Vṛndāvana. When Kṛṣṇa expanded Himself in this way, the parents of the boys and calves felt increased love for their offspring. Upon hearing the account of this miraculous pastime, Mahārāja Parīkṣit asked, "When Kṛṣṇa expanded Himself, why is it that the boys' parents became more loving toward Him than toward their own sons? Also, why did the cows become so loving toward the calves, more so than toward their own calves?" Śukadeva replied that since what is most attractive to the living being is his own self, and since Kṛṣṇa, as the Supersoul, is the Self of all selves, He is the all-attractive center for everyone. Therefore, when He expanded Himself as the calves and boys of Vṛndavāna, the calves' and boys' parents were more affectionate toward Kṛṣṇa's expansions than toward their own offspring.

By loving Kṛṣṇa, a person realizes his love for all living beings. In other words, universal love is a part of God consciousness. This is expressed in two great commandments of the Bible: "Thou shalt love the Lord thy God with all thine heart, and with all thy soul, and with all thy might" (Deuteronomy 6:5); and "Thou shalt love they neighbor as thyself" (Matthew 19:19). Prabhupāda would give a homely example to show how love of God implies universal love: When a man marries a woman, he also gains a relationship with her whole family and may quickly develop affection for his new in-laws. Similarly, if one develops love for Kṛṣṇa, the father of all living beings, one immediately becomes aware of one's loving relationship with all Kṛṣṇa's children. A devotee who even partially realizes his love for Kṛṣṇa wants to work to fulfill Kṛṣṇa's mission in this world, which is to help all living beings end their suffering and go back to Godhead. When one does this not for fame as a preacher and not as a professional business—but as a humble servant meeting all difficulties for the sake of spreading Kṛṣṇa consciousness—he becomes the dearmost servant of the Lord. This is the perfection of happiness in spiritual love, and it is completely unlike lust, the desire for one's own pleasure.

SŪTRA 25

सा तु कर्मज्ञानयोगेभ्योऽप्यधिकतरा ॥२५॥

sā tu karma-jñāna-yogebhyo 'py adhikatarā

sā—it; *tu*—but; *karma*—to fruitive work; *jñāna*—speculative knowledge; *yogebhyaḥ*—and mystic meditation; *api*—indeed; *adhikatarā*—superior.

TRANSLATION

Pure devotional service, on the other hand, is far superior to fruitive work, philosophical speculation, and mystic meditation.

PURPORT

Having described the *gopīs* of Vraja as the topmost example of *parā bhakti,* Nārada now turns his attention to *bhakti-yoga* in general. Here Nārada asserts that all *bhaktas* are categorically superior to other Vedic practitioners. The classification of human beings into *karmīs, jñānīs, yogīs,* and *bhaktas* is itself a brilliant gift of Vedic knowledge. Let us see why, out of the full range of possible activities, *bhakti* is the highest.

Karma refers in the broadest sense to any activity, but it often means activities performed within the bounds of Vedic injunctions with the intention of enjoying the results. (Another term, *vikarma,* is used for activity forbidden by the *Vedas.*) So *karma,* although having religious stature, is still material. The *karmī* is interested in rewards like money, sense pleasure, and fame in this life, and he also seeks promotion to higher planets in the next life. The great defect of *karma* is that it always results in reactions, which force the *karmī* to take another material birth by the process of transmigration of the soul. Therefore, whether "good" or "bad," pious or impious, all *karma* keeps one bound within the cycle of birth and death.

Jñāna refers to the cultivation of knowledge. The *jñānī* sees the shortcomings of *karma* and begins to inquire into higher truth. *Jñānīs* are generally philosophers and meditators. They are not interested merely in material results, but in knowledge for its own sake. By cultivating *jñāna* through the study of Vedic *śāstras* or through meditation, the *jñānī* can come to the brink of spiritual knowledge, awareness of eternal Brahman. But unless he goes further and understands his relationship with the Supreme Personality of Godhead, he will suffer the same defeat as the *karmī*—confinement within the cycle of birth and death. A prayer to Kṛṣṇa by the demigods points up the *jñānīs'* shortcoming:

> O lotus-eyed Lord, although nondevotees who accept severe austerities and penances to achieve the highest position may think themselves liberated, their intelligence is impure. They fall down from their position of imagined superiority because they have no regard for Your lotus feet. [*Bhāg.* 10.2.32]

The third category of human endeavor is *yoga*. Lord Kṛṣṇa describes the *yogī* as follows: "A *yogī* is greater than the ascetic, greater than the empiricist, and greater than the fruitive worker. Therefore, O Arjuna, in all circumstances be a *yogī*" (Bg. 6.46). There are many types of *yoga*, such as *haṭha-yoga, aṣṭāṅga-yoga, rāja-yoga, dhyāna-yoga,* and *bhakti-yoga*. Rudimentary *haṭha-yoga* has become very popular as a form of exercise and relaxation, but real *yoga*—as taught by Patañjali in his *Yoga-sūtra* or by Kṛṣṇa in the Sixth Chapter of *Bhagavad-gītā*—is an eightfold system of meditation for attaining *samādhi,* or complete absorption of the mind in the Supreme. The eightfold *yoga* process is very difficult to perform, and even Arjuna decided it was too difficult for him. And those few who *can* practice it often become captivated by the *siddhis,* or perfections, that one can gain through this *yoga,* such as the ability to walk on water, become extremely small, and control other people's minds. So the mystic *yoga* process, being very difficult and full of many possible distractions, is not recommended in this age.

Activities of *karma, jñāna,* and *yoga* are not condemned as such by those practicing *bhakti,* devotional service. Rather, when these lesser activities are dovetailed in the service of the Supreme Lord, they are favorable methods of devotional service. For example, when *karma,* or activity, is joined with devotional service, it becomes *karma-yoga,* action in Kṛṣṇa consciousness. Lord Kṛṣṇa recommends this in the *Bhagavad-gītā* (9.27):

yat karoṣi yad aśnāsi yaj juhoṣi dadāsi yat
yat tapasyasi kaunteya tat kuruṣva mad-arpaṇam

"Whatever you do, whatever you eat, whatever you offer or give away, and whatever austerities you perform—do that, O son of Kuntī, as an offering to Me" (Bg. 9.27).

Those who cultivate knowledge (*jñāna*) are often very proud and consider themselves superior to devotees. But the perfection of knowledge is to surrender to the Supreme Personality of Godhead and realize that He is everything. Then *jñāna* becomes *jñāna-yoga* and is purified of mental speculation. As Kṛṣṇa says in the *Bhagavad-gītā* (7.19),

bahūnāṁ janmanām ante jñānavān māṁ prapadyate
vāsudevaḥ sarvam iti sa mahātmā su-durlabhaḥ

"After many births and deaths, he who is actually in knowledge surrenders unto Me, knowing Me to be the cause of all causes and all that is. Such a great soul is very rare" (Bg. 7.19).

Similarly, Kṛṣṇa tells Arjuna at the end of the Sixth Chapter of the *Gītā* that absorption in Kṛṣṇa consciousness is the ultimate *yoga:*

yoginām api sarveṣāṁ mad-gatenāntar ātmanā
śraddhāvān bhajate yo māṁ sa me yuktatamo mataḥ

"And of all *yogīs,* the one with great faith who always abides in Me, thinks of Me within himself, and renders transcendental loving service to Me—he is the most intimately united with Me in *yoga* and is the highest of all. That is My opinion" (Bg. 6.47).

So *karma, jñāna,* and *yoga* can become favorable for Kṛṣṇa consciousness. But direct *parā bhakti* is the conclusion of Lord Kṛṣṇa's teachings in the *Bhagavad-gītā:*

man-manā bhava mad-bhakto mad-yājī māṁ namas-kuru
mām evaiṣyasi satyaṁ te pratijāne priyo 'si me

sarva-dharmān parityajya mām ekaṁ śaraṇaṁ vraja
ahaṁ tvāṁ sarva-pāpebhyo mokṣayiṣyāmi mā śucaḥ

"Always think of Me, become My devotee, worship Me, and offer your homage unto Me. Thus you will come to Me without fail. I promise you this because you are My very dear friend. Abandon all varieties of religion and just surrender unto Me. I shall deliver you from all sinful reactions. Do not fear" (Bg. 18.65–66).

Thus in the *Bhagavad-gītā* Lord Kṛṣṇa confirms Nārada's assertion here that *bhakti* is supreme.

SŪTRA 26

फलरूपत्वात् ॥२६॥

phala-rūpatvāt

phala—of the fruit; *rūpatvāt*—because of being the form.

TRANSLATION

After all, *bhakti* is the fruit of all endeavor.

PURPORT

Bhakti is more than a process leading to a result: it is the constitutional nature of the living being. As Lord Caitanya states in the *Caitanya-caritāmṛta* (*Madhya* 20.108), *jīvera 'svarūpa' haya—kṛṣṇera 'nitya-dāsa'*: "It is the living entity's constitutional position to be an eternal servant of Kṛṣṇa." Even in the beginning stages, *bhakti* is both the means and the end. To explain this, Śrīla Prabhupāda gives the example of a mango. In its unripe stage, a mango is a mango, and when it becomes ripe and relishable, it is still a mango. So even neophyte activities of *bhakti* are within the realm of love of God and are pleasing to Kṛṣṇa. But activities of *karma, jñāna,* and *yoga* are not pleasing to Kṛṣṇa unless they are dovetailed with *bhakti.*

When one begins devotional service, the emphasis is on performing obligatory practices ordered by the spiritual master. But even at this stage *bhakti-yoga* is based on the soul's dormant inclinations. Śrīla Prabhupāda explains in *The Nectar of Devotion* (p. 20):

> [The practice of devotional service] is not for developing something artificial. For example, a child learns or practices to walk. This walking is not unnatural. The walking capacity is there originally in the child, and simply by a little practice he walks very nicely. Similarly, devotional service to the Supreme Lord is the natural instinct of every living entity.

Nārada has defined *bhakti* as superior to other processes because it is both the means and the end, whereas other processes must ultimately lead to *bhakti* to have any value. This is one important reason why *bhakti* is superior, and now Nārada will offer further evidence.

SŪTRA 27

इश्वरस्याप्यभिमानिद्वेषित्वाद्दैन्यप्रियत्वाच्च ॥२७॥

īśvarasyāpy abhimāni-dveṣitvād dainya-priyatvāc ca

īśvarasya—of the Supreme Lord; *api*—also; *abhimāni*—of those who are proud; *dveṣitvāt*—because of being one who dislikes; *dainya*—of humility; *priyatvāt*—because of being fond; *ca*—and.

TRANSLATION

Furthermore, the Lord dislikes the proud but is pleased with the humble.

PURPORT

The humility Nārada praises here is not ordinary modesty but is in relationship to the Supreme Lord. The whole point is that the *bhakta* does what Kṛṣṇa likes. In the *Hari-bhakti-vilāsa* (11.417), Sanātana Gosvāmī describes six symptoms of a surrendered soul, and each of them involves humility before the Lord:

ānukūlyasya saṅkalpaḥ prātikūlyasya varjanam
rakṣiṣyatīti viśvāso goptṛtve varaṇaṁ tathā
ātma-nikṣepa-kārpaṇye ṣaḍ-vidhā śaraṇāgatiḥ

"The six aspects of full surrender to Kṛṣṇa are (1) accepting things favorable for devotional service, (2) rejecting things unfavorable for devotional service, (3) believing firmly in the Lord's protection, (4) feeling exclusively dependent on the mercy of the Lord for one's maintenance, (5) having no interest separate from that of the Lord, and (6) always feeling meek and humble before the Lord."

Humility is pleasing to Kṛṣṇa, and therefore the devotee is humble.

If Lord Kṛṣṇa had said He preferred pride, the devotee would be proud. In fact, sometimes the Lord likes His intimate friends to show a kind of transcendental pride and reprimand Him. By the influence of the Lord's *yogamāyā* potency, Kṛṣṇa's cowherd boyfriends think themselves His equals and sometimes challenge Him. A boy will climb on His back and say, "What kind of a big man are You?" Similarly, when mother Yaśodā or Śrīmatī Rādhārāṇī chides Kṛṣṇa, He likes it. These are examples of proud behavior in *prema-bhakti,* but Nārada is discussing a more basic instruction—that pride in one's self and one's activities is not pleasing to the Lord.

Everyone should acknowledge that the Supreme Lord has given him whatever opulence he has. Whatever prowess, wealth, beauty, fame, or learning we possess is nothing to be proud of because it is all "borrowed plumes." Even when we receive Kṛṣṇa's favor in devotional service, we should know that it is due to His mercy and not our own greatness. Sometimes when a devotee displays pride, Kṛṣṇa personally crushes it, as at the beginning of the *rāsa* dance:

> The *gopīs* . . . soon began to feel very proud, thinking themselves to be the most fortunate women in the universe by being favored by the company of Kṛṣṇa. Lord Kṛṣṇa, who is known as Keśava, could immediately understand their pride caused by their fortune of enjoying Him personally, and in order to show them His causeless mercy and to curb their false pride, He immediately disappeared from the scene, exhibiting His opulence of renunciation. [*Kṛṣṇa,* p. 253]

The more power one has, the more one is liable to become puffed up. Demigods like Brahmā and Indra sometimes become proud and forget Kṛṣṇa's supreme position. Once when Indra became envious of Kṛṣṇa, he tried to punish the residents of Vṛndāvana by sending torrential rainfall, but Kṛṣṇa protected the Vraja-vāsīs by lifting Govardhana Hill. Indra then approached Kṛṣṇa and sought forgiveness:

> [Indra said,] "Within this material world there are many fools like myself who consider themselves to be the Supreme Lord or the all-in-all within the universe. You are so merciful that without punishing their offenses, You devise means so that their false prestige is subdued and they can know that You, and no one else, are the Supreme Personality of Godhead." [*Kṛṣṇa,* p. 226]

Lord Caitanya considered humility essential for one who is aspiring to chant the holy names of God. He wrote in His *Śikṣāṣṭaka* (3),

> *tṛṇād api su-nīcena taror iva sahiṣṇunā*
> *amāninā māna-dena kīrtanīyaḥ sadā hariḥ*

"One who thinks himself lower than the grass, who is more tolerant than a tree, and who does not expect honor but is always prepared to give all respect to others can very easily always chant the holy name of the Lord." Vaiṣṇavas offer respect not only to the Supreme Lord and His direct representatives, but to all living beings. The more one advances spiritually, the more humble one becomes. The greatest devotee, the *mahā-bhāgavata,* sees everyone except himself as a servant of Lord Kṛṣṇa. As said in the *Caitanya-caritāmṛta* (*Antya* 20.25), "Although a Vaiṣṇava is the most exalted person, he is prideless and gives all respect to everyone, knowing everyone to be the resting place of Kṛṣṇa."

If at any point a devotee becomes proud of being a distinguished Vaiṣṇava, then he has developed an *anartha* (unwanted thing). This is confirmed in the *Caitanya-caritāmṛta* (*Antya* 20.28): "Wherever there is a relationship of love of Godhead, its natural symptom is that the devotee does not think himself a devotee. Instead, he always thinks that he has not even a drop of love for Kṛṣṇa" (Cc. *Antya* 20.28).

Although all transcendentalists may aspire to humility, *bhakti-yoga* is the best way to cultivate it. In *bhakti-yoga* one cannot advance without pleasing Lord Kṛṣṇa by acts of humility, whereas *karma, jñāna,* and *yoga* do not directly culture humility. Therefore a person who follows these other processes is more likely to think he is advancing by his own effort. The *karmī* may think he is accumulating wealth by his hard endeavor, the *jñānī* that he is gaining knowledge by his tedious study, and the *yogī* that he has attained mystic powers by long years of austerity. By contrast, the pure *bhakta* knows that the bliss he feels in the course of his devotional service is due simply to the mercy of the Supreme Lord. Thus the devotee alone is always aware that his advancement depends on his humility before Kṛṣṇa. One cannot be puffed up and at the same time be a devotee.

Lord Kṛṣṇa is attracted to the humble. For example, He was very pleased by the unpretentious behavior of Sudāmā Vipra, and He blessed him in many ways. Similarly, Lord Caitanya showed special mercy to a devotee named Kālīdāsa, who worshiped all Vaiṣṇavas with great respect and love. But Lord Caitanya was not pleased by the proud scholarship of Vallabha Bhaṭṭa.

Nārada's statement here—that the Supreme Lord is pleased with the humble and displeased with the proud—does not mean Kṛṣṇa is partial. Lord Kṛṣṇa does not withhold His love from anyone; rather, it is we who withhold our love from Him out of pride and ignorance and thus become unqualified to experience His presence and reciprocate His love. The sun shines for the benefit of all living beings, but creatures like owls hide themselves from its rays. The great devotee Prahlāda Mahārāja puts it this way in the *Śrīmad-Bhāgavatam* (7.9.27):

> Unlike an ordinary living entity, my Lord, You do not discriminate between friends and enemies, the favorable and the unfavorable, because for You there is no conception of higher and lower. Nonetheless, You offer Your benedictions according to the level of one's service, exactly as a desire tree delivers fruits according to one's desires and makes no distinction between lower and higher.

SŪTRA 28

तस्या ज्ञानमेव साधनमित्येके ॥२८॥

tasyā jñānam eva sādhanam ity eke

tasyāḥ—of it (*bhakti*); *jñānam*—knowledge; *eva*—alone; *sādhanam*—the means; *iti*—thus; *eke*—some.

TRANSLATION

Some say that knowledge is the means for developing devotion.

PURPORT

In this and the following two *sūtras* Nārada discusses the relation between knowledge and *bhakti*.

Is *bhakti* based on knowledge? Acquiring knowledge is certainly an important part of Kṛṣṇa consciousness. In the beginning of the *Bhagavad-gītā,* Kṛṣṇa reprimands Arjuna for "speaking learned words" but acting like one in ignorance. Kṛṣṇa thus becomes the *guru* of

Arjuna and begins by teaching him about the immortality of the soul. Indeed, throughout the *Bhagavad-gītā* Kṛṣṇa gives Arjuna essential knowledge concerning devotional service. Lord Caitanya also took the role of teacher in His pastimes with Sārvabhauma Bhaṭṭācārya, Prakāśānanda Sarasvatī, and Rūpa and Sanātana Gosvāmīs.

Kṛṣṇa conscious knowledge is not *jñāna* in the impersonal sense but is rather knowledge of the soul, God, and God's energies, with a *bhakti* conclusion. It is obvious, therefore, that knowledge helps one practice *bhakti*. Sometimes Śrīla Prabhupāda was asked, "How can a person without knowledge know if a spiritual master is bona fide?" Śrīla Prabhupāda replied that to know who a *bona fide* spiritual master is, one must first have some idea of what a *spiritual master* is. He gave the example that if someone wants to buy gold, he had better learn about gold and the gold market. Otherwise, he will be easily cheated. Or if someone wants to attend a college, he has to research the qualifications of various universities, their entrance requirements, and so on. So knowledge is certainly an important component of *bhakti*. Śrīla Prabhupāda wrote his books with the aim of distributing transcendental knowledge, and in his *Bhagavad-gītā* he wrote, "Religion without philosophy is sentiment, or sometimes fanaticism, while philosophy without religion is mental speculation."

Yet although knowledge is important, it is not an absolute requisite for *bhakti*. If Kṛṣṇa likes, He can immediately bestow enlightenment upon any person, regardless of his education. And in the *Śrīmad-Bhāgavatam* (1.2.7), Sūta Gosvāmī declares,

vāsudeve bhagavati bhakti-yogaḥ prayojitaḥ
janayaty āśu vairāgyaṁ jñānaṁ ca yad ahaitukam

"By rendering devotional service unto the Personality of Godhead, Kṛṣṇa, one immediately acquires causeless knowledge and detachment."

Therefore, while knowledge may help one to take up and prosecute *bhakti*, the contention that knowledge is the source of *bhakti* is false.

SŪTRA 29

अन्योन्याश्रयत्वमित्येके ॥२९॥

anyonyāśrayatvam ity eke

anyonya—mutual; *āśrayatvam*—dependency; *iti*—thus; *eke*—some.

TRANSLATION

Others consider *bhakti* and knowledge interdependent.

PURPORT

The spiritual harmony of knowledge and devotion is well expressed in the phrase *bhakti-vedānta.* Some observers think of *bhakti* and *jñāna* as separate or in opposition to each other. The Advaitins claim a monopoly on *jñāna* through the study of the *Vedānta-sūtra* according to the commentary of Śaṅkara. But Vedāntic study is not in opposition to *bhakti-yoga.* The author of the *Vedānta-sūtra* is Śrīla Vyāsadeva, who also compiled the *Śrīmad-Bhāgavatam,* which is a masterpiece of *bhakti* as well as the natural commentary on the *Vedānta-sūtra.* The Vaiṣṇava *ācāryas* Rāmānuja, Madhva, and Baladeva Vidyābhūṣaṇa all wrote commentaries on the *Vedānta-sūtra* and proved Vedānta to be harmonious with devotional service. So when a Vaiṣṇava studies the *Vedānta-sūtra* and other Vedic literatures in order to understand the glories of the Supreme Lord, then we have *bhakti-vedānta.*

Knowledge is especially required by the Kṛṣṇa conscious preacher, who has to meet opposing arguments. The Vaiṣṇava *ācāryas* were all highly learned in Sanskrit, philosophy, and logic, but they were never dry speculators like the academic or impersonalist scholars. They knew that Kṛṣṇa is the conclusion of the *Vedas.* As Śrī Kṛṣṇa says in the *Bhagavad-gītā* (15.15), *vedaiś ca sarvair aham eva vedyaḥ/ vedānta-kṛd veda-vid eva cāham:* "By all the *Vedas,* I am to be known. Indeed, I am the compiler of *Vedānta,* and I am the knower of the *Vedas.*"

Knowledge and devotion are harmonious, but to say that they are interdependent is too strong. Love of Kṛṣṇa often arises without a long development of *jñāna.* Nārada Muni once blessed a sadistic hunter with pure devotion to Kṛṣṇa. This type of spontaneous development of *bhakti* is known as *kṛpā-siddhi,* perfection via the good graces of the Lord and the Vaiṣṇavas.

In the eternal pleasure pastimes of the Lord, Yogamāyā sometimes covers the devotee's knowledge that Kṛṣṇa is God. This is another example of how knowledge and *bhakti* are not always interdependent. Sometimes the eternal associates of Kṛṣṇa remember that He is the Supreme Lord, and sometimes they forget, depending on the requirements of their particular devotional mood, or *rasa*. At Kṛṣṇa's name-giving ceremony, the sage Garga said, "This child will grow in power, beauty, opulence—everything—on the level of Nārāyaṇa, the Supreme Personality of Godhead." Still, mother Yaśodā treated Kṛṣṇa as her dependent child. Once Yaśodā ordered Kṛṣṇa to open His mouth so she could see if He had eaten dirt. Kṛṣṇa obeyed, and when mother Yaśodā looked into her child's mouth, she saw the universal form, including all time, space, and planets. Realizing that Kṛṣṇa was the Supreme Person, she prayed,

> Let me offer my respectful obeisances unto the Supreme Personality of Godhead, . . . under whose illusory energy I am thinking that Nanda Mahārāja is my husband and Kṛṣṇa is my son, that all the properties of Nanda Mahārāja belong to me, and that all the cowherd men and women are my subjects. [*Kṛṣṇa*, p. 84]

But then Lord Kṛṣṇa expanded His internal energy to cover mother Yaśodā's sense of awe and reverence with maternal affection. She immediately forgot that Kṛṣṇa was God and again accepted Him as her child. In cases like these, in the eternal pastimes of the Lord, knowledge of Kṛṣṇa's divinity comes and goes, but always in the service of *bhakti*.

SŪTRA 30

स्वयं फलरूपेति ब्रह्मकुमारः ॥३०॥

svayaṁ phala-rūpeti brahma-kumāraḥ

svayam—itself; *phala-rūpā*—manifesting as its fruit; *iti*—thus; *brahma-kumāraḥ*—the son of Brahmā (Nārada).

TRANSLATION

But the son of Brahmā says that *bhakti* is its own fruit.

PURPORT

Nārada now gives his opinion—that *bhakti* is not dependent on anything else for nourishment. In other words, Kṛṣṇa consciousness is the natural, transcendental state of the living being, and this state manifests automatically when we take up the process of *bhakti-yoga*. As Śrīla Prabhupāda puts it in his lecture entitled "On Chanting Hare Kṛṣṇa," "Kṛṣṇa consciousness is not an artificial imposition on the mind. This consciousness is the original energy of the living entity." The chanting of Hare Kṛṣṇa, Śrīla Prabhupāda says, "is directly enacted from the spiritual platform, surpassing all lower stages of consciousness—namely, sensual, mental, and intellectual."

In His *Śikṣāṣṭaka* (1), Lord Caitanya declares that the chanting of the holy name of Kṛṣṇa cleans the mirror of the mind. When the mirror of the mind is clean, one can see one's original, spiritual self along with the Supreme Lord. The initial activities of *bhakti*, therefore, clear away ignorance and false ego and reveal to the living entity his eternal state of devotional service. So *bhakti* is not produced by something else; rather, the practices of *sādhana-bhakti* remove the obstacles to our original loving relationship with the Lord.

Śrīla Prabhupāda would sometimes say that Kṛṣṇa consciousness is causeless. For example, "Revival of the dormant affection or love of Godhead does not depend on the mechanical system of hearing and chanting, but it solely and wholly depends on the causeless mercy of the Lord" (*Bhāg.* 1.7.6, purport). This means that the Lord freely bestows *bhakti* upon the devotee. The Supreme Lord is not bound to respond to any religious act or austerity we may perform, as if in mechanical obedience to law. This theory, put forward by the Karma-mīmāṁsakas, is rejected in *bhakti-yoga*. Kṛṣṇa is *svarāṭ*, supremely independent, and so is *bhakti*. In other words, one's advancement in devotional service does not depend on any of the various departments of human accomplishment, such as *karma, jñāna,* or *yoga*. If a person happens to be lacking in any department—even in devotion itself—Lord Kṛṣṇa can supply the requirements as He likes.

In a purport describing the free wandering of Nārada Muni, Śrīla

Prabhupāda gives an eloquent expression of the independence of *bhakti-yoga:*

> There is no reason or obligation for [Nārada's] traveling, and no one can stop him from his free movement. Similarly, the transcendental system of devotional service is also free. It may or may not develop in a particular person even after he undergoes all the detailed formulas. Similarly, the association of the devotee is also free. One may be fortunate to have it, or one may not have it even after thousands of endeavors. Therefore, in all spheres of devotional service, freedom is the main pivot. [*Bhāg.* 1.6.37, purport]

The Māyāvādīs sometimes twist a *sūtra* like this one in an attempt to prove that the individual *ātmā* needs no assistance to attain self-realization. They say that the scriptures and *gurus* and even God Himself are just inventions that may help us achieve self-realization but that then must be thrown away, just as one may remove a thorn in his flesh with another thorn and then throw them both away. The misconception here is that the *bhakti-śāstras* and pure devotees are finite products of the material world. In truth, the *śāstras* are eternal manifestations of the Supreme Personality of Godhead, as stated in the *Bhagavad-gītā* (3.15): *brahmākṣara-samudbhavam.* Elsewhere it is stated that the *Vedas* are the "breathing of Nārāyaṇa." The Vedic scriptures are sometimes manifest and sometimes not, but they exist eternally. Similarly, the Supreme Lord and His eternal associates sometimes appear within the material world, and after a time they disappear, but they are always manifest in the spiritual world, where they engage in unlimited varieties of pastimes. Śrīla Prabhupāda writes,

> Persons with a poor fund of knowledge conclude that a place devoid of material qualities must be some sort of formless nothingness. In reality, however, there are qualities in the spiritual world, but they are different from the material qualities because everything there is eternal, unlimited, and pure. [Cc. *Ādi* 5.22, purport]

Lord Kṛṣṇa, His expansions, and His devotees are not "dispensable," as the Māyāvādīs contend. On the contrary, it is the Māyāvāda doctrine that is a temporary creation, introduced at a certain time for a special purpose but intended to be discarded later. Śrīla Kṛṣṇadāsa Kavirāja writes,

Śaṅkara, who was an incarnation of Lord Śiva, is faultless because he is a servant carrying out the orders of the Lord. But those who follow his Māyāvāda philosophy are doomed. They will lose all their advancement in spiritual knowledge. One who considers the transcendental body of Lord Viṣṇu to be made of material nature is the greatest offender at the lotus feet of the Lord. There is no greater blasphemy against the Supreme Personality of Godhead. [Cc. *Ādi* 7.114–15]

The opinion of Nārada Muni, here describing himself as "the son of Lord Brahmā," is that *bhakti* is eternal and self-manifested, not dependent on any lesser process. When such devotional service is revealed to a sincere devotee, he realizes that its nature is like the Lord's—*sac-cid-ānanda,* full of eternity, bliss, and knowledge.

SŪTRAS 31–32

राजगृहभोजनादिषु तथैव दृष्टत्वात् ॥३१॥
न तेन राजपरितोषः क्षुच्छान्तिर्वा ॥३२॥

rāja-gṛha-bhojanādiṣu tathaiva dṛṣṭatvāt.

na tena rāja-paritoṣaḥ kṣuc-chāntir vā

rāja—royal; *gṛha*—in a residence; *bhojana*—in a meal: *ādiṣu*—and so on; *tathā eva*—just like this; *dṛṣṭatvāt*—because of its being seen; *na*—not; *tena*—by that; *rāja*—of the king; *paritoṣaḥ*—satisfaction; *kṣut*—of hunger; *śāntiḥ*—pacification; *vā*—or.

TRANSLATION

This is illustrated by the examples of a royal palace, a meal, and so on. A king is not really satisfied just by seeing a palace, nor can someone placate his hunger just by looking at a meal.

PURPORT

By these worldly examples, Nārada helps us understand the actual experience of *bhakti.* Nārada has said that some philosophers think knowledge is the means for developing *bhakti,* whereas others say that knowledge and *bhakti* are interdependent. But Nārada's conclusion is that *bhakti* is its own fruit. This means that *bhakti,* being an intimate exchange between the Lord and His devotees, does not depend on any other process. Only the Lord's pure devotees can enter into and understand such an exchange.

The examples Nārada gives illustrate the difference between *jñāna* (theoretical knowledge) and *vijñāna* (realized knowledge). It is especially important to hear from a spiritual master who has *vijñāna.* We will have to experience *vijñāna* for ourselves, but if the spiritual master is not self-realized, how can he guide us? Only those who have confidential knowledge can convey it to others. For example, Lord Brahmā, the first enlightened living being, received Vedic knowledge directly from Lord Kṛṣṇa. If one hears Brahmā's realized knowledge from someone in disciplic succession who has also realized it, then one is in a position to receive *vijñāna.*

Much depends on the quality of submissive hearing. These *sūtras* of the *Nārada-bhakti-sūtra* dealing with the examples of a king's palace and a feast give us a remarkable inside look at spiritual life. If we listen with sensitivity and faith, then even before the stage of full realization we can begin to get an inkling of what it is like. We hear that spiritual perfection will be like going home, and our attraction for this develops. One thinks, "Yes I too would like to go home, back to Godhead." Faithful hearing can produce realization. Śrīla Prabhupāda writes,

> For topics concerning Uttama-śloka, the Supreme Personality of Godhead, the spiritual master speaks, and the disciple hears with attention. . . . The spiritual master and disciple do not need to understand more than Kṛṣṇa because simply by understanding Kṛṣṇa and talking about Kṛṣṇa, one becomes a perfectly learned person. [*Bhāg.* 10.1.4, purport]

Throughout the Vedic literature we find a strong emphasis on hearing about Kṛṣṇa. Śrīla Prabhupāda states, "Whenever offenseless hearing and glorification of God are undertaken, it is to be understood that Lord Kṛṣṇa is present there in the form of transcendental sound, which is as powerful as the Lord personally" (*Bhāg.* 1.2.17, purport). Unless one experiences it, one cannot understand the powerful purification engendered by hearing from a bona fide spiritual master. As Śrīla Prabhupāda further writes:

> Human reason fails to understand how by serving the devotee *bhāgavata* or the book *bhāgavata* one gets gradual promotion on the path of devotion. But actually these are facts explained by Śrīla Nāradadeva, who happened to be a maidservant's son in his previous life. [*Bhāg.* 1.2.18, purport]

Effective hearing must be accompanied by surrender to the Lord and the Lord's devotee. It is not idle armchair talk. One has to be serious about inquiring into the Absolute Truth, prepared to hear submissively, and ready to serve the learned spiritual master.

Here Nārada's analogies of a king looking at a palace and a hungry man looking at a meal point up the fact that *bhakti* has to be practiced wholeheartedly if one wants to fully appreciate it. The other processes—*karma, jñāna,* and *yoga*—even if practiced well, cannot bring the taste of *kṛṣṇa-bhakti.* They are compared to the nipples on a goat's neck, which look promising but which cannot yield milk, no matter how much you try to milk them. Nor can mere academic knowledge of *bhakti* produce any real understanding of it. Prabhupāda liked to compare academics who study *bhakti* to bees who lick the outside of a bottle of honey: a lot of energy expended, but all for naught.

The example of eating is also a metaphor to help us understand what it is like to attain Kṛṣṇa consciousness:

bhaktiḥ pareśānubhavo viraktir
anyatra caiṣa trika eka-kālaḥ
prapadyamānasya yathāśnataḥ syus
tuṣṭiḥ puṣṭiḥ kṣud-apāyo 'nu-ghāsam

"Devotion, direct experience of the Supreme Lord, and detachment from other things—these three occur simultaneously for one who has taken shelter of the Supreme Personality of Godhead, in the same way that pleasure, nourishment, and relief from hunger come simultaneously and increasingly with each bite for a person engaged in eating" (*Bhāg.* 11.2.42).

Śrīla Prabhupāda used to say that no one has to give you a certificate to state that you are now Kṛṣṇa conscious. You will know it for yourself, and in fact, *only* you can know it for yourself. Similarly, if you are hungry and you begin to appease your hunger by eating, no one has to tell you, "Now you're satisfied." So, even the most vivid analogies cannot enlighten us beyond our realization. Ultimately, we have to go to the spiritual world to see it for ourselves. During the 1960's in America, at the time of the Vietnam War, a new devotee asked Śrīla Prabhupāda, "What is it like in Kṛṣṇaloka?" Śrīla Prabhupāda replied, "You won't be bothered by the draft board." That was a suitable (and humorous) reply for a person plagued with that particular fear, but there is of course much more to Kṛṣṇaloka than "no draft board." Sometimes when Prabhupāda was pressed with inquiries about the spiritual world, he would reply, "You will know when you go there."

The conclusion is that Nārada and the *ācāryas* are inviting us to get off the mental platform and to actually participate in *bhakti-yoga*—if we want to know what it really is and taste its fruit, going back to Godhead.

SŪTRA 33

अस्मात् सैव ग्राह्या मुमुक्षुभिः ॥३३॥

asmāt saiva grāhyā mumukṣubhiḥ

asmāt—therefore; *sā*—it; *eva*—only; *grāhyā*—should be accepted; *mumukṣubhiḥ*—by persons desiring liberation.

TRANSLATION

Therefore seekers of liberation should take to devotional service alone.

PURPORT

As stated in the *Śrīmad-Bhāgavatam* (10.2.32), those who pursue liberation but do not take shelter of the Supreme Lord in devotional service may think that they have attained the highest position and been liberated, but eventually they fall down to materialistic activities. Because the impersonalist meditator fails to develop his loving relationship with the Supreme Person, he must return from his sojourn in Brahman and come back into the material world to fulfill his personal desires. Therefore eternal liberation, freedom from repeated birth and death, is achieved only in the spiritual world, when one is fixed in one's eternal relationship of loving devotional service to the Supreme

Personality of Godhead. In previous *sūtras* Nārada mentioned that pure devotional service is not performed for any reward, including release from birth and death. Lord Caitanya also expressed this idea in His *Śikṣāṣṭaka* (4):

na dhanaṁ na janaṁ na sundarīṁ
kavitāṁ vā jagad-īśa kāmaye
mama janmani janmanīśvare
bhavatād bhaktir ahaitukī tvayi

"O almighty Lord, I have no desire for accumulating wealth, nor do I have any desire to enjoy beautiful women, nor do I want many followers. All I want is Your causeless devotional service in my life, birth after birth." By saying "birth after birth," Lord Caitanya implies that He does not seek liberation, either. All He desires is continuous service and remembrance of the Lord, in any sphere of life.

And yet although a pure devotee never aspires for *mukti,* he automatically achieves it. By Kṛṣṇa's desire, he is promoted to Kṛṣṇaloka or to a Vaikuṇṭha planet, depending on his *rasa* with the Lord. Or, like Nārada, he may remain in the material world to preach Kṛṣṇa consciousness. Śrīla Prabhupāda used to say that liberation doesn't mean one has to develop four arms and four heads. If one is purely Kṛṣṇa conscious one may continue to live in the material world and be fully liberated. As Śrīla Rūpa Gosvāmī says in his *Bhakti-rasāmṛta-sindhu* (1.2.187):

īhā yasya harer dāsye karmaṇā manasā girā
nikhilāsv apy avasthāsu jīvan-muktaḥ sa ucyate

"A person acting in the service of Kṛṣṇa with his body, mind, intelligence, and words is a liberated person even within the material world, although he may engage in many apparently material activities."

CHAPTER 3

The Means of Achievement

SŪTRA 34

तस्याः साधनानि गायन्त्याचार्याः ॥३४॥

tasyāḥ sādhanāni gāyanty ācāryāḥ

tasyāḥ—of it; *sādhanāni*—the means of development; *gāyanti*—sing; *ācāryāḥ*—the great teachers.

TRANSLATION

Standard authorities have described the methods for achieving devotional service.

PURPORT

Having described the essence of *parā bhakti,* the highest stage of devotional service, Nārada now turns to the practices one must perform to reach that stage. The practice stage of *bhakti* is called *sādhana-bhakti.* Nārada previously stated that *bhakti* was its own means, that it does not depend on anything else—specifically *jñāna,* or knowledge. And as Śrīla Prabhupāda points out, *bhakti* doesn't even depend on the devotee's practice:

> Kṛṣṇa consciousness cannot be aroused simply by practice. Actually there is no such practice. When we wish to develop our innate capacity for devotional service, there are certain processes which, by our accepting and executing them, will cause that dormant capacity to be invoked. Such practice is called *sādhana-bhakti.* [*The Nectar of Devotion,* p. 20]

The rules and regulations of *bhakti* are meant to cure a conditioned soul of the madness that causes his bondage and suffering. Śrīla Prabhupāda writes (*The Nectar of Devotion,* p. 21), "As a man's mental disease is cured by the directions of a psychiatrist, so this *sādhana-bhakti* cures the conditioned soul of his madness under the spell of *māyā,* material illusion."

Nārada says that the methods he will teach have been given by the *ācāryas,* those who teach by both word and deed. *Bhakti* can be taught only by Vaiṣṇava *ācāryas* and their representatives, not by teachers of comparative religion or impersonalists in the guise of *bhaktas.* Nārada himself is one of the greatest *ācāryas,* and so his own sayings are sufficient. Still, following the *paramparā* tradition, he quotes previous *ācāryas* and also gives his own insights. Thus his teachings are acceptable to all, regardless of *sampradāya* or particular founder-*ācārya.* Here Nārada uses the word *gāyanti,* "they sing," because the *ācāryas* joyfully teach the principles of *bhakti.*

SŪTRA 35

तत्तु विषयत्यागात् संगत्यागाच्च ॥३५॥

tat tu viṣaya-tyāgāt saṅga-tyāgāc ca

tat—that; *tu*—and; *viṣaya*—of sense gratification; *tyāgāt*—by rejection; *saṅga*—of (material) association; *tyāgāt*—by rejection; *ca*—and.

TRANSLATION

One achieves *bhakti* by giving up sense gratification and mundane association.

PURPORT

Viṣaya refers to the objects of sense enjoyment, and one who indulges in sense enjoyment is called a *viṣayī.* A *viṣayī* cannot succeed in devotional service. The *ācāryas* therefore set down regulations for eating, mating, and so on. Nārada states that one should not only give up gross practices of sense indulgence but should even stop thinking of sense gratification. The word *saṅga-tyāga* indicates that one should refrain from associating with sense objects even within the mind and heart. The *ācāryas* of all religions so consistently recommend such renunciation of sense pleasure that the need for it may seem a truism. But to practice it is not easy. And yet if we want to advance in *bhakti-yoga,* practice it we must. As Lord Kṛṣṇa says, "What is called renunciation you should know to be the same as *yoga*, or linking oneself with the Supreme, O son of Pāṇḍu, for one can never become a *yogī* unless he renounces the desire for sense gratification" (Bg. 6.2).

The Kṛṣṇa conscious method of renunciation is to engage the mind and senses in devotional service. As Śrīla Rūpa Gosvāmī says in his *Bhakti-rasāmṛta-sindhu* (2.255),

anāsaktasya viṣayān yathārham upayuñjataḥ
nirbandhaḥ kṛṣṇa-sambandhe yuktaṁ vairāgyam ucyate

"When one is not attached to anything but simultaneously accepts everything in relation to Kṛṣṇa, one is situated above possessiveness."

An active devotee is more complete in his renunciation than one who rejects material things without knowledge of their relationship to Kṛṣṇa. This method of *yukta-vairāgya* gives one great freedom, but it must be done rightly. Śrīla Prabhupāda writes, "One should, however, note that after doing something whimsically he should not offer the results to the Supreme Lord. That sort of duty is not in the devotional service of Kṛṣṇa consciousness. One should act according to the order of Kṛṣṇa, [which] comes through disciplic succession from the bona fide spiritual master" (Bg. 18.57, purport). In short, sinful activity cannot be brought under the purview of "offering everything to Kṛṣṇa." Indeed, Śrīla Prabhupāda would not accept disciples unless they agreed to follow the four regulative principles—no illicit sex, no intoxication, no gambling, and no meat-eating.

Renunciation is possible because of the higher pleasure attainable in spiritual life. As Kṛṣṇa states in the *Bhagavad-gītā* (2.59),

viṣayā vinivartante nirāhārasya dehinaḥ
rasa-varjaṁ raso 'py asya paraṁ dṛṣṭvā nivartate

"Although the embodied soul may be restricted from sense enjoyment, the taste for sense objects remains. But ceasing such engagements by experiencing a higher taste, he is fixed in consciousness." In his purport to this verse, Śrīla Prabhupāda compares the restriction from sense enjoyment mystic *yogīs* observe to the restrictions a doctor places upon a patient that forbid him from taking certain types of food. In neither instance is the taste for the forbidden pleasures lost.

"But," Śrīla Prabhupāda writes, "one who has tasted the beauty of the Supreme Lord, Kṛṣṇa, in the course of his advancement in Kṛṣṇa consciousness no longer has a taste for dead, material things. Therefore, restrictions are there for the less intelligent neophytes in the spiritual advancement of life, but such restrictions are good only until one actually has a taste for Kṛṣṇa consciousness."

Previously Nārada has stated that it is not sufficient merely to hear about spiritual life or to tell others about it without actually practicing it and realizing its fruits oneself. And so the *sādhana-bhakta* actually practices—he avoids lusty attachments on the strength of his vows, and Kṛṣṇa helps him from within. Eventually he relishes a higher taste and loses the desire for sense gratification. *Bhakti-yoga,* being a transcendental science, yields the expected results when carefully followed.

The phrase *saṅga-tyāgāt,* which Nārada uses here, also appears in Śrīla Rūpa Gosvāmī's *Upadeśāmṛta* (3). According to Rūpa Gosvāmī, *saṅga-tyāga,* by which he means "abandoning the association of nondevotees," is one of the most important requirements for the execution of pure devotional service. When Lord Caitanya was asked to define a Vaiṣṇava, He replied, *asat-saṅga-tyāga—ei vaiṣṇava ācāra:* "Characteristically, a Vaiṣṇava is one who gives up the association of worldly people, or nondevotees" (Cc. *Madhya* 22.87). Just as *asat-saṅga* increases our material attachment and impedes our devotional service, so *sādhu-saṅga* furthers our devotional service by helping us become attached to Lord Kṛṣṇa and detached from the practices of nondevotees.

In the *Śrīmad-Bhāgavatam* Lord Kapila advises His mother, Devahūti, that while material attachment is the greatest entanglement for the spirit soul, "that same attachment, when applied to the self-realized devotees, opens the door of liberation" (*Bhāg.* 3.25.20). In his purport, Śrīla Prabhupāda writes, "This indicates that the propensity for attachment cannot be stopped; it must be utilized for the best purpose. Our attachment for material things perpetuates our conditioned state, but the same attachment, when transfered to the Supreme Personality of Godhead or His devotee, is the source of liberation."

This *sūtra* contains a stern order for the aspiring devotee: "If you want to progress in *bhakti,* you must give up sense gratification and material association." In his *Bhagavad-gītā* purports, Śrīla Prabhupāda tells us how we should approach such orders: "The Lord instructs that one has to become fully Kṛṣṇa conscious to discharge duties, as if in military discipline. Such an injunction may make things a little difficult; still, duties must be carried out, with dependence on Kṛṣṇa, because that is the constitutional position of the living entity" (Bg. 3.30, purport). Lethargy in the face of these orders should be thrown off. The alternative is great unhappiness, more than we can imagine, as the soul falls down into lower species of life, birth after birth.

SŪTRA 36

अव्यावृत्तभजनात् ॥३६॥

avyāvṛtta-bhajanāt

avyāvṛtta—uninterrupted; *bhajanāt*—by worship.

TRANSLATION

One achieves *bhakti* by worshiping the Lord ceaselessly.

PURPORT

Nārada has given a negative order—to restrain the mind and senses; he now gives the positive method for engaging the mind and senses in Kṛṣṇa consciousness. Śrīla Prabhupāda compared Kṛṣṇa conscious activity to placing an iron rod in fire. As the rod stays steadily within the flames, it becomes hotter and hotter, until eventually it becomes fiery. In the same way, the devotee who steadily engages in Kṛṣṇa consciousness gradually becomes transformed, until eventually he becomes fully Kṛṣṇa conscious. If one is completely absorbed in Kṛṣṇa's service, there is no scope for the activities of *māyā*.

The *Śrīmad-Bhāgavatam* (1.2.6) also recommends uninterrupted devotional service:

> *sa vai puṁsāṁ paro dharmo yato bhaktir adhokṣaje*
> *ahaituky apratihatā yayātmā suprasīdati*

"The supreme occupation for all humanity is that by which one can attain to loving devotional service unto the transcendental Lord. Such devotional service must be unmotivated and uninterrupted to completely satisfy the self."

In this *sūtra* Nārada uses the word *bhajana,* which also appears, in a slightly different form, in the *Bhagavad-gītā* (6.47). In concluding His instructions on *aṣṭāṅga-yoga* in the Sixth Chapter of the *Gītā,* Lord Kṛṣṇa says that one who serves Him with devotion and faith (*śraddhāvān bhajate yo mām*) is the highest *yogī.* Śrīla Prabhupāda explains that the word *bhaj* means "service":

> Service with love and faith is especially meant for the Supreme Personality of Godhead. One can avoid worshiping a respectable man or demigod and may be called discourteous, but one cannot avoid serving the Supreme Lord without being thoroughly condemned. [Bg. 6.47, purport]

This passage indicates that *bhakti* is not a spiritual recreation for a few people but is intended for all, and it cannot be avoided without dire consequences.

Nārada says *bhakti* is attained by uninterrupted loving service. But does he mean that one must be flawless, that one must never slip? No, Lord Kṛṣṇa allows for mistakes, provided one is determined to serve Him. He says in the Ninth Chapter of the *Gītā,*

api cet su-durācāro bhajate mām ananya-bhāk
sādhur eva sa mantavyaḥ samyag vyavasito hi saḥ

"Even if one commits the most abominable action, if he is engaged in devotional service he is to be considered saintly because he is properly situated in his determination" (Bg. 9.30). Śrīla Prabhupāda warns us, however, not to take advantage of this statement and think we can intentionally violate the rules of devotional life and still be a devotee. The blessing from the Lord expressed here is that if we go on serving the spiritual master and Kṛṣṇa with determination—especially by chanting Hare Kṛṣṇa, Hare Kṛṣṇa, Kṛṣṇa Kṛṣṇa, Hare Hare/ Hare Rāma, Hare Rāma, Rāma Rāma, Hare Hare—then Lord Kṛṣṇa will accept us as His devotee, despite our imperfections.

But exactly what does one do to always keep busy in Kṛṣṇa consciousness and avoid becoming bored or restless? Prahlāda Mahārāja taught a ninefold process of *bhakti* for maintaining full engagement in the Lord's service: (1) hearing about the Lord, (2) chanting His name and glories, (3) remembering Him, (4) serving His lotus feet, (5) worshiping the Deity, (6) offering prayers to the Lord, (7) becoming His servant, (8) becoming His friend, and (9) offering Him everything. While the first two of these processes are extremely important, any one of them is sufficient for achieving perfection. Śrīla Prabhupāda writes:

> The nine different processes enunciated by Prahlāda Mahārāja, who learned them from Nārada Muni, may not all be required for the execution of devotional service; if a devotee performs only one of these nine without deviation, he can attain the mercy of the Supreme Personality of Godhead. [*Bhāg.* 7.5.24, purport]

In early 1968 I wrote a letter to Śrīla Prabhupāda saying that sometimes I couldn't decide which service I should do at a given moment. Should I wash the dishes or chant Hare Kṛṣṇa? Prabhupāda replied:

> There isn't any difference between chanting the Holy Name [and] washing the dishes of the Temple. So do not be worried when you are attracted for doing other work in the Temple. There is variegatedness in transcendental activities. Sometimes we like to chant, sometimes we like to wash dishes. There is no difference on the Absolute plane.

SŪTRA 37

लोकेऽपि भगवद्गुणश्रवणकीर्तनात् ॥३७॥

loke 'pi bhagavad-guṇa-śravaṇa-kīrtanāt

loke—in the world; *api*—even; *bhagavat*—of the Supreme Lord; *guṇa*—about the qualities; *śravaṇa*—by hearing; *kīrtanāt*—and chanting.

TRANSLATION

One achieves *bhakti* by hearing and chanting about the Supreme Lord's special qualities, even while engaged in the ordinary activities of life in this world.

PURPORT

Someone might say that Nārada is being unreasonable in advocating "uninterrupted loving service." How can those who are busy with duties in the world maintain constant *bhajana*? But Nārada, like all *ācāryas,* is well aware of the worldly situation and the *jīva's* predicament. Thus he recommends *śravaṇaṁ kīrtanam,* hearing and chanting about the Lord, for all persons at all times. An outstanding example of a Kṛṣṇa conscious devotee who was busy in the world is Arjuna, Kṛṣṇa's friend. And it was Lord Kṛṣṇa Himself who insisted that Arjuna not renounce the battlefield in favor of meditation:

tasmāt sarveṣu kāleṣu mām anusmara yudhya ca
mayy arpita-mano-buddhir mām evaiṣyasy asaṁśayaḥ

"Therefore, Arjuna, you should always think of Me in the form of Kṛṣṇa and at the same time carry out your prescribed duty of fighting. With your activities dedicated to Me and your mind and intelligence fixed on Me, you will attain Me without doubt" (Bg. 8.7).

Śrīla Prabhupāda writes, "The Lord never suggests anything impractical. . . . If he [Arjuna] doesn't practice remembering Kṛṣṇa while he is struggling for existence, then it will not be possible for him to remember Kṛṣṇa at the time of death" (Bg. Introduction, pp. 27–28). Lord Caitanya also advises, *kīrtanīyaḥ sadā hariḥ:* "One should always chant the names of the Lord."

Still the question remains, How can an active person perform double duty—work and chant at the same time? But it is possible, through love. Prabhupāda gave the example of a man who goes to work in an office while his young son is very ill at home. Out of natural affection, the father is always thinking, "How is the boy?" Another example, given by the *ācāryas,* concerns a married woman's attachment for her paramour. The wife always thinks of her lover, even while doing her household chores. In fact, she does her housework even more carefully so that her husband will not suspect her. In the same way, we should always remember the supreme lover, Śrī Kṛṣṇa, even while meticulously discharging our material duties. If we say, "But I lack strong love for Kṛṣṇa," the only remedy is *vaidhi-bhakti.* The very purpose of this training stage of *bhakti* is to bring out our original love for God, just as striking a match brings out a flame. And among all the devotional practices, the foremost are *śravaṇaṁ kīrtanaṁ viṣṇoḥ*, hearing and chanting the glories of the Lord.

No one can honestly say he has absolutely *no* time to devote to *śravaṇaṁ kīrtanam.* Even the busiest people find time daily to go through newspapers or magazines, and almost everyone finds some time for television, as well as for idle talk. Much of this time could be spared for *bhakti-yoga.* And even when we are working at the office or factory, if we are donating a portion of our earnings to Kṛṣṇa we may think, "Kṛṣṇa has assigned me this particular duty."

If despite his best efforts a devotee finds his social and occupational duties overwhelming, he should consider living in a different way. One should avoid *ugra-karma,* work that completely saps one of all higher energy and pious inclination. In the *Śrīmad-Bhāgavatam,* Nārada Muni advised Mahārāja Yudhiṣṭhira that one should work "to earn his livelihood as much as necessary to maintain body and soul together. . . . An intelligent man in human society should make his program of activities very simple" (*Bhāg.* 7.14.5–6).

Śrīla Prabhupāda, who worked for many years as a Kṛṣṇa conscious businessman, addressed the problem realistically. He said that there was no question of stopping all activities, just as there is no question of wiping out one's temperature altogether when trying to recover from a fever. If one has a fever of 105°F, one should carefully decrease it to the normal temperature, 98.6°, and maintain it there. Śrīla Prabhupāda writes, "The great sages and saints of India wanted to maintain the normal temperature by a balanced program of material and spiritual knowledge. They never allowed the misuse of human intelligence for diseased sense gratification" (*Īśopaniṣad* 11, purport). Most people give the highest priority to economic development and sense gratification, relegating religion to a support activity. But actual religion—self-realization—should come first. Economic development is required only to maintain the body in a sound, healthy condition.

Understanding the awkward position of people in the Kali-yuga, the Supreme Lord has given us the chanting of the holy names as the *yuga-dharma,* the religion of the age:

harer nāma harer nāma harer nāmaiva kevalam
kalau nāsty eva nāsty eva nāsty eva gatir anyathā

"In this age of quarrel and hypocrisy, the only means of deliverance is the chanting of the holy names of the Lord. There is no other way. There is no other way. There is no other way" (*Bṛhan-nāradīya Purāṇa*).

Śrīla Prabhupāda formed the International Society for Krishna Consciousness on the basis of the *yuga-dharma* and Nārada Muni's instructions in this *sūtra*. Throughout the world, many of Prabhupāda's followers chant sixteen rounds of the Hare Kṛṣṇa *mantra* daily, attend a morning and evening program of *kīrtana* and scriptural discourse, and follow the four rules prohibiting sinful life—even while pursuing active professional careers. Lord Kṛṣṇa has personally promised Nārada Muni that whoever chants His glories will attain the Lord's mercy, despite social or occupational status:

nāhaṁ tiṣṭhāmi vaikuṇṭhe yogināṁ hṛdayeṣu vā
yatra gāyanti mad-bhaktāḥ tatra tiṣṭhāmi nārada

"My dear Nārada, I do not dwell in Vaikuṇṭha or in the hearts of the *yogī*, but wherever My devotees sing My glories" (*Padma Purāṇa*).

SŪTRA 38

मुख्यतस्तु महत्कृपयैव भगवत्कृपालेशाद्वा ॥३८॥

mukhyatas tu mahat-kṛpayaiva bhagavat-kṛpā-leśād vā

mukhyataḥ—primarily; *tu*—but; *mahat*—of great souls; *kṛpayā*—by the mercy; *eva*—indeed; *bhagavat*—of the Supreme Lord; *kṛpā*—of the mercy; *leśāt*—by a trace; *vā*—or.

TRANSLATION

Primarily, however, one develops *bhakti* by the mercy of great souls, or by a small drop of the Lord's mercy.

PURPORT

Nārada has outlined the main practices for a devotee-in-training (*sādhaka*). Now he emphasizes that the devotee cannot succeed simply on the strength of his own endeavor, but only when he receives the mercy of Kṛṣṇa's representative or a drop of the Lord's direct mercy.

Unless one seeks out the association of a *sādhu, bhakti* will remain distant. But who is a *sādhu*? Śrīla Prabhupāda explains:

> A *sādhu* is not just an ordinary man with a saffron robe or long beard. A *sādhu* is described in *Bhagavad-gītā* as one who unflinchingly engages in devotional service. Even though one is found not to be following the strict rules and regulations of devotional service, if one simply has unflinching faith in Kṛṣṇa, the Supreme Person, he is understood to be a *sādhu*. . . . If one associates with a *sādhu,* the result will be that the *sādhu* will teach him how to become a devotee, a worshiper and sincere servitor of the Lord. These are the gifts of a *sādhu*. [*Bhāg.* 3.25.20, purport]

The *Caitanya-caritāmṛta* and the *Bhakti-rasāmṛta-sindhu* state that the acceptance of a spiritual master is absolutely essential for advancement in devotional service. Śrīla Prabhupāda writes:

> Without the attentive service of his parents, a child cannot grow to manhood; similarly, without the care of the spiritual master one cannot rise to the plane of transcendental service. . . . One should always remember that a person who is reluctant to accept a spiritual master and be initiated is sure to be baffled in his endeavor to go back to Godhead. [Cc. *Ādi* 1.46, purport, and 1.35, purport]

And so by the grace of the spiritual masters, all the aforementioned practices taught by Nārada—the chanting and hearing of the holy names, avoiding sense gratification, and so on—will come naturally to one who serves and inquires from devotees.

Conditioned souls are brought to the path of *bhakti* by the help of the Vaiṣṇavas, and also by the direct guidance of the Supreme Lord. *Harim vinā naiva sṛtim taranti:* "Without the blessings of Hari, the Supreme Personality of Godhead, one cannot stop the continuous chain of birth and death within this material world." Lord Kṛṣṇa, as the Supersoul within everyone's heart, directly gives us guidance. When a soul cries out for spiritual guidance, the Lord as the *caitya-guru,* or the spiritual master in the heart, gives direct inspiration. Kṛṣṇa states,

teṣām evānukampārtham aham ajñāna-jaṁ tamaḥ
nāśayāmy ātma-bhāva-stho jñāna-dīpena bhāsvatā

"To show them special mercy, I, dwelling in their hearts, destroy with the shining lamp of knowledge the darkness born of ignorance" (Bg. 10.11).

In the purport to the previous verse (Bg. 10.10), Śrīla Prabhupāda explains, "A person may have a bona fide spiritual master and may be attached to a spiritual organization, but still, if he is not intelligent enough to make progress, then Kṛṣṇa from within gives him instructions so that he may ultimately come to Him without difficulty."

The Lord's mercy is therefore available both in the form of the instructing spiritual masters and the Supersoul within the heart. The appearance of the spiritual master within the life of the conditioned soul is the direct mercy of the Lord. Prabhupāda writes that "the great sage Śukadeva Gosvāmī was certainly inspired by Lord Kṛṣṇa to appear voluntarily before Mahārāja Parīkṣit, the great devotee of the Lord, just to give him the teachings of *Śrīmad-Bhāgavatam*" (*Bhāg.* 1.19.36).

It is truly a sign of the Lord's mercy when one meets His pure representative, the bona fide spiritual master. But how effective this mercy is depends on one's sincerity. As soon as the Lord finds that a soul has developed eagerness to go back to Godhead, the Lord sends a bona fide spiritual master, and if one takes full advantage of the instructions of such a spiritual master, one is guaranteed success. Śrīla Prabhupāda writes, "The conclusion is that to get the . . . help of a bona fide spiritual master means *to receive the direct help of the Lord Himself*" (*Bhāg.* 1.19.36, purport; italics in original).

SŪTRA 39

महत्संगस्तु दुर्लभोऽगम्योऽमोघश्च ॥३९॥

mahat-saṅgas tu durlabho 'gamyo 'moghaś ca

mahat—of great souls; *saṅgaḥ*—the association; *tu*—but; *durlabhaḥ*—difficult to achieve; *agamyaḥ*—difficult to understand; *amoghaḥ*—infallible; *ca*—also.

TRANSLATION

The association of great souls is rarely obtained, difficult to understand, and infallible.

PURPORT

In His instructions to Śrīla Rūpa Gosvāmī (Cc. *Madhya* 19.138–48), Lord Caitanya graphically describes the rarity of gaining the association of a pure devotee. The Lord tells Rūpa Gosvāmī that there are unlimited living entities among 8,400,000 species, and all these living entities are wandering from body to body, planet to planet, within this universe. The few living entities in human bodies may be divided into the uncultured and the cultured—those who are ignorant of the Vedic principles and those who know them. Among those who know the Vedic principles, roughly half simply give lip service to these principles while committing all kinds of sins in violation of these principles. Out of those who actually follow the Vedic principles, most seek material rewards like wealth, good birth, or elevation to heaven. Among millions of pious followers of the Vedic injunctions, one may be actually wise (a *jñānī*). Out of many millions of such *jñānīs,* Lord Caitanya says, one may actually become liberated from birth and death, and out of many millions of such liberated persons, a devotee of the Lord is very difficult to find.

Lord Kṛṣṇa makes the same point:

manuṣyāṇāṁ sahasreṣu kaścid yatati siddhaye
yatatām api siddhānāṁ kaścin māṁ vetti tattvataḥ

"Out of many thousands of men, one may endeavor for perfection, and of those who have achieved perfection, hardly one knows Me in truth" (Bg. 7.3). This indicates that even one who has attained Brahman realization falls far short of knowledge of the Supreme Personality of Godhead. We should not be misled, therefore, about who is a "great soul" or think that any "swami" or "*guru*" will be able to deliver us from material entanglement. As the *Śrīmad-Bhāgavatam* says (6.14.5),

muktānām api siddhānāṁ nārāyaṇa-parāyaṇaḥ
su-durlabhaḥ praśantātmā koṭiṣv api mahā-mune

"O great sage, out of many millions of materially liberated people who are free from ignorance, and out of many millions of *siddhas* who have nearly attained perfection, there is hardly one pure devotee of Nārāyaṇa. Only such a devotee is actually completely satisfied and peaceful."

Even when *mahātmās* do appear in human society, they are often not appreciated or understood. Śrīla Prabhupāda writes,

> Sometimes devotees are personally attacked with violence. Lord Jesus Christ was crucified, Haridāsa Ṭhākura was caned in twenty-two marketplaces, and Lord Caitanya's principal assistant, Nityānanda, was violently attacked by Jagāi and Mādhāi. . . . Although a *sādhu* is not inimical toward anyone, the world is so ungrateful that even a *sādhu* has many enemies. [*Bhāg.* 3.25.21, purport]

But if one gets the association of a *mahātmā* and is receptive to his blessings, one will infallibly be benefited. Nārada is an excellent example of a *mahātmā* who transformed the lives of many. He once turned a hunter into a pure Vaiṣṇava. The hunter was so cruel that he used to half kill animals because he enjoyed their pain. But as soon as he met Nārada and began to hear from him, the hunter became afraid of his sins. Nārada assured him, "If you follow my instructions, you can be liberated." Nārada then instructed the hunter to worship Lord Kṛṣṇa by chanting the Hare Kṛṣṇa *mantra.* A *mahātmā* never says, "Surrender to me," but he advises everyone to surrender to Lord Kṛṣṇa, the Supreme Personality of Godhead. This is his infallibility.

The power of the Vaiṣṇavas is expressed in a Bengali song beginning *gaurāṅgera bhakta-gaṇi jani jani śakti dhare:* "The devotees of Lord Caitanya are very powerful, and every one of them can deliver the whole world." But the disciple has to do his part also. On receiving the grace of a Vaiṣṇava, one must agree to give up his sinful activities. Then the spiritual master can take care of him and elevate him to spiritual emancipation. Devotees who may not be on the level of a *paramahaṁsa* like Nārada Muni, but who strictly follow in his disciplic succession, can also deliver infallible knowledge. Śrīla Prabhupāda writes:

> The spiritual master, being in the disciplic succession stemming from Nārada Muni, is in the same category with Nārada Muni. A person can be relieved of his sinful activity if he surrenders to the lotus feet of a person who actually represents Nārada Muni. [Cc. *Madhya* 24.258, purport]

Another proof of the power of the *mahātmā* is his ability to convert nondevotees into saintly persons. Śrīla Bhaktivinoda Ṭhākura stated that a Vaiṣṇava can be tested by seeing how good a "touchstone" he is—by seeing how many Vaiṣṇavas he has made during his life. Lord Caitanya desired that as many persons as possible should repeat the message of Kṛṣṇa and convince others to take up Kṛṣṇa consciousness, following in the footsteps of Nārada Muni and other great *ācāryas*.

In conclusion, the association of a *mahātmā* is very rare, and yet it is available to a sincere seeker. Upon contacting a great soul, one should realize one's good fortune, and with a joyful but serious attitude one should surrender unto his lotus feet. How one should regard a *mahātmā* upon meeting him is exemplified in this quote from the *Hari-bhakti-sudhodaya* (13.2), spoken by Lord Caitanya to Sanātana Gosvāmī:

> My dear Vaiṣṇava, seeing a person like you is the perfection of one's eyesight, touching your lotus feet is the perfection of the sense of touch, and glorifying your good qualities is the tongue's real activity, for in the material world it is very difficult to find a pure devotee of the Lord.

SŪTRA 40

लभ्यतेऽपि तत्कृपयैव ॥४०॥

labhyate 'pi tat-kṛpayaiva

labhyate—it is gained; *api*—yet; *tat*—of Him (the Supreme Lord); *kṛpayā*—by the mercy; *eva*—only.

TRANSLATION

The association of great souls can be attained—but only by the Lord's mercy.

PURPORT

Although the pure devotee is rarely found in the world, the Supreme Lord directly helps a sincere seeker of the truth. As Lord Caitanya declared to Śrīla Rūpa Gosvāmī:

brahmāṇḍa bhramite kona bhāgyavān jīva
guru-kṛṣṇa-prasāde pāya bhakti-latā-bīja

"According to their *karma,* all living entities are wandering throughout the entire universe. Some of them are being elevated to the upper planetary systems, and some are going down to the lower planetary systems. Out of many millions of wandering living entities, one who is very fortunate gets an opportunity to associate with a bona fide spiritual master by the grace of Kṛṣṇa. By the mercy of both Kṛṣṇa and the spiritual master, such a person receives the seed of the creeper of devotional service" (Cc. *Madhya* 19.151).

In His Paramātmā feature, Lord Kṛṣṇa is situated in everyone's heart, and He fulfills our desires in accordance with what we deserve, which is based on our previous activities. (Even sinful desires must be sanctioned by Kṛṣṇa before one can fulfill them.) Śrīla Prabhupāda writes, "If the living entity by chance or fortune comes in contact with the Kṛṣṇa consciousness movement and wishes to associate with that movement, Kṛṣṇa, who is situated in everyone's heart, gives him the chance to meet a bona fide spiritual master" (Cc. *Madhya* 19.151, purport). If one doesn't know exactly what or who he is looking for, but he calls out to God and asks to be delivered, the Lord will bestow His mercy—the chance to surrender to a great soul.

Nārada's disciple Dhruva Mahārāja is an example of one who was helped by God. Dhruva was insulted by his stepmother, and on the advice of his mother he went to seek God in the forest. Although the boy desired an exalted position and revenge, his determination appealed to the Supreme Lord. Dhruva wandered in the forest asking the animals, "Where is God? Are you God?"—and suddenly the great sage Nārada appeared before him. Śrīla Prabhupāda explains,

> The Supreme Personality of Godhead is present in everyone's heart, and as soon as He understands that the living entity is serious about entering devotional service, He sends His representative. In this way Nārada was sent to Dhruva Mahārāja. [*Bhāg.* 4.8.25, purport]

SŪTRA 41

तस्मिंस्तज्जने भेदाभावात् ॥४१॥

tasmiṁs taj-jane bhedābhāvāt

tasmin—in Him; *tat*—His; *jane*—in the people; *bheda*—of difference; *abhāvāt*—because of the absence.

TRANSLATION

[One can attain *bhakti* either by the association of the Lord's pure devotees or directly by the Lord's mercy because] the Lord and His pure devotees are nondifferent.

PURPORT

The mercy of the Lord and that of His pure devotees are equally potent because the devotee and the Supreme Lord impart the same teachings. Śrī Kṛṣṇa says, "Surrender to Me," and the pure devotee says, "Yes, I surrender to You," and tells others, "Surrender to Kṛṣṇa." Thus the mercy of the Lord and that of His loving servants have the same effect: the seed of devotion is planted in the hearts of receptive conditioned souls.

The Māyāvādīs are always seeking an opportunity to annihilate God's personal identity, and so they interpret this *sūtra* in the following way: "Just as a river loses its name and form after it enters the ocean, so a devotee loses his individuality when he merges himself in the Lord." Impersonalists consider annihilation of the self and merging with the Lord as the last word in divine love. As for the meaning intended by Nārada and the scriptures, the Māyāvādīs say that this is a concession "for the ordinary devotees."

Vaiṣṇavas, however, do not tolerate such blasphemous word jugglery. The oneness of God and *guru* (or God and all living beings) is a oneness in quality. The living entities are small samples of the original Supreme Personality of Godhead, who is full, powerful, and opulent. The living beings tend to forget their qualitative oneness with the Lord, and so He appears in the form of scriptures, great souls, and the *caitya-guru* (Supersoul) to remind us of our spiritual identity. The Supersoul doesn't have to be reminded of His own divinity, because He is never designated by a material body. This is another difference between the *jīvas* and the Lord: The Lord is always self-enlightened in His spiritual form, while the *jīvas* are always prone to come under the influence of *māyā*. Another difference between the two is that the Supersoul is present in everyone's body, whereas the individual conditioned soul is present in one particular body.

The *sac-cid-ānanda* form of Godhead is different from that of the living entity in both his conditioned and liberated states. Although the Māyāvādīs will continue to misunderstand the philosophy of spiritual oneness, a *kavi,* or learned person, doesn't commit such mistakes. Śrīla Prabhupāda describes the position of the Māyāvādīs and those they influence:

> Only atheists consider the living entity and the Personality of Godhead equal in all respects. Caitanya Mahāprabhu therefore says, *māyāvādi-bhāṣya śunile haya sarva-nāśa:* "If one follows the instructions of Māyāvādī philosophers and believes that the Supreme Personality of Godhead and the individual soul are one, his understanding of real philosophy is forever doomed." [*Bhāg.* 4.28.63, purport]

SŪTRA 42

तदेव साध्यतां तदेव साध्यताम् ॥४२॥

tad eva sādhyatāṁ tad eva sādhyatām

tat—that; *eva*—only; *sādhyatām*—should be strived for; *tat*—that; *eva*—only; *sādhyatām*—should be strived for.

TRANSLATION

Strive, strive only for the association of pure devotees.

PURPORT

Nāradadeva blesses the hearers of the *Nārada-bhakti-sūtra* with his advice, repeated twice here for emphasis—strive, strive for attaining the lotus feet of *guru* and Kṛṣṇa via the association of pure devotees. When the Lord and His devotees see our sincere efforts, they will give us all required assistance.

The best expression of single-minded devotion to Kṛṣṇa was given by Śrī Caitanya Mahāprabhu. Let us strive to follow in His footsteps, always asking for direction from His well-wishing followers and always praying as He showed us in His *Śikṣāṣṭaka* (4):

na dhanaṁ na janaṁ na sundarīṁ
kavitāṁ vā jagad-īśa kāmaye
mama janmani janmanīśvare
bhavatād bhaktir ahaitukī tvayi

"O almighty Lord, I have no desire to accumulate wealth, nor do I desire beautiful women, nor do I want any number of followers. I only want Your causeless devotional service, birth after birth."

SŪTRA 43

दुःसंगं सर्वथैव त्याज्यः ॥४३॥

duḥsaṅgaṁ sarvathaiva tyājyaḥ

duḥsaṅgam—bad association; *sarvathā*—in all its aspects; *eva*—indeed; *tyājyaḥ*—to be given up.

TRANSLATION

One should give up all kinds of degrading association.

PURPORT

After stating that the association of pure devotees is as good as being with the Supreme Lord, Nārada informs us of the destructive effects of bad company. As we mentioned previously, Lord Caitanya once defined a Vaiṣṇava as one who gives up the association of worldly people and nondevotees: *asat-saṅga-tyāga—ei vaiṣṇava ācāra.* Caitanya Mahāprabhu specifically enumerated different types of *asat-saṅga: strī-saṅgī, eka asādhu krsnābhakta āra* (Cc. *Madhya* 22.87). A Vaiṣṇava should avoid *strī-saṅgī,* those who associate loosely with women, and he should also shun the *kṛṣṇa-abhaktas,* those who are not devotees of Kṛṣṇa. This especially refers to Māyāvādīs.

Lord Kapila states, "The infatuation and bondage that accrue to a man from attachment to any other object is not as complete as that resulting from an attachment to a woman or to the fellowship of men who are fond of women" (*Bhāg.* 3.31.35). In the Kali-yuga, we are constantly invited to partake in illicit sex through advertising and television. Unrestricted social mixing between men and women is a major distraction from the spiritual path.

The statements about women should not be taken as a criticism of women as a class. Just as woman is often the symbol of *māyā* for a man, so attachment to men is also the main entanglement for a woman. As Lord Kapila states, "A woman, therefore, should consider her husband, her house, and her children to be the arrangement of the external energy of the Lord for her death, just as the sweet singing of the hunter is death for the deer" (*Bhāg.* 3.31.42). Of course, it is not possible to completely restrict the sexes from associating with each other, and so the positive approach is to put Kṛṣṇa in the center of one's life. If a man and a woman live in a Kṛṣṇa conscious marriage, transferring their main attachment to Kṛṣṇa, then their relationship may become a source of spiritual rejuvenation.

When Lord Caitanya says that one should avoid the non-*sādhus,* he means persons who don't follow basic principles of religious life. For example, every Kṛṣṇa conscious devotee follows the four rules, but the non-*sādhus* always indulge in illicit sex, meat-eating, intoxication, and gambling. If a devotee begins to intensively associate with non-*sādhus,* he will eventually pick up their habits, despite all his knowledge and training. As stated in the *Hari-bhakti-sudhodaya,* "Association is very important. It acts just like a crystal stone, which will reflect anything put before it" (*The Nectar of Devotion,* p. 106). And as Lord Caitanya taught Sanātana Gosvāmī, "One should not even see those who are bereft of devotional service in Kṛṣṇa consciousness and who are therefore devoid of pious activities" (Cc. *Madhya* 22.92).

When the demon Hiraṇyakaśipu sarcastically inquired from his son about Kṛṣṇa consciousness, Prahlāda explained why the demons cannot possibly know about Kṛṣṇa:

matir na kṛṣṇe parataḥ svato vā
mitho 'bhipadyeta gṛha-vratānām
adānta-gobhir viśatāṁ tamisraṁ
punaḥ-punaś-carvita-carvaṇānām

"[Prahlāda Mahārāja said:] Because of their uncontrolled senses, persons too addicted to materialistic life make progress toward hellish conditions and repeatedly chew that which has already been chewed.

Their inclinations toward Kṛṣṇa are never aroused, either by the instructions of others, by their own efforts, or by a combination of both" (*Bhāg.* 7.5.30).

Those with uncontrolled senses can never know Kṛṣṇa themselves, and if an aspiring devotee associates with them, he will also lose his ability to know Kṛṣṇa.

Association with nondevotees takes place in many ways, aside from face-to-face encounters. Through books, movies, gathering places—the possibilities of contact are unlimited. Especially nowadays, a person may apparently live alone in a city apartment and yet be completely immersed in bad association through mass media and technological entertainment. It takes deliberate cultivation, and a fight, to remove oneself from bad influences.

One may object to these injunctions and claim, "God is everywhere! Why say that certain people are bad?" The topmost devotee, the *mahā-bhāgavata,* can see all persons as perfect servants of God. He humbly thinks that everyone is a servant of the Lord except himself. But another qualification of a *mahā-bhāgavata* is that he always thinks of Kṛṣṇa and never forgets Him for a moment. One should not imitate one aspect of the *mahā-bhāgavata's* activities while lacking his qualifications. In other words, on the plea of following the example of the great devotees, one should not indulge in bad association and claim, "It's all Kṛṣṇa."

The great majority of devotees have to make an effort to come up from the lower (*kaniṣṭha*) stage of devotion, where one sees God only in the temple. They have to strive to reach the second stage (*madhyama*), where one acknowledges that God is in everyone's heart and yet discriminates in his relationships. The *madhyama-bhakta* saves his love for the Supreme Lord, makes friendships with like-minded devotees, shows compassion to innocent persons, and avoids the demons. He takes seriously the following injunction from the *Kātyāyana-saṁhitā:* "It is better to accept the miseries of being encaged within bars and surrounded by burning flames than to associate with those bereft of Kṛṣṇa consciousness. Such association is a very great hardship" (Cc. *Madhya* 21).

SŪTRA 44

कामक्रोधमोहस्मृतिभ्रंशबुद्धिनाशसर्वनाशकारणत्वात् ॥४४॥

kāma-krodha-moha-smṛti-bhraṁśa-buddhi-nāśa-sarva-nāśa-kāraṇatvāt

kāma—of lust; *krodha*—anger; *moha*—bewilderment; *smṛti-bhraṁśa*—failure of memory; *buddhi-nāśa*—loss of intelligence; *sarva-nāśa*—and total loss; *kāraṇatvāt*—because of being the cause.

TRANSLATION

Material association is the cause of lust, anger, confusion, forgetfulness, loss of intelligence, and total calamity.

PURPORT

One may wonder why Nārada is dwelling on the effects of bad association after having discussed advanced subjects in *bhakti-yoga*. But who else will heed the warnings except those who are serious about crossing the ocean of birth and death? Even one who is practicing devotional service in the renounced order can fall down. As stated in *Caitanya-candrodaya-nāṭaka* (8.23),

niṣkiñcanasya bhagavad-bhajanonmukhasya
pāraṁ paraṁ jigamiṣor bhava-sāgarasya
sandarśanaṁ viṣayiṇām atha yoṣitāṁ ca
hā hanta hanta viṣa-bhakṣaṇato 'py asādhu

"Alas, for a person who is seriously desiring to cross the material ocean and engage in the transcendental loving service without material motives, seeing a materialist engaged in sense gratification and seeing a woman who is similarly interested are more abominable than drinking poison willingly." And so the advice against bad association is intended for all, including those transcendentalists who wish to progress without impediment.

In the *Bhagavad-gītā* (2.62–63), Lord Kṛṣṇa analyzes the soul's downfall due to bad association:

dhyāyato viṣayān puṁsaḥ saṅgas teṣūpajāyate
saṅgāt sañjāyate kāmaḥ kāmāt krodho 'bhijāyate

krodhād bhavati sammohaḥ sammohāt smṛti-vibhramaḥ
smṛti-bhraṁśād buddhi-nāśo buddhi-nāśāt praṇaśyati

"While contemplating the objects of the senses, a person develops attachment for them, and from such attachment lust develops, and from lust anger arises. From anger complete delusion arises, and from delusion bewilderment of memory. When memory is bewildered, intelligence is lost, and when intelligence is lost one falls down again into the material pool."

Bad association (*duḥsaṅga)* brings out the stored karmic tendencies for sin, thus activating one's lower propensities. If an aspiring devotee hears the hedonists talk of lusty enjoyments, he may easily become agitated, since until he becomes pure he has many tendencies to enjoy worldly pleasures. As soon as he begins to think about the objects of pleasure, he will begin to desire them. Then he will attempt to fulfill his desires, and on being frustrated he will become angry. Thereafter he will lose his discrimination, become deluded, and so on. By keeping company with nondevotees, therefore, bad habits crop up one after another, and good qualities become ruined. As Lord Kapiladeva states (*Bhāg.* 3.31.32–33):

> If, therefore, the living entity again associates with the path of unrighteousness, influenced by sensually-minded people engaged in the pursuit of sexual enjoyment and the gratification of the palate, he again goes to hell as before. He becomes devoid of truthfulness, cleanliness, mercy, gravity, spiritual intelligence, shyness, austerity, fame, forgiveness, control of the mind, control of the senses, fortune, and all such opportunities.

Not only "coarse fools" but even austere ascetics—if they are not devotees—are considered *duḥsaṅga.* Mental speculators, impersonal *yogīs, jñānīs,* and voidists may all adversely influence a devotee and turn him toward nondevotional paths. Bhagavān Ācārya, a follower of Lord Caitanya's, insisted that he was immune to contamination because he was a fixed-up devotee of the Lord. But Svarūpa Dāmodara Gosvāmī replied that hearing talks on Māyāvāda philosophy "breaks the heart and life of a devotee" and should not be indulged in. Śrīla Prabhupāda writes:

> The Māyāvādī philosophers have presented their arguments in such attractive, flowery language that hearing Māyāvāda philosophy may sometimes change the mind of even a *mahā-bhāgavata,* or very advanced devotee. An actual Vaiṣṇava cannot tolerate any philosophy that claims God and the living being to be one and the same. [Cc. *Ādi* 7.110, purport]

Considering the dangers of *duḥsaṅga,* even for a fully engaged *sādhaka,* we can see that Nārada has not exaggerated these dangers or given a warning only for neophytes.

SŪTRA 45

तरंगिता अपीमे संगात् समुद्रायन्ति ॥४५॥

taraṅgitā apīme saṅgāt samudrāyanti

taraṅgitāḥ—forming waves; *api*—indeed; *ime*—these; *saṅgāt*—from material association; *samudrāyanti*—create an ocean.

TRANSLATION

Rising like waves from material association, these bad effects mass into a great ocean of misery.

PURPORT

The deluding potency, *māyā,* is the Lord's own energy and can thus overcome even a powerful sage. As Lord Kapila declares, "Among all kinds of living entities begotten by Brahmā, namely men, demigods, and animals, none but the sage Nārāyaṇa is immune to the attraction of *māyā* in the form of a woman" (*Bhāg.* 3.31.37). One should not flirt with *māyā,* thinking that one can transgress a little and then pull back later if it gets too rough. Until we are completely liberated we maintain seeds of destruction within us, and we should not allow them to grow by bad association.

Once Śrīla Prabhupāda learned that some of his initiated disciples had indulged in their former habits of smoking marijuana. Prabhupāda said that this was due to bad association, and he gave the example of bedbugs. During winter, bedbugs seem to disappear from your bed, but in due time they emerge and again bite you and grow fat on your blood. Similarly, a transcendentalist's *kāma* may seem to be entirely subdued, but it is actually present in a very reduced state. If given a fresh opportunity, his material desires will strike again. On another occasion, Śrīla Prabhupāda referred to "hippy seeds." Having noticed one of his *brahmacārī* disciples with long hair, he said the disciple's old hippy tendencies were now sprouting in the form of long hair.

So it is good to be afraid of even a little bad association and avoid it at all costs. But one may question whether this attitude is at odds with the compassionate mood of the preacher. If the preacher associates with materialists, won't he become like them? The answer is that a preacher must be strong in his Kṛṣṇa consciousness to prevent becoming contaminated. If he follows the rules and regulations of *bhakti-yoga*—including association with devotees, chanting and hearing the Lord's glories, avoiding sense gratification, and so on—then he will be able to preach without falling down. Acting as the spiritual master of Lord Caitanya, Īśvara Purī gave him instructions that in truth are directed at us: "My dear child, continue dancing, chanting, and performing *saṅkīrtana* in association with devotees. Furthermore, go out and preach the value of chanting *kṛṣṇa-nāma,* for by this process You will be able to deliver all fallen souls" (Cc. *Ādi* 7.92). Similarly, Śrīla Prabhupāda instructed his disciples to be compassionate preachers:

> One who is not very expert in preaching may chant in a secluded place, avoiding bad association, but for one who is actually advanced, preaching and meeting people who are not engaged in devotional service are not disadvantages. A devotee gives the nondevotees his association but is not affected by their misbehavior. Thus by the activities of a pure devotee even those who are bereft of love of Godhead get a chance to become devotees of the Lord one day. [Cc. *Ādi* 7.92, purport]

Śrīla Prabhupāda sometimes told the following story to illustrate how one may mix with nondevotees and yet keep one's devotional integrity:

Once a crocodile invited a monkey in a tree to come and ride on his back. The foolish monkey jumped down from the tree and soon found himself clinging to the crocodile's back in the middle of the river.

The monkey asked the crocodile, "Where are we going?"

The crocodile replied, "I'm going to take you home, where my wife will cut out your heart and we will eat you for lunch!"

The monkey replied, "But I left my heart back on shore in the tree. Will you please let me get it?"

The crocodile thought this was a good proposal and allowed the monkey to touch shore. But the monkey jumped into his tree and refused to accept further invitations from the crocodile.

The moral of this story: You may associate with the nondevotee, but don't give him your heart.

Preachers living in ISKCON temples follow this advice daily. They rise early and gather for *maṅgala-ārati* before the temple Deities, chant *kīrtana* and *japa*, hear *Śrīmad-Bhāgavatam* class, and honor *prasādam* in the association of devotees. Strengthened by this morning program, they go out to preach in the most materialistic places in the world, offering people a chance to receive Kṛṣṇa's mercy in the form of literature, *prasādam*, or *hari-nāma*. In the early evening the preachers return to the temple for more chanting and hearing. While they are with the nondevotees, they do not compromise their devotional principles, and thus they keep their hearts aloof from the modes of material nature and bad association.

Of course, if a preacher finds himself being overwhelmed by the material energy, he should save himself instead of allowing *māyā* to swallow him up while he's trying to save others. But Nārada's advice against bad association does not mean that those who are strong enough to preach should not approach the Jagāis and Mādhāis of this world and humbly offer them the holy name and transcendental literature. If devotees don't approach them, how will the fools and rascals be saved?

SŪTRA 46

कस्तरति कस्तरति मायां यः संगं त्यजति
यो महानुभावं सेवते निर्ममो भवति ॥४६॥

kas tarati kas tarati māyāṁ yaḥ saṅgaṁ tyajati yo mahānubhāvaṁ sevate nirmamo bhavati

kaḥ—who; *tarati*—crosses beyond; *kaḥ*—who; *tarati*—crosses beyond; *māyām*—illusion; *yaḥ*—he who; *saṅgam*—material association; *tyajati*—abandons; *yaḥ*—who; *mahā-anubhāvam*—the wise person; *sevate*—serves; *nirmamaḥ*—free from false proprietorship; *bhavati*—becomes.

TRANSLATION

Who can cross beyond illusion? One who abandons material association, serves the sages, and becomes selfless.

PURPORT

Crossing over *māyā* is sometimes compared to crossing an ocean. At the time of death the conditioned soul has to transmigrate to another material body, and even if he is born in a higher planet, he still has to suffer repeated birth and death. To cross the limits of this ocean of *saṁsāra,* he has to go back to Godhead. But this is very difficult, because any material desires, whether sinful or pious, will plunge the conditioned soul back into *saṁsāra.*

However, Lord Kṛṣṇa makes the process easy. In the *Bhagavad-gītā* (7.14) He states,

daivī hy eṣā guṇa-mayī mama māyā duratyayā
mām eva ye prapadyante māyām etāṁ taranti te

"This divine energy of mine, consisting of the three modes of material nature, is difficult to overcome. But those who have surrendered unto Me can easily cross beyond it."

Nārada is now giving detailed information on how to surrender to Kṛṣṇa and cross over the powerful ocean of illusion. In this *sūtra* he mentions renouncing attachment, associating with great souls, and becoming free of possessiveness. One has to attempt all these and other favorable methods, but at the same time one must understand that he cannot swim across the ocean on his own. By one's sincere acts of devotion, Kṛṣṇa is moved to come to the rescue. Lord Kṛṣṇa tells Arjuna, "But those who worship Me, giving up all their activities unto Me and being devoted to Me without deviation, engaged in devotional service—for them I am the swift deliverer from the ocean of birth and death" (Bg. 12.6–7). In his purport Śrīla Prabhupāda states, "Simply by chanting the holy name of Kṛṣṇa—Hare Kṛṣṇa, Hare Kṛṣṇa, Kṛṣṇa Kṛṣṇa, Hare Hare/ Hare Rāma, Hare Rāma, Rāma Rāma, Hare Hare—

a devotee of the Lord can approach the supreme destination easily and happily, but this destination cannot be approached by any other process of religion."

As already stated, the mercy of the Lord is best obtained from His pure devotees. They enable one to take shelter of the Lord's lotus feet, which act like a boat to carry one across the vast ocean of *māyā:*

> O lotus-eyed Lord, by concentrating one's meditation on Your lotus feet, which are the reservoir of all existence, and by accepting those lotus feet as the boat by which to cross the ocean of nescience, one follows in the footsteps of *mahā-janas* [great saints, sages, and devotees]. By this simple process, one can cross the ocean of nescience as easily as one steps over the hoofprint of a calf. [*Bhāg.* 10.2.30]

SŪTRA 47

यो विविक्तस्थानं सेवते यो लोकबन्धमुन्मूलयति
निस्त्रैगुण्यो भवति यो योगक्षेमं त्यजति ॥४७॥

yo vivikta-sthānaṁ sevate yo loka-bandham unmūlayati nistraiguṇyo bhavati yo yoga-kṣemaṁ tyajati

yaḥ—who; *vivikta*—secluded; *sthānam*—a place; *sevate*—serves; *yaḥ*—who; *loka*—of mundane society; *bandham*—the bondage; *unmūlayati*—uproots; *nistrai-guṇyaḥ*—free from the influence of the three modes of material nature; *bhavati*—becomes; *yaḥ*—who; *yoga*—(desire for) gain; *kṣemam*—and security; *tyajati*—gives up.

TRANSLATION

[Who can cross beyond illusion?] That person who stays in a secluded place, cuts off at the root his attachment to mundane society, becomes free from the influence of the three modes of nature, and gives up hankering for material gain and security.

PURPORT

Nārada is giving more ways to cross beyond *māyā.* The first is solitude (*vivikta-sthānaṁ sevate*). Several times in the *Bhagavad-gītā* Lord Kṛṣṇa advises that one practice spiritual life alone. Solitude is particularly stressed in meditative *yoga,* which requires that one live alone in a secluded place (*rahasi sthitaḥ ekākī*) (Bg. 6.10). And in the Thirteenth Chapter, when listing the items of knowledge, Lord Kṛṣṇa includes *vivikta-deśa-sevitvam,* "aspiring to live in a solitary place" (Bg. 13.11). Again, in the Eighteenth Chapter, when describing a person who has been elevated to the position of self-realization, Lord Kṛṣṇa says that he "lives in a solitary place" (*vivikta-sevī*) (Bg. 18.52).

Neophyte devotees, however, are not advised to live alone. Although solitary *bhajana* was practiced by Nāmācārya Haridāsa Ṭhākura, and sometimes by Lord Caitanya, Bhaktisiddhānta Sarasvatī Ṭhākura criticized devotees who prematurely wanted to chant in a solitary place. He wrote, "My dear mind, why are you so proud of being a Vaiṣṇava? Your solitary worship and chanting of the holy name of the Lord are based on a desire for cheap popularity, and therefore your chanting of the holy name is only a pretension" (quoted in *Kṛṣṇa,* p. 882).

A sacred and solitary place, as mentioned in the *Gītā,* also refers to a place of pilgrimage. Śrīla Prabhupāda writes, "In India the *yogīs*—the transcendentalists or the devotees—all leave home and reside in sacred places such as Prayāga, Mathurā, Vṛndāvana, Hṛṣīkeśa, and Hardwar and in solitude practice *yoga* where the sacred rivers like the Yamunā and Ganges flow" (Bg. 6.11–12, purport). For devotees of Kṛṣṇa, the most sacred place of pilgrimage is Mathurā-maṇḍala, the district that includes Mathurā and Vṛndāvana. Rūpa Gosvāmī recommends living in Mathurā-maṇḍala as one of the five main principles of *bhakti-yoga,* and Śrīla Prabhupāda praises Mathurā-maṇḍala as follows in his summary study of Rūpa Gosvāmī's *Bhakti-rasāmṛta-sindhu:*

> A pure devotee of Lord Kṛṣṇa resides in the district of Mathurā or Vṛndāvana and visits all the places where Kṛṣṇa's pastimes were performed. . . . Actually, if someone goes to Vṛndāvana, he will immediately feel separation from Kṛṣṇa, who performed such nice activities when He was present there. [*The Nectar of Devotion,* p. 139]

Śrīla Prabhupāda worked hard for many years to establish temples in Vṛndāvana and in Māyāpura, the birthplace of Lord Caitanya, so that Westerners could come and be purified by living in the *dhāma.* Of Vṛndāvana Śrīla Prabhupāda states, "The places in the eighty-four-square-mile district of Mathurā are so beautifully situated on the banks of the river Yamunā that anyone who goes there will never want to return to this material world. . . . Transcendental feelings are aroused immediately without fail after one arrives in Mathurā or Vṛndāvana" (*The Nectar of Devotion,* p. 111). The essential benefit of a solitary place is that it provides freedom from worldly people and passions. For devotees, this can best be attained in the *dhāma,* in the association of like-minded souls.

Nārada also says that one who wants to overcome *māyā* must break the bonds of material attachment and live above the modes of nature. These are some of the natural results of Kṛṣṇa conscious life. In the Fourteenth Chapter of the *Bhagavad-gītā* Lord Kṛṣṇa describes how the three modes of nature—goodness, passion, and ignorance—bind the living entity in *saṁsāra.* To become free of the modes, one has to hear the truth from the spiritual master. Then one will gradually understand his original spiritual nature and how one is entrapped by the modes. If one lives in the association of transcendentalists and serves Lord Kṛṣṇa along with them, one will not be controlled by the modes of goodness, passion, and ignorance. The *ācāryas* tell us that living in the forest is in the mode of goodness, living in a town is in the mode of passion, and living in a brothel is in the mode of ignorance—but to live in a temple of Viṣṇu, in the society of devotees, is Vaikuṇṭha. Indeed, another meaning of "secluded and sacred place" is the temple of the Lord. Śrīla Prabhupāda writes, "In this *bhakti-yoga* system, the temple is considered the sacred place. The temple is *nirguṇa,* transcendental" (*The Path of Perfection,* p. 38).

Nārada also recommends renouncing anxieties for acquisition and maintenance: *yoga-kṣemaṁ tyajati.* Lord Kṛṣṇa also mentions *yoga-kṣema* in the *Bhagavad-gītā* (9.22):

ananyāś cintayanto māṁ ye janāḥ paryupāsate
teṣāṁ nityābhiyuktānāṁ yoga-kṣemaṁ vahāmy aham

"But those who always worship Me with exclusive devotion, meditating on My transcendental form—to them I carry what they lack, and I preserve what they have."

Dependence on the Lord for maintenance is an advanced stage of spiritual life, but it is not based on imagination. The principle is that one should not want more than what is absolutely necessary. Wanting anything beyond that will simply cause anxiety. In any case, whether one is a poor *brāhmaṇa,* a mendicant *sannyāsī,* a businessman, or an administrator in a religious institution, he or she should realize that the Supreme Lord is the actual maintainer. If we live simply, engaging in Kṛṣṇa's service and not creating unnecessary demands, we will be able to reduce concerns for maintenance and enter the spirit of *yoga-kṣemaṁ tyajati,* as recommended by Nārada Muni.

SŪTRA 48

यः कर्मफलं कर्माणि सन्यस्यति ततो निर्द्वन्द्वो भवति ॥४८॥

yaḥ karma-phalaṁ karmāṇi sanyasyati tato nirdvandvo bhavati

yaḥ—who; *karma-phalam*—the fruit of material work; *karmāṇi*—his material activities; *sanyasati*—resigns; *tataḥ*—thus; *nirdvandvaḥ*—unaffected by dualities; *bhavati*—becomes.

TRANSLATION

[Who can cross beyond illusion?] That person who renounces material duties and their profits, thus transcending duality.

PURPORT

A devotee has faith that Lord Kṛṣṇa will supply his needs. But this does not mean that he becomes lazy or inactive. He works for Kṛṣṇa. By dedicating all acts to the Lord, the devotee becomes free from karmic reactions. As long as one continues to work under the influence of the modes of nature, one must experience duality—good and bad, hot and cold, rich and poor, pleasure and pain, and so on. As Lord Kṛṣṇa states in *Bhagavad-gītā* (7.28),

icchā-dveṣa-samutthena dvandva-mohena bhārata
sarva-bhūtāni sammohaṁ sarge yānti paran-tapa

"O scion of Bhārata, O conqueror of foes, all living entities are born into delusion, bewildered by dualities arisen from desire and hate." And in his purport, Prabhupāda explains,

> Deluded persons, symptomatically, dwell in dualities of dishonor and honor, misery and happiness, woman and man, good and bad,

pleasure and pain, etc., thinking, "This is my wife; this is my house; I am the master of this house; I am the husband of this wife." These are the dualities of delusion. Those who are so deluded by dualities are completely foolish and therefore cannot understand the Supreme Personality of Godhead.

The delusion of duality stems from identifying the self with the body. When a person understands that he is not the body but an eternal servant of Kṛṣṇa, the delusion of duality ceases for him. A devotee can break the bonds of duality even while living in the material world. When a devotee feels bodily heat or cold, pleasure or pain, he sees it in terms of the body, and he continues to perform his service without distraction. Early in the *Bhagavad-gītā,* Lord Kṛṣṇa advises Arjuna to remain equipoised in both happiness and distress. Later, Kṛṣṇa expresses His pleasure with the devotee who transcends duality: "One who neither rejoices nor grieves, who neither laments nor desires, and who renounces both auspicious and inauspicious things—such a devotee is very dear to Me" (Bg. 12.17).

It should be obvious by now that *bhakti* is not merely pious thoughts of "love" but rather fearless action. Nārada asks nothing less of the *bhakta* than complete surrender and complete dedication unto the will of Bhagavān. But if at any point one feels himself unable to reach the ideals taught by Nārada, he is not condemned. Lord Kṛṣṇa also says that if we cannot achieve the topmost surrender, then we should do what we can and try to progress gradually (see *Bhagavad-gītā* 12.8–12). But we should be humble about our inability to fully surrender to Lord Kṛṣṇa. We should not attempt to change the uncompromising teachings in order to justify our weakness. Nārada and the Vaiṣṇava *ācāryas* are asking us to change our lives in order to become *bhaktas,* because that alone will make us eternally happy. The difficulties we feel in making these changes are due to our material attachments.

Lord Kṛṣṇa gives a stern order in *Bhagavad-gītā* (3.30):

mayi sarvāṇi karmāṇi sannyasyādhyātma-cetasā
nirāśīr nirmamo bhūtvā yudhyasva vigata-jvaraḥ

"O Arjuna, surrendering all your works unto Me, with full knowledge of Me, without desires for profit, with no claims to proprietorship, and free from lethargy, fight." And Śrīla Prabhupāda was also stern, cautioning his followers, "An easy-going life and Kṛṣṇa consciousness go ill together." *Māyā* dictates to us to take it easy and stay in the material world, but her suggestions are only a deception. She will tell us not to perform austerities in devotional service, but if we fall under her influence, we will be forced to labor and suffer in lower species of life, birth after birth. Nārada is asking us to undergo a little trouble now in order to cross over the ocean of *māyā* and be free of all suffering forever.

SŪTRA 49

यो वेदानपि सन्यस्यति केवलमविच्छिन्नानुरागं लभते ॥४९॥

yo vedān api sanyasyati kevalam avicchinnānurāgaṁ labhate

yaḥ—who; *vedān*—the *Vedas;* *api*—even; *sanyasyati*—renounces; *kevalam*—exclusive; *avicchinna*—uninterrupted; *anurāgam*—loving attraction; *labhate*—obtains.

TRANSLATION

That person who renounces even the *Vedas* obtains exclusive and uninterrupted attraction for God.

PURPORT

By "renouncing the *Vedas*" Nārada means renouncing the fruitive sacrifices recommended in the *Vedas' karma-kāṇḍīya* portions, which are for those pursuing fruitive results. Lord Kṛṣṇa advises Arjuna, "The *Vedas* deal mainly with the subject of the three modes of material nature. O Arjuna, become transcendental to these three modes. . . . All purposes served by a small well can at once be served by a great reservoir of water. Similarly, all the purposes of the *Vedas* can be served to one who knows the purpose behind them" (Bg. 2.45–46). The *karma-kāṇḍīya* instructions are for gradual development, but the ultimate goal is to know Lord Kṛṣṇa, the cause of all causes (see *Bhagavad-gītā* 15.15). If one is attached only to the rituals and not the goal, then he cannot rise to the transcendental stage.

Similarly, the study of the *Vedānta-sūtra* is meant for understanding

Lord Kṛṣṇa. Śrīla Prabhupāda writes, "Vedānta is the last word in Vedic wisdom, and the author and knower of the Vedānta philosophy is Lord Kṛṣṇa; and the highest Vedāntist is the great soul who takes pleasure in chanting the holy name of the Lord" (Bg. 2.46, purport).

Śrīla Vyāsadeva begins the *Śrīmad-Bhāgavatam* (1.1.2) with the declaration that no lesser forms of religion will be taught: *dharmaḥ projjhita-kaitavaḥ.* Only pure devotional service is taught in the *Bhāgavata Purāṇa.* Lord Kṛṣṇa also concludes His instructions to Arjuna by advising him, *sarva-dharmān parityajya mām ekaṁ śaraṇaṁ vraja:* "Abandon all varieties of religion and just surrender unto Me." (Bg. 18.66)

Still, although a pure devotee ignores the *karma-kāṇḍīya* portion of the *Vedas* and gives up all forms of *dharma* save *bhakti,* he never defies the *bhakti-śāstras* or gives up following their injunctions. In fact, liberated souls always relish hearing the pastimes of the Personality of Godhead from transcendental books like the *Śrīmad-Bhāgavatam,* the *Caitanya-caritāmṛta,* and the works of the six Gosvāmīs of Vṛndāvana. Śrīla Prabhupāda writes, "The *Śrīmad-Bhāgavatam* . . . is purely transcendental literature which can be understood only by the pure devotees of the Lord who are transcendental to competitive sense gratification" (*Bhāg.* 1.1.2, purport). Śrīla Vyāsadeva says, "O thoughtful devotees, as long as you are not absorbed in transcendental bliss, you should continue tasting the *Śrīmad-Bhāgavatam,* and when you are fully absorbed in bliss you should go on tasting its mellows forever" (*Bhāg.* 1.1.3). The sages at Naimiṣāraṇya declare, "We never tire of hearing the transcendental pastimes of the Personality of Godhead, who is glorified by hymns and prayers. Those who enjoy association with Him relish hearing His pastimes at every moment" (*Bhāg.* 1.1.19).

Even great souls who were liberated in Brahman realization became attracted to the narrations of Kṛṣṇa in *Śrīmad-Bhāgavatam.* As Śukadeva Gosvāmī told Mahārāja Parīkṣit, "My dear King, although I was fully situated in the transcendental position, I was nonetheless attracted to the pastimes of Lord Kṛṣṇa. Therefore I studied *Śrīmad-Bhāgavatam* from my father." (*Bhāg.* 2.1.9) And Lord Caitanya, though God Himself, constantly relished hearing the *Bhāgavatam* and other Vaiṣṇava literatures, as well as the poetry of Vaiṣṇava saints, which He discussed among His intimate devotees. So renouncing the *karma-kāṇḍīya* rituals of the *Vedas* does not mean giving up the eternal pastimes of Lord Kṛṣṇa.

For those who are striving for perfection, certainly the relevant part of the *Vedas* is not to be rejected. But sometimes devotees in the spon-taneous stage appear to come into conflict with Vedic customs. Once Sārvabhauma Bhaṭṭācārya had to explain this stage of spontaneous love to King Pratāparudra. The king had observed the devotees of Lord Caitanya arriving in Purī without following some of the customary rules. The king asked Sārvabhauma, "Why have they not observed the regulations for visiting the pilgrimage place, such as fasting and shaving the head? Why have they first eaten *prasādam*?" Sārvabhauma replied to the king, "What you have said is right according to the regulative principles governing the visiting of holy places, but there is another path, which is the path of spontaneous love. According to those principles, there are subtle intricacies involved in the execution of religious principles" (Cc. *Madhya* 11.111–12). Because Lord Caitanya was personally present and distributing *prasādam* from His own hand, His intimate devotees neglected the regulative principle of fasting.

Nārada uses the word *kevalam,* which indicates that one's love for Kṛṣṇa must be undivided and unalloyed. *Bhakti* as taught by Nārada is not part-time service, or devotion only up to a certain point. In the spontaneous stage, all considerations except *bhakti* are unimportant, as in the *gopīs'* rejection of family and social considerations. The *gopīs* did not disregard their duties consciously, but they were simply unable to think of anything but going to Kṛṣṇa.

When a devotee reaches the stage Nārada describes here, his devotional service flows uninterruptedly. Queen Kuntī aspired for that stage: "O Lord of Madhu," she prayed, "as the Ganges ever flows to the sea without hindrance, let my attraction be constantly drawn unto You without being diverted to anyone else" (*Bhāg.* 1.8.42). Śrīla Prabhupāda describes Nārada Muni's own flow of devotional service:

> Such a flow of devotional service cannot stop. On the contrary, it increases more and more without limitation. The flow of devotional service is so potent that any onlooker also becomes liberated from the influence of the modes of passion and ignorance. [*Bhāg.* 1.5.28, purport]

Neophyte devotees complain of sporadic enthusiasm. They are sometimes eager to chant and hear of Kṛṣṇa, but at other times they are troubled by thoughts of sense pleasure and a lack of taste for Kṛṣṇa consciousness. This up-and-down syndrome is not unusual for beginners. Every soul's original state is to experience a spontaneous flow of love of God, but this love has been covered by countless millions of years of conditioning in the material world. This conditioning is not easy to overcome. In the early stages of *bhakti,* therefore, determination is of the utmost importance. At the same time, we may be inspired by the reality of spontaneous love as described by Nārada and exhibited by devotees who serve the Lord in *prema-bhakti.*

SŪTRA 50

स तरति स तरति लोकांस्तारयति ॥५०॥

sa tarati sa tarati lokāṁs tārayati

saḥ—he; *tarati*—crosses beyond; *saḥ*—he; *tarati*—crosses beyond; *lokān*—the people of this world; *tārayati*—he makes cross beyond.

TRANSLATION

Such a person, indeed, is delivered, and he also delivers the rest of the world.

PURPORT

Nārada repeats "He crosses *māyā*" so that there will be no doubt. The skeptic questions, "Has anyone really crossed over *māyā?*" Don't doubt, Nārada says: The pure devotee crosses *māyā,* and he can deliver you, too.

Many disciples of Śrīla Prabhupāda attest to the fact that he personally picked them up from *māyā.* When I first met Śrīla Prabhupāda, I asked him, "Is there a stage in spiritual advancement from which one won't fall back?" Prabhupāda replied, "Yes." And his answer convinced me. The perfect answer in a book would not have been enough for me. Although great souls are not self-assertive, they personally demonstrate that liberated persons do exist, and that they can help us. As the demigods stated in their prayers to Kṛṣṇa as He lay in the womb of Devakī, "When *ācāryas* completely take shelter under Your lotus feet in order to cross the fierce ocean of nescience, they leave behind on earth the method by which they cross, and because You are very merciful to Your other devotees, You accept this method to help them" (*Bhāg.* 10.2.31). Śrīla Prabhupāda writes,

> If things are made easy, this affords facility for the person who has made them easy and also for others who follow the same principles. The process recommended for crossing the ocean of nescience is easy not only for the devotee but for common persons who follow the devotee (*mahā-jano yena gataḥ sa panthāḥ*). [*Bhāg.* 10.2.30, purport]

Pure devotees help others in many ways. Sometimes they give lectures, and at other times they meet with both devotees and nondevotees. When persons come forward for more serious instruction, the pure devotee acts as spiritual master and trains disciples to render service to the Personality of Godhead. Sometimes pure devotees become authors. Śrīla Prabhupāda writes, "It is the duty of the *ācārya* to publish books that will help future candidates take up the method of service and become eligible to return home, back to Godhead, by the mercy of the Lord." Sometimes the liberated souls recruit disciples who then go out and preach, following the example of their spiritual master. Great souls sometimes begin movements or societies in which devotees can live and practice *bhakti.* And sometimes they construct temples where the public can come to see the Deity form of Lord Kṛṣṇa and taste His *prasādam,* the remnants of food offered to Him. Thus both by personal example and by precept, and even after their disappearance from the mortal world, the great souls help the conditioned souls who have forgotten their love for Kṛṣṇa. As Śrīla Bhaktivinoda Ṭhākura so eloquently put it:

> He reasons ill who says that Vaiṣṇavas die,
> When thou art living still in sound!
> The Vaiṣṇavas die to live, and living try
> To spread the holy name around.

CHAPTER 4

Pure and Mixed Devotion

SŪTRA 51

अनिर्वचनीयं प्रेमस्वरूपम् ॥५१॥

anirvacanīyaṁ prema-svarūpam

anirvacanīyam—beyond description; *prema*—of mature love of God; *svarūpam*—the essential identity.

TRANSLATION

The true nature of pure love of God is beyond description.

PURPORT

Although Nārada has been expertly analyzing *bhakti* from the beginning stages up to *parā bhakti,* he now says that it is inexpressible. *Bhakti* is particularly inexplicable to unqualified persons. Until a person practices devotion with faith, how can he know of it just by inquiring from a sage? Sometimes when devotees would ask Śrīla Prabhupāda questions on subjects that were beyond their ability to understand, he would give the analogy of a small boy trying to understand sexual pleasure. Because the child is physically immature, he cannot know what sex is, but once he reaches puberty, he automatically understands. When I first began typing Prabhupāda's manuscript of *Teachings of Lord Caitanya,* I was curious about some esoteric aspects of *parā bhakti.* Lord Caitanya described that when a devotee reaches perfection, he chooses to follow a particular eternal resident of Vṛndāvana and learn of his own *rasa* from that resident. In March of 1967 I wrote to Prabhupāda asking more about this subject. He replied as follows:

> When we are in the perfect stage of devotional service, we can know our eternal relation with Krishna, and as such one of the

associates of Lord Krishna becomes our ideal leader. This acceptance of leadership by one of the eternal associates of the Lord is not artificial. Do not therefore try it at present; it will be automatically revealed to you at the proper time.

It is not only immature young *bhaktas* who are barred from understanding *parā bhakti*. This advanced stage of devotion is even beyond the ability of erudite scholars to fathom. Kṛṣṇadāsa Kavirāja writes, "The pastimes of Lord Kṛṣṇa are uncommonly full of transcendental potency. It is characteristic of such pastimes that they do not fall within the jurisdiction of experimental logic and arguments" (Cc. *Antya* 19.103). Rūpa Gosvāmī echoes this statement: "The activities and symptoms of that exalted personality in whose heart love of Godhead has awakened cannot be understood even by the most learned scholar" (*Bhakti-rasāmṛta-sindhu* 1.4.17).

To say that *bhakti* is inexpressible is not merely an evasive reply given to an outsider. In the higher stages especially, *bhakti* is inconceivable. The most intense expression of love of Godhead was displayed by Lord Caitanya. As described in *Caitanya-caritāmṛta*, Śrī Kṛṣṇa wanted to know the love that Śrīmatī Rādhārāṇī felt for Him, and so He appeared as Lord Caitanya. Lord Caitanya's ecstatic feelings and expressions were recorded in notes kept by Svarūpa Dāmodara Gosvāmī, memorized by Raghunātha dāsa Gosvāmī, and related by Raghunātha dāsa to Kṛṣṇadāsa Kavirāja Gosvāmī. But in telling these pastimes in the *Caitanya-caritāmṛta*, Kṛṣṇadāsa Kavirāja confessed his limitations:

> Even Anantadeva, who possesses thousands of mouths, cannot fully describe the ecstatic transformations that Lord Caitanya experienced in a single day. What can a poor creature like me describe of those transformations? I can give only a hint of them, as if showing the moon through branches of a tree. This description, however, will satisfy the mind and ears of anyone who hears it, and he will be able to understand these uncommon activities of deep ecstatic love for Kṛṣṇa. Ecstatic love for Kṛṣṇa is wonderfully deep. By personally tasting the glorious sweetness of that love, Śrī Caitanya Mahāprabhu showed us its extreme limits. [Cc. *Antya* 17.64–67]

Although *prema-bhakti* is beyond words, whatever can be conveyed by authorized devotees is appreciated by those who are sincere and faithful. Kṛṣṇadāsa Kavirāja says,

Just try to hear these topics with faith, for there is great pleasure even in hearing them. That hearing will destroy all miseries pertaining to the body, mind, and other living entities, and the unhappiness of false arguments as well. [Cc. *Antya* 19.110]

A Vaiṣṇava compares the pastimes of Lord Kṛṣṇa or Lord Caitanya to the unlimited sky. Many birds fly in the sky, but some fly higher according to their abilities. In the society of devotees, realized souls share their realizations, but no one presumes to describe *all* the qualities or pastimes of Kṛṣṇa. *Bhakti* can therefore be partially expressed, but its totality is inconceivable and inexpressible. When Lord Caitanya was about to teach Rūpa Gosvāmī, He said,

My dear Rūpa, please listen to Me. It is not possible to describe devotional service completely; therefore I am just trying to give you a synopsis of the symptoms of devotional service. The ocean of the transcendental mellow of devotional service is so big that no one can estimate its length and breadth. However, just to help you taste it, I am describing but one drop. [Cc. *Madhya* 19.136–37]

SŪTRA 52

मूकास्वादनवत् ॥५२॥

mūkāsvādana-vat

mūkā—of a mute; *āsvādana*—the tasting; *vat*—like.

TRANSLATION

[Trying to describe the experience of pure love of God] is like a mute's effort to describe what he tastes.

PURPORT

Even a qualified devotee may not be able to put his exact experience of love of God into words. Language has its limits for conveying experience, but it may function like the branch of the tree that helps us locate the moon in the sky. In describing the gradual development of *bhakti* to Rūpa Gosvāmī, Lord Caitanya compared it to an intensifying taste of sweetness:

> Gradual development of love of God may be compared to different states of sugar. First there is the seed of the sugar cane, then sugar cane, and then the juice extracted from the cane. When this juice is boiled, it forms liquid molasses, then solid molasses, then sugar, candy, rock candy, and finally lozenges. [Cc. *Madhya* 19.179]

Lord Caitanya went on to describe the combination of devotional ecstasies known as *sāttvika* and *vyabhicārī:* "These tastes are like a combination of yogurt, sugar candy, ghee, black pepper, and camphor, and are as palatable as sweet nectar" (Cc. *Madhya* 19.182). There is nothing deceptive or incomplete in this language, and yet it is language—the branch pointing to the moon in the sky. After hearing of the taste of love of Godhead, a devotee should aspire for that love and practice devotional service so that he may taste it for himself.

Nārada does not say that the subject matter of *bhakti* is something so vague and inconceivable that it can never be known or spoken of. His point is that the individual and ultimate experience is so wonderful that it is very hard to describe. One should not glibly say, "I know everything about love of Kṛṣṇa." Although the *gopīs* always chanted the glories of Lord Kṛṣṇa, they were sometimes struck dumb. Śrīla Prabhupāda writes,

> Spiritual feelings of happiness and intense ecstasies have no mundane comparison. Therefore it is very difficult to give expression to such feelings. We can have just a glimpse of such ecstasy in the words of Śrī Nārada Muni. [*Bhāg.* 1.6.17, purport]

SŪTRA 53

प्रकाश्यते क्वापि पात्रे ॥५३॥

prakāśyate kvāpi pātre

prakāśyate—it is revealed; *kva api*—sometimes; *pātre*—to a fit recipient.

TRANSLATION

Nonetheless, from time to time pure love of God is revealed to those who are qualified.

PURPORT

A *mahā-bhāgavata* devotee, or the Lord Himself, is pleased to find a fit candidate for understanding the inexpressible meanings of *bhakti-yoga*. The transference of knowledge in Kṛṣṇa consciousness is, in one sense, very straightforward. Śrīla Prabhupāda used to criticize the story of a disciple who said that he received knowledge from his *guru* by a method similar to receiving an electric shock. Lord Kṛṣṇa taught Arjuna by the process of question and answer, and one may still faithfully study Kṛṣṇa's lucid words for enlightenment in *bhakti-yoga*. As always, therefore, the process of receiving the teachings of *bhakti-yoga* is to serve the spiritual master, inquire from him, and hear his *paramparā* instructions.

And yet learning the science of *bhakti-yoga* is not an ordinary transference of knowledge, as when a professor writes lessons on a blackboard and his students write them down. Only if the spiritual teacher is actually potent and the students are purely receptive can the teacher plant the seed of *bhakti* (the *bhakti-latā-bīja*) in their hearts. How that seed fructifies in a student's heart is not understandable by material calculations. Śrīla Prabhupāda writes,

> Human reason fails to understand how by serving the devotee *bhāgavata* or the book *bhāgavata* one gets gradual promotion on the path of devotion. But actually these are the facts explained by Śrīla Nāradadeva, who happened to be a maidservant's son in his previous life. [*Bhāg.* 1.2.18, purport]

Although the *guru*-disciple relationship is a subtle one, it can be understood by the standard qualifications of both persons. For example, although Nārada was a young boy, the *bhaktivedānta* sages who visited his home found him a fit candidate, and so they blessed him. Nārada recalls the incident:

> Although they were impartial by nature, those followers of the Vedānta blessed me with their causeless mercy. As far as I was concerned, I was self-controlled and had no attachment for sports, even though I was a boy. In addition, I was not naughty and I did not speak more than required. [*Bhāg.* 1.5.24]

The sages at Naimiṣāraṇya praised the speaker Sūta Gosvāmī in a similar way:

> And because you are submissive, your spiritual masters have endowed you with all the favors bestowed upon a gentle disciple. Therefore you can tell us all that you have scientifically learned from them. [*Bhāg.* 1.1.8]

For realization of the most advanced spiritual knowledge, such as the pastimes of Lord Caitanya, the devotee has to be extremely well qualified. As Kṛṣṇadāsa Kavirāja says, "Unto one who is able to understand, Śrī Caitanya Mahāprabhu has shown mercy by giving him the association of the servant of His own servant" (Cc. *Madhya* 2.83). The spiritual knowledge Lord Caitanya conveyed to Rāmānanda Rāya was so completely out of the range of mundane vision that Lord Caitanya said that "only a madman can understand it." Lord Caitanya confided to Rāmānanda:

> Please rest assured that I have nothing to hide from you. Even if I do try to hide something from you, you are such an advanced devotee that you can understand all My secrets. . . . The facts which I have disclosed to you cannot be understood by materialistic people. When they hear of this, they will simply laugh at Me. You can understand this yourself and keep it to yourself. [*Teachings of Lord Caitanya,* p. 346]

In his later years, when Lord Caitanya exhibited His pastimes of entering intensely into the mood of Rādhārāṇī in separation from Kṛṣṇa, He shared this *rasa* only with His most intimate devotees, such as Rāmānanda Rāya and Svarūpa Dāmodara. They could understand the Lord's moods, which sometimes produced displays of seeming madness and which ordinary words or behavior could not express. "Only a person on the level of Svarūpa Dāmodara Gosvāmī can fully know what Lord Śrī Caitanya Mahāprabhu tastes in His love for Kṛṣṇa" (Cc. *Antya* 18.22).

Nārada Muni's point in this *sūtra* is that even when *bhakti* cannot be expressed in words, its essence can be manifest by the ecstatic symptoms of one great soul and appreciated by other great souls. When Lord Caitanya felt an ecstatic mood coming on but there were nondevotees present, He would try to restrain His outward manifestations of ecstatic love. For example, when Lord Caitanya first met Rāmānanda Rāya, they embraced and almost lost consciousness, overwhelmed by the ecstatic love of Kṛṣṇa and the *gopīs*. But some stereotyped, ritualistic *brāhmaṇas* were present at that time, and they doubted the propriety of the interaction between the Lord and Rāmānanda. According to Kṛṣṇadāsa Kavirāja, "While the *brāhmaṇas* were thinking in this way about the activities of Śrī Caitanya Mahāprabhu and Rāmānanda Rāya, Lord Caitanya saw the *brāhmaṇas* and restrained His transcendental emotions" (Cc. *Madhya* 8.28).

We should not think that only a fixed number of intimate devotees can receive the *bhakti-śakti,* and that we are obviously not among the chosen. The *ācāryas* advise us that if we keep striving, one day each one of us may uncover our original, dormant Kṛṣṇa consciousness. Moreover, Lord Caitanya surpassed all previous *ācāryas, bhaktas,* and incarnations by very liberally distributing intimate love of God. Anyone who is receptive to the *saṅkīrtana* movement of Lord Caitanya can therefore be quickly elevated to the platform where he can understand the inexpressible experiences of *bhakti-yoga*. In appreciation for this liberality of Lord Caitanya, Rūpa Gosvāmī composed a prayer:

namo mahā-vadānyāya kṛṣṇa-prema-pradāyate
kṛṣṇāya kṛṣṇa-caitanya nāmne gaura-tviṣe namaḥ

"I offer my respectful obeisances unto the Supreme Lord, Śrī Kṛṣṇa Caitanya, who is more magnanimous than any other *avatāra,* even Kṛṣṇa Himself, because He is bestowing freely what no one else has ever given—pure love of Kṛṣṇa."

SŪTRA 54

गुणरहितं कामनारहितं प्रतिक्षणवर्धमानमविच्छिन्नं
सूक्ष्मतरमनुभवरूपम् ॥५४॥

guṇa-rahitaṁ kāmanā-rahitaṁ pratikṣaṇa-vardhamānam avicchinnaṁ sūkṣma-taram anubhava-rūpam

guṇa—material qualities; *rahitam*—devoid of; *kāmanā*—material desire; *rahitam*—devoid of; *prati-kṣaṇa*—at every moment; *var-*

dhamānam—increasing; *avicchinnam*—uninterrupted; *sūkṣma-taram*—most subtle; *anubhava*—consciousness; *rūpam*—as its form.

TRANSLATION

Pure love of God manifests as the most subtle consciousness, devoid of material qualities and material desires, increasing at every moment, and never interrupted.

PURPORT

What passes for love in the material world often sounds and appears like *bhakti,* at least to those who are untrained in devotional service. But Nārada Muni makes it clear in this *sūtra* that *bhakti* is always different from material loving affairs.

The word *guṇa-rahitam* means "above the modes of nature." Nārada has already mentioned this quality of *bhakti* in Sūtra 47. *Bhakti* is not like any kind of behavior governed by the modes of ignorance, passion, or goodness. We should never think that Lord Kṛṣṇa's pastimes with the *gopīs* and cowherd boys are mundane. Kṛṣṇa's pastimes are, in fact, the original activities of love, and whatever resembles love in any way within this material world comes originally from Kṛṣṇa. As Śrīla Prabhupāda explains in *Kṛṣṇa,* p. 27:

> If there is any opulence within this material world, the cause of the opulence is Kṛṣṇa. If there is any reputation within this material world, the cause of the reputation is Kṛṣṇa. If there is any strength within this material world, the cause of such strength is Kṛṣṇa. If there is any wisdom and education within this material world, the cause of such wisdom and education is Kṛṣṇa. Therefore Kṛṣṇa is the source of all relative truths. [*Kṛṣṇa,* p. 27]

The word *kāmanā-rahitam* means "without selfish desire." This quality, too, has appeared before—in Sūtra 27, where Nārada said, "There is no question of lust in the execution of devotional service in pure love of God, because in it all material activities are renounced."

Unlike the pleasure that comes from exchanges of material so-called love, the pleasure of *bhakti* is *pratikṣaṇa-vardhamānam* (increasing at every moment) and *avicchinnam* (uninterrupted). This is the nature of the Lord's spiritual pleasure potency, known as *hlādinī-śakti,* which conducts the loving exchanges between Kṛṣṇa and His devotees. In sex passion, satiation soon brings an end to the mounting feelings of pleasure, but in the loving exchanges between Kṛṣṇa and His eternal associates there is an eternal competition, bringing ever-increasing pleasure. Kṛṣṇa is very pleased to see the beauty of His *gopīs,* and when the *gopīs* see that Kṛṣṇa is pleased with them they become many times more happy, and this increases their beauty. In turn, this increases Kṛṣṇa's beauty and pleasure. And so the devotee and the Lord enjoy loving exchanges, but without interruption.

Unlike mortal love affairs, in *bhakti* the love does not break by quarrel or death of one of the partners. Lord Caitanya describes the bliss of *saṅkīrtana* as *ānandāmbudhi-vardhanam,* "increasing the ocean of transcendental bliss." Because the Supreme Lord is Himself ever increasing and always fresh, the devotee is never bored or unfaithful and is never cheated.

Bhakti is also *sūkṣma-taram,* subtler than the subtlest thing. As described in the *Bhagavad-gītā* (3.42): "The working senses are superior to dull matter; mind is higher than the senses; intelligence is still higher than the mind; and he (the soul) is even higher than the intelligence." So the subtle exchanges of loving emotion between the pure souls and their beloved Lord are completely unlike material love, which is really nothing but lust.

SŪTRA 55

तत्प्राप्य तदेवावलोकयति तदेव शृणोति तदेव चिन्तयति ॥५५॥

tat prāpya tad evāvalokayati tad eva śṛṇoti tad eva cintayati

tat—it; *prāpya*—having obtained; *tat*—Him; *eva*—alone; *avalokayati*—one looks at; *tat*—Him; *eva*—alone; *śṛṇoti*—one hears about; *tat*—Him; *eva*—alone; *cintayati*—one thinks about.

TRANSLATION

Having obtained pure love of God, one looks only at the Lord, hears only about Him, and thinks only about Him.

PURPORT

Lord Kṛṣṇa describes this stage of perfection in the *Bhagavad-gītā* (6.30),

yo māṁ paśyati sarvatra sarvaṁ ca mayi paśyati
tasyāhaṁ na praṇaśyāmi sa ca me na praṇaśyati

"For one who sees Me everywhere and sees everything in Me, I am never lost, nor is he ever lost to Me." Śrīla Prabhupāda writes,

> Such a person may appear to see all the separate manifestations of the material nature, but in each and every instance he is conscious of Kṛṣṇa, knowing that everything is a manifestation of Kṛṣṇa's energy." [Bg. 6.30, purport]

This is *samādhi,* or trance, and whether one achieves it by the eightfold *yoga* system or by *bhakti-yoga,* it is the same. In the case of the *bhakti-yogī,* he is fixed in devotional service at all times, and whatever he sees contributes to his meditation on Kṛṣṇa.

To help us understand pure Kṛṣṇa consciousness, the *ācāryas* give us examples of *samādhi*-like states, even in ordinary affairs. When a mother sees the shoes of her little child, she doesn't just perceive them as neutral objects: she feels protection and love for her child. Similarly, when a lover picks up his beloved's comb (especially if he is in separation from her) he may feel intense emotions of love. In the case of Śrī Kṛṣṇa, the Supreme Personality of Godhead, *everything* is His energy. So wherever the *bhakta* goes or whatever he perceives throughout the universe, he is reminded of the Lord. Moreover, this recognition is not merely an intellectual habit but a total, overpowering state of love.

In his *Brahma-saṁhitā* (5.38), Lord Brahmā describes the devotional qualification for seeing Kṛṣṇa always and everywhere:

premāñjana-cchurita-bhakti-vilocanena
santaḥ sadaiva hṛdayeṣu vilokayanti
yaṁ śyāmasundaram acintya-guṇa-svarūpaṁ
govindam ādi-puruṣaṁ tam ahaṁ bhajāmi

"I worship Govinda, the primeval Lord, who is Śyāmasundara, Kṛṣṇa

Himself, with inconceivable, innumerable attributes, and whom the pure devotees see in their heart of hearts with the eye of devotion tinged with the salve of love."

In his purport, Śrīla Bhaktisiddhānta Sarasvatī writes,

> The eye of devotion is nothing but the eye of the pure unalloyed spiritual self of the *jīva.* The form of Kṛṣṇa is visible to that eye in proportion to its purification by the practice of devotion.

What prevents most of us from seeing Kṛṣṇa with eyes of love? We have a "cataract" on our eyes that consists of our material attachments. As Śrī Kṛṣṇa states,

nāhaṁ prakāśaḥ sarvasya yoga-māyā-samāvṛtaḥ
mūḍho 'yaṁ nābhijānāti loko mām ajam avyayam

"I am never manifest to the foolish and unintelligent. For them I am covered by My internal potency, and therefore they do not know that I am unborn and infallible" (Bg. 7.25). Lord Kṛṣṇa does not hide from us; He wants us to be with Him. He is like the sun that always blazes in the sky. No cloud is big enough to cover the sun, but from our earthly vantage point even a small cloud can block our view of the sun. In the same way, the clouds of our desire and hatred prevent us from seeing our beloved Lord and block us from enjoying the happiness and peace that come from serving Him. To realize Kṛṣṇa consciousness, therefore, we have to rise above our *upādhis,* the false designations that make us think the body is the self and make us identify with our mental concoctions.

Nārada is describing the ultimate stage of *bhakti.* This stage is rare, but one can achieve it by the mercy of the Vaiṣṇavas who teach *bhakti-yoga.* One who reads the Vedic literature with a speculative attitude will never know Kṛṣṇa. But we can attain His grace if we work in *bhakti-yoga,* guided by His representatives. Śrīla Prabhupāda writes,

> When one is fully engaged in Kṛṣṇa consciousness, beginning by chanting the *mahā-mantra*—Hare Kṛṣṇa, Hare Kṛṣṇa, Kṛṣṇa Kṛṣṇa, Hare Hare/ Hare Rāma, Hare Rāma, Rāma Rāma, Hare Hare—then only can one understand the Supreme Personality of Godhead. [Bg. 7.24, purport]

SŪTRA 56

गौणी त्रिधा गुणभेदादार्तादिभेदाद्वा ॥५६॥

gauṇī tridhā guṇa-bhedād ārtādi-bhedād vā

gauṇī—secondary, mixed with the material modes; *tridhā*—threefold; *guṇa*—of the material modes; *bhedāt*—by the differentiation; *ārta*—of the one who is distressed; *ādi*—and so on; *bhedāt*—by differentiation; *vā*—or.

TRANSLATION

Secondary devotional service is of three kinds, according to which of the three material modes predominates, or according to which material motivation—distress and so on—brings one to *bhakti*.

PURPORT

It may seem as if we have been suddenly dropped from the heights. Nārada has been describing the highest stage of Kṛṣṇa consciousness, and now he is discussing secondary devotion. But Nārada's course of instruction is well planned, practical, and realistic. He wants us to attain the higher stages, but, as Lord Kṛṣṇa says, *vāsudevaḥ sarvam iti sa mahātmā su-durlabhaḥ:* "The great soul who can see Kṛṣṇa everywhere is very rare" (Bg. 7.19). Nārada is therefore bringing our attention to the *anarthas* within the minds and habits of aspiring *bhaktas* so that we can work toward the higher stages and not consider pure love of Kṛṣṇa an unattainable dream. On the other hand, if one tries to jump to the higher stages as if such a leap were easy, that is another mistake (committed by the *prākṛta-sahajiyās*), which causes a great disturbance to both oneself and society.

The preparatory stages of *bhakti* are called secondary devotion, and they are necessary for those who are still affected by the modes of nature. Lord Kṛṣṇa describes the motivations for such secondary devotion in the *Bhagavad-gītā* (7.16):

catur-vidhā bhajante māṁ janā sukṛtino 'rjuna
ārto jijñāsur arthārthī jñānī ca bharatarṣabha

"O best among the Bhāratas, four kinds of pious men begin to render devotional service unto Me: the distressed, the desirer of wealth, the inquisitive, and he who is searching for knowledge of the Absolute."

This *Bhagavad-gītā* verse occurs just after Lord Kṛṣṇa describes the four kinds of persons who never surrender to the Lord. Those who are devoted to the Supreme Lord, even while seeking to fulfill material desires, are called *sukṛtinaḥ*, or pious souls. Their good qualification is that they have turned to God. In the *Śrīmad-Bhāgavatam* (2.3.10), Śukadeva Gosvāmī encourages everyone, no matter what his present condition, to take up *kṛṣṇa-bhakti:*

akāmaḥ sarva-kāmo vā mokṣa-kāma udāra-dhīḥ
tīvreṇa bhakti-yogena yajeta puruṣaṁ param

"A person who has broader intelligence, whether he be full of all material desire, without any material desire, or desiring liberation, must by all means worship the supreme whole, the Personality of Godhead."

The *sukṛtīs* who are not yet on the platform of unalloyed devotion can be purified by association with pure devotees. Of course, if one remains stuck in this lower stage, then he will be discontented. What prevents a devotee from advancing is the desire for *bhukti* (enjoyment of material objects) or *mukti* (liberation). In the *Bhakti-rasāmṛta-sindhu* (1.2.22), Śrīla Rūpa Gosvāmī describes *bhukti* and *mukti* as two witches who haunt the conditioned souls and keep them from experiencing the bliss of *bhakti.* Actual devotional service is *anyābhilāṣitā-śūnya,* service rendered favorably to the Lord without desire for material profit or speculation (see *Bhagavad-gītā* 7.16, purport).

The devotees who serve Kṛṣṇa in order to satisfy selfish desires are called *sakāma-bhaktas.* Those who serve purely, without such desires, are *akāma* devotees. When a *sakāma* devotee continues to render devotional service, the Supreme Lord turns him from a *sakāma-* into an *akāma-bhakta.* The devotee begins to realize that the taste of serving Kṛṣṇa is the real goal and pleasure, and his desires for other things begin to dwindle. This auspicious change of heart occurs by the potency of Śrī Kṛṣṇa working through the process of *bhakti.* As stated in the *Śrīmad-Bhāgavatam* (5.19.27),

> The Supreme Personality of Godhead fulfills the material desires of a devotee who approaches Him with such motives, but He does not bestow benedictions upon the devotee that will cause him to demand benedictions again. However, the Lord willingly gives the devotee

> shelter at His feet, even though such a person does not aspire for it, and that shelter satisfies all his desires. That is the Supreme Personality's special mercy.

Lord Kṛṣṇa substitutes the nectar of His service for one's attraction to petty things. Who else could do this but the merciful and all-knowing Personality of Godhead? The stage of secondary devotion, therefore, is not meant for permanent residence; rather, it is an auspicious stage from which to go forward. Since any progress the conditioned soul makes toward the lotus feet of the Supreme Lord is favorable for him, secondary devotional service is not unimportant, just as the first steps a baby takes as he attempts to walk are crucial for his development.

SŪTRA 57

उत्तरस्मादुत्तरस्मात्पूर्वपूर्वो श्रेयाय भवति ॥५७॥

uttarasmād uttarasmāt pūrva-pūrvo śreyāya bhavati

uttarasmāt uttarasmāt—than each later one; *pūrva-pūrvaḥ*—each earlier one; *śreyāya bhavati*—is to be considered better.

TRANSLATION

Each earlier stage should be considered better than the one following it.

PURPORT

Worship of the Lord in the mode of goodness (*sattva*) is better than worship in passion (*rajas*), and worship in the mode of passion is better than worship in ignorance (*tamas*). In His teachings to His mother, Lord Kapiladeva explains devotional service executed under the influence of the three modes:

> O noble lady, there are multifarious paths of devotional service in terms of the different qualities of the executor. Devotional service executed by a person who is envious, hypocritical, violent, and angry, and who is a separatist, is considered to be in the mode of darkness. The worship of Deities in the temple by a separatist, with a motive for

material enjoyment, fame, and opulence, is devotion in the mode of passion. When a devotee worships the Supreme Personality of Godhead and offers Him the results of his activities in order to free himself from the inebrieties of fruitive activities, his devotion is in the mode of goodness. [*Bhāg.* 3.29.7–10]

In his purport to this passage, Śrīla Prabhupāda explains the key word *bhinna-dṛk,* meaning "possessed of a separatist vision":

> The word "separatist" must be understood carefully. . . . A separatist is one who sees his interest as separate from that of the Supreme Lord. Mixed devotees, or devotees in the modes of passion and ignorance, think that the interest of the Supreme Lord is supplying the orders of the devotee; the interest of such devotees is to draw from the Lord as much as possible for their sense gratification. This is the separatist mentality.

Still, despite their separatist mentality, such mixed devotees are blessed, for if they begin executing devotional service under the guidance of teachers who are in pure goodness (*śuddha-sattva*), they can be gradually elevated to pure *bhakti.* As stated in the verse previously quoted (*Bhāg.* 2.3.10), all classes of worshipers are encouraged to turn to the supreme father, even with their material desires. In his purport Śrīla Prabhupāda writes, "As the unmixed sun ray is very forceful and is therefore called *tīvra,* similarly unmixed *bhakti-yoga* of hearing, chanting, etc. (*tīvreṇa bhakti-yogena*), may be performed by one and all, regardless of inner motive."

SŪTRA 58

अन्यस्मात् सौलभ्यं भक्तौ ॥५८॥

anyasmāt saulabhyaṁ bhaktau

anyasmāt—than anything else; *saulabhyam*—ease of attainment; *bhaktau*—in devotional service.

TRANSLATION

Success is easier to attain by devotional service than by any other process.

PURPORT

Nārada assures us that everyone can speedily advance by practicing *bhakti-yoga*—because it is the easiest way. This is an extremely important qualification, especially for us in the present age, the Age of Kali. As stated in the *Śrīmad-Bhāgavatam* (1.1.10),

> *prāyeṇālpāyuṣaḥ sabhya kalāv asmin yuge janāḥ*
> *mandāḥ su-manda-matayo manda-bhāgyā hy upadrutāḥ*

"O learned one, in this iron age of Kali men have but short lives. They are quarrelsome, lazy, misguided, unlucky, and, above all, always disturbed."

The characteristics of the people of this age are all disqualifications for spiritual life. In previous millennia the human condition was much more favorable for spiritual advancement. In the Satya-yuga almost all people were in the mode of goodness, and society was peaceful and religious. At that time the recommended form of religion was meditation. The sage Vālmīki is said to have meditated sixty thousand years before writing the *Rāmāyaṇa,* and Kardama Muni meditated ten thousand years. As the millennia proceeded from Tretā to Dvāpara, human society degraded more and more. Five thousand years ago, when Lord Kṛṣṇa recommended *aṣṭāṅga-yoga* to Arjuna, Arjuna rejected it, saying it was impractical and impossible for him. We should not maintain grandiose conceptions of what we are able to perform nowadays but should face the facts of our near-bankrupt condition of spirituality. "Here is the easiest path," says Nārada, and we should grab at his offer as a drowning man grabs for a life raft.

Even in former ages, when more difficult processes were recommended, the goal was always *bhakti,* or devotion to the Supreme Lord. In this age the most accessible form of *bhakti* is *saṅkīrtana,* or congregational chanting of the holy names of God. It is recommended as the *yuga-dharma,* or religion of the age. As stated in the *Bṛhan-nāradīya Purāṇa,* "In the Age of Kali no effective means of God realization is possible except the chanting of the holy names." The same thing is recommended in the *Śrīmad-Bhāgavatam,* where the nine sages known as the Yogendras declare that in Kali-yuga intelligent persons will take to the process of *saṅkīrtana.* And Śukadeva Gosvāmī tells Mahārāja Parīkṣit that the chanting of the holy names is the saving grace of this age:

kaler doṣa-nidhe rājan asti hy eko mahān guṇaḥ
kīrtanād eva kṛṣṇasya mukta-saṅgaḥ paraṁ vrajet

"My dear king, although Kali-yuga is full of faults, there is still one good quality about this age: simply by chanting the Hare Kṛṣṇa *mahā-mantra,* one can become free from material bondage and be promoted to the transcendental kingdom" (*Bhāg.* 12.3.51).

In ignorance and defiance of the recommended *yuga-dharma,* unauthorized teachers make a business of teaching *yoga* and meditation. But since almost no one is qualified to practice the severe austerities of meditation, streamlined versions are taught, which are mostly a form of cheating. Even if a person seriously takes up the path of *karma-yoga, jñāna-yoga,* or *aṣṭāṅga-yoga,* he will meet with many difficulties. For example, the *jñānī* may become very attached to accumulating knowledge for its own sake, up to the point where he tries to merge with the Absolute Truth. The *karma-yogī,* or man of action, too often forgets to dedicate his activities to God and instead becomes attached to the fruits of his work or to fame. The *aṣṭāṅga-yogīs,* if they are able to progress at all in the eightfold system, are liable to get sidetracked by the *siddhis,* or powers, that come to them. But *bhakti,* by its very nature, purifies one's senses, actions, and motives. Moreover, one doesn't have to go painfully and slowly through every single step on the *yoga* ladder from *karma* to *jñāna* to *bhakti.* At any moment, whenever one decides to surrender, and wherever one gets the association of pure devotees, one can take the express elevator of *bhakti-yoga.* As Lord Kṛṣṇa recommends,

daivī hy eṣā guṇa-mayī mama māyā duratyayā
mām eva ye prapadyante māyām etāṁ taranti te

"This divine energy of Mine, consisting of the three modes of material nature, is difficult to overcome. But those who have surrendered unto Me can easily cross beyond it" (Bg. 7.14).

SŪTRA 59

प्रमाणान्तरस्यानपेक्षत्वात् स्वयं प्रमाणत्वात् ॥५९॥

pramāṇāntarasyānapekṣatvāt svayaṁ pramāṇatvāt

pramāṇa—means of valid knowing; *antarasya*—another; *an-apekṣatvāt*—because of not being dependent on; *svayam*—in its own right; *pramāṇatvāt*—because of being a valid authority.

TRANSLATION

The reason devotional service is the easiest of all spiritual processes is that it does not depend on any other authority for its validity, being itself the standard of authority.

PURPORT

Pramāṇa means proof. Vaiṣṇava philosophers condense all the different types of *pramāṇas* into three: *pratyakṣa, anumāna,* and *śabda. Pratyakṣa* means direct evidence by the senses. But since the senses are imperfect, *pratyakṣa* often has to be corrected by higher knowledge. *Anumāna* refers to deductive and inductive logic, which depends on the validity of its premises and reasons, and so cannot prove anything with final certainty. *Śabda* means receiving knowledge from authoritative sources. Vedic knowledge is *śabda-pramāṇa.* This is particularly applicable to transcendental subject matter, which cannot be understood by the empirical and theorizing methods. Even in ordinary affairs, there are many things we have to accept on authority. We can learn the identity of our father from our mother, the only foolproof authority. Aside from the mother there is no way to know for sure who our father is. When the source of information is perfect, as in Vedic knowledge, then *śabda-pramāṇa,* or *śabda-brahma,* becomes the ultimate proof. As Śrīla Prabhupāda states, "As far as the soul's existence is concerned, no one can establish his existence experimentally beyond the proof of *śruti,* or Vedic wisdom" (Bg. 2.25, purport).

Aside from the proof of *śāstra* and *guru,* Nārada has taught that the truth of *bhakti* is proven by one's directly experiencing its fruits in one's own life. In Sūtras 31 and 32, Nārada gives the analogy of how a man's hunger cannot be appeased just by looking at a meal. It is not enough to hear that a particular food preparation has a very sweet and delicious flavor. Even if you know all the dish's ingredients, that knowledge will not satisfy your hunger. In the same way, mere theoretical knowledge of God does not bring pleasure—either to God or to the individual soul. *Bhakti* has to be directly perceived. Śrīla Prabhupāda used to say that when you become Kṛṣṇa conscious no one has to give you a certificate or diploma saying, "You are now Kṛṣṇa conscious." You'll know it for yourself.

The potency of *bhakti* to purify one's heart is proved by the loss of material desires. Those who come to Kṛṣṇa consciousness after years of sinful life know this proof very well. Their renunciation of meat-eating, intoxicants, and illicit sex is not an act of repression but is based on tasting a higher pleasure. And so *bhakti* is its own proof.

Nondevotees may ask for empirical proof: "Show us your Kṛṣṇa. Prove that He is God. We want to see Him lift Govardhana Hill." But their demand for proof cannot be satisfied in that way. Lord Kṛṣṇa reveals Himself in His original form only to His devotees:

nāhaṁ prakāśaḥ sarvasya yoga-māyā-samāvṛtaḥ
mūḍho 'yaṁ nābhijānāti loko mām ajam avyayam

"I am never manifest to the foolish and unintelligent. For them I am covered by My internal potency, and therefore they do not know that I am unborn and infallible" (Bg. 7.25).

To the atheists, God gives proof of His existence when He appears as death and takes everything away. But God does not manifest His internal potency to the faithless. Śrīla Prabhupāda writes, "Even if one is perfected by realization of impersonal Brahman or localized Paramātmā, he cannot possibly understand the Supreme Personality of Godhead, Śrī Kṛṣṇa, without being in Kṛṣṇa consciousness" (Bg. 7.26, purport).

SŪTRA 60

शान्तिरूपात्परमानन्दरूपाच्च ॥६०॥

śānti-rūpāt paramānanda-rūpāc ca

śānti—of peace; *rūpāt*—because of (being) the form; *parama*—topmost; *ānanda*—of pleasure; *rūpāt*—because of (being) the form; *ca*—and.

TRANSLATION

Furthermore, *bhakti* is the embodiment of peace and supreme ecstasy.

PURPORT

This *sūtra* is further proof that *bhakti* is the best process for spiritual advancement. Lord Kṛṣṇa's personal form, name, and varied activities attract His devotees, who experience a love filled with *śānti* (peace) and *paramānanda* (supreme ecstasy). Indeed, the very nature of *bhakti* is peace and happiness.

In the *Bhagavad-gītā,* Lord Kṛṣṇa tells us who is eligible for *śānti:*

bhoktāraṁ yajña-tapasāṁ sarva-loka-maheśvaram
suhṛdaṁ sarva-bhūtānāṁ jñātvā māṁ śāntim ṛcchati

"One in full consciousness of Me, knowing Me to be the ultimate beneficiary of all sacrifices and austerities, the Supreme Lord of all planets and demigods, and the benefactor and well-wisher of all living entities, attains peace from the pangs of material miseries" (Bg. 5.29).

Śrīla Prabhupāda calls this verse "the peace formula," the sure method for achieving both individual and collective tranquillity. When people who temporarily control some property ignore the Lord's proprietorship over all that be and claim that they themselves are the sole proprietors and enjoyers of the world, and when people in positions of leadership claim to be the best friends of their dependents but fail to give them a chance to acquire transcendental knowledge, then the result is not peace but agitation, chaos, and war. Peace comes when we recognize Lord Kṛṣṇa as the supreme ruler, proprietor, and friend.

Regarding happiness, Śrīla Rūpa Gosvāmī defines three types: "(1) happiness derived from material enjoyment, (2) happiness derived by identifying oneself with the Supreme Brahman, and (3) happiness derived from Kṛṣṇa consciousness" (*The Nectar of Devotion,* p. 10). Rūpa Gosvāmī's conclusion is that happiness derived from pure *bhakti* is the highest because it is eternal, whereas material enjoyment and even oneness with Brahman are bound to be disrupted. Happiness in devotional service is open to all, but those who try to increase their own importance cannot know the sweet taste of Kṛṣṇa consciousness. Happiness comes not by trying to be the master but by becoming the servant of the servant of the supreme master. While praying to the Supreme Lord for relief from his suffering, Gajendra praised the happiness of the devotees:

Unalloyed devotees, who have no desire other than to serve the Lord, worship Him in full surrender and always hear and chant about His activities, which are most wonderful and auspicious. Thus they always merge in an ocean of transcendental bliss. Such devotees never ask the Lord for any benediction. [*Bhāg.* 8.3.20]

SŪTRA 61

लोकहानौ चिन्ता न कार्या निवेदितात्मलोकवेदत्वात् ॥६१॥

loka-hānau cintā na kāryā niveditātma-loka-vedatvāt

loka—of the world; *hānau*—about loss; *cintā*—worry; *na kāryā*—should not be done; *nivedita*—because of having surrendered; *ātma*—one's own; *loka*—mundane affairs; *vedatvāt*—and Vedic duties.

TRANSLATION

After consigning to the Lord all one's mundane and Vedic duties, one no longer need worry about worldly loss.

PURPORT

This *sūtra* holds various meanings. First, the devotee should not worry about his worldly situation. Having surrendered to Lord Kṛṣṇa, he is on the most auspicious path, going back to Godhead. Even if he suffers financial loss or ill health, he realizes that Lord Kṛṣṇa is giving him token punishment for his past sinful activities. And so he converts the losses into spiritual assets by remaining steadfast in devotional service, despite the disturbances (see *Bhāgavatam* 10.14.8).

In the beginning of his commitment, a devotee may fear that he is somehow jeopardizing his future by fully surrendering to Lord Kṛṣṇa. Arjuna worried that if he took up the meditative *yoga* process Kṛṣṇa outlined in the Sixth Chapter of the *Bhagavad-gītā* he might become an "unsuccessful transcendentalist, who in the beginning takes to the process of self-realization with faith but who later desists due to worldly-mindedness" (Bg. 6.37). If that were to happen, Arjuna reasoned, he would have "no position in any sphere" and could thus enjoy neither material success nor spiritual profit. But Lord Kṛṣṇa assured His disciple, "A transcendentalist engaged in auspicious activities does not meet with destruction either in this world or in the spiritual world; one who does good, My friend, is never overcome by evil" (Bg. 6.40). Even if a devotee does fall short in his attempt at full surrender, whatever devotional service he performs is eternally counted in his favor. At the time of death, one's material success is taken away, but whatever devotional service one has performed, even if "unsuccessfully," is a profit for the next life. As Nārada Muni himself states in the *Śrīmad-Bhāgavatam* (1.5.17),

tyaktvā sva-dharmaṁ caraṇāmbujaṁ harer
bhajann apakvo 'tha patet tato yadi
yatra kva vābhadram abhūd amuṣya kiṁ
ko vārtha āpto 'bhajatāṁ sva-dharmataḥ

"One who has forsaken his material occupation to engage in the devotional service of the Lord may sometimes fall down while in an immature stage, yet there is no danger of his being unsuccessful. On the other hand, a nondevotee, though fully engaged in occupational duties, does not gain anything" (*Bhāg.* 1.5.17).

Not only should a devotee reject the idea that he is somehow missing out on material happiness, but he should also be free of worry that he is neglecting his worldly responsibilities. It is a fact that everyone born into the material world has many obligations and moral debts. But a life of dedication to the Supreme Lord frees one—at least from the Lord's point of view—from all other duties:

devarṣi-bhūtāpta-nṛṇāṁ pitṝṇāṁ
na kiṅkaro nāyam ṛṇī ca rājan
sarvātmanā yaḥ śaraṇaṁ śaraṇyaṁ
gato mukundaṁ parihṛtya kartam

"Anyone who has taken shelter of the lotus feet of Mukunda, the giver of liberation, giving up all other obligations, and has taken to the path in all seriousness, owes neither duties nor obligations to the demigods, sages, general living entities, family members, humankind, or forefathers" (*Bhāg.* 11.5.41).

If a sincere devotee is accused of being irresponsible, or if his life is endangered and it seems as though the cause is his attempt to surrender to Lord Kṛṣṇa, he has no recourse but to pray for the mercy of the

Lord. The devotee has surrendered to the Supreme Personality of Godhead, and he cannot take back that surrender in a misguided effort to "save" himself. As Bhaktivinoda Ṭhākura sings,

mārabi rākhabi—yo icchā tohārā
nitya-dāsa prati tuā adhikārā

"Now if You like You can kill me, or if You like You can give me protection. Whatever You like You can do. I am Your eternal servitor. You have every right to deal with me in any way You please."

SŪTRA 62

न तत्सिद्धौ लोकव्यावहारो हेयः
किन्तु फलत्यागस्तत्साधनं च कार्यमेव ॥६२॥

na tatsiddhau loka-vyāvahāro heyaḥ kintu phala-tyāgas tat-sādhanaṁ ca kāryam eva

na—not; *tat*—of it (devotional service); *siddhau*—in the achievement; *loka*—mundane; *vyāvahāraḥ*—business; *heyaḥ*—to be abandoned; *kintu*—rather; *phala*—of the results; *tyāgaḥ*—abandonment; *tat*—of it (devotional service); *ca*—and; *kāryam*—must be done; *eva*—indeed.

TRANSLATION

Even after one has achieved devotional service, one should not abandon one's responsibilities in this world but should rather continue surrendering the results of one's work to the Lord. And while still trying to reach the stage of pure devotion, one must certainly continue executing prescribed duties.

PURPORT

Lord Kṛṣṇa has strongly criticized the pseudo renunciants who live at the cost of society: "One who restrains the senses of action but whose mind dwells on sense objects certainly deludes himself and is called a pretender" (Bg. 3.7). Śrīla Prabhupāda states that it is better to work in *karma-yoga* (Kṛṣṇa consciousness) within one's *varṇa* and *āśrama* designation:

A householder can also reach this destination [Viṣṇu, or Kṛṣṇa] by regulated service in Kṛṣṇa consciousness. For self-realization, one can live a controlled life, as prescribed in the *śāstras,* and continue carrying out his business without attachment, and in that way make progress. A sincere person who follows this method is far better situated than the false pretender who adopts show-bottle spiritualism to cheat the innocent public. A sincere sweeper in the street is far better than the charlatan meditator who meditates only for the sake of making a living. [Bg. 3.7, purport]

This does not mean, however, that ordinary work is itself the fulfillment of human life. The *karmī* slogan "Work is worship" is not the same as working in Kṛṣṇa consciousness. But one has to do both: work to earn one's living and at the same time work for the satisfaction of Viṣṇu, or Kṛṣṇa. Śrīla Prabhupāda writes, "Any other work done in this material world will be a cause of bondage, for both good and evil work have their reactions, and any reaction binds the performer."

How to maintain oneself and one's family and at the same time work for Kṛṣṇa is a great art, and as such it requires the guidance of the Lord's devotee. If obligations to family and society conflict with one's basic spiritual vows, then one must give first priority to the spiritual duties. One who has taken initiation into spiritual life should never give up his vow to chant a quota of holy names daily and to fulfill the basic orders of the spiritual master.

Whether a Vaiṣṇava works in the business world or lives as a renunciant, he should never be embarrassed to preach Kṛṣṇa consciousness or doubt the value of preaching. Even if we consider preaching work a debt to humanity, it is a crucial social commitment. Once the mother and father of a young devotee complained to Śrīla Prabhupāda that their son was a full-time student in the Kṛṣṇa consciousness movement. They said they wanted him to become a doctor. Prabhupāda replied that they should let the young man decide for himself, and that in any case, there were many doctors in the world but few serious devotees. Prabhupāda said that the work of the devotee was more important than the work of a physician. A doctor can repair the health of a few hundred people, but even that is temporary. Medical cures do not free the patient from his *karma,* which forces him to take rebirth and suffer again in another material body. But a devotee who successfully distributes Kṛṣṇa consciousness can help people achieve liberation from birth and death. So his work is the most important in the world.

Although he may not be an expert politician or economist, a *bhakta* knows the real cause of people's suffering—forgetfulness of their relationship with Kṛṣṇa, which leads to their becoming conditioned by the modes of material nature. Knowing that *bhakti-yoga* is the only way to extricate oneself from material conditioning and reestablish one's relationship with God, the devotee tries to distribute knowledge of Kṛṣṇa consciousness. Śrīla Prabhupāda writes, "Since the [devotee] tries to broadcast the importance of becoming Kṛṣṇa conscious, he is the best philanthropist in the world" (Bg. 6.32, purport).

The preacher stays connected to the world, yet he is transcendental to worldly concerns. Although some *yogīs* abandon society and cultivate their own spiritual salvation, the *bhakti-yogī* who follows Prahlāda Mahārāja, Lord Caitanya, and Śrīla Prabhupāda keeps a compassionate connection with the people of the world. As Lord Caitanya stated to His followers, "Distribute this Kṛṣṇa consciousness movement all over the world. Let people eat these fruits [of love of God] and ultimately become free from old age and death" (Cc. *Ādi* 9.39).

The surrendered devotee, therefore, does not worry about his worldly situation, nor does he support mundane welfare causes. But to satisfy Lord Caitanya and the spiritual masters descending from Him in disciplic succession, he works magnanimously on behalf of all living beings by spreading Kṛṣṇa consciousness.

SŪTRA 63

स्त्रीधननास्तिकचरित्रं न श्रवणीयम् ॥६३॥

strī-dhana-nāstika-caritraṁ na śravaṇīyam

strī—of women; *dhana*—wealth; *nāstika*—and atheists; *caritram*—stories; *na śravaṇīyam*—should not be listened to.

TRANSLATION

One should not find entertainment in news of women, money, and atheists.

PURPORT

Nārada has said that a *bhakta* may discharge his duties in the world as long as he is God-centered and offers the results of his work to the Lord in devotional service. But while living in the world he must avoid sinful life and persons who indulge in it (see Sūtras 43 and 44). Now he says we should avoid not only associating with sinful persons but even *hearing* about them.

If we want to be free from *māyā,* we cannot take Nārada's advice lightly or dismiss it as old fashioned. Māyā is not a lightweight contender. She has been placed in charge of imprisoning all the conditioned souls in the universe, and some of her principal weapons are indicated in this *sūtra*—sex, wealth, and atheism. With a healthy respect for her power, we should give a wide berth to the māyic talks concerning these topics.

Mundane talks are also known as *prajalpa.* In his *Upadeśāmṛta,* Śrīla Rūpa Gosvāmī mentions *prajalpa* as one of the main impediments to devotional service. And Lord Caitanya instructed Sanātana Gosvāmī, "A devotee should avoid reading or hearing newspapers or mundane books that contain stories of love affairs between men and women or subjects palatable to the senses" (Cc. *Madhya* 22.120).

In the modern age these injunctions have become more difficult than ever to follow. The airwaves are filled with *prajalpa,* and by pressing a button we can turn on a television set and plunge ourselves into a visual and aural phantasmagoria. While writing his purports on the *Bhāgavatam* verses describing the life of Ajāmila, Śrīla Prabhupāda responded to our predicament. Ajāmila was a pious young *brāhmaṇa,* but one day, while traveling along the public way, he came upon a low-class man embracing a prostitute and was overcome by lust. Prabhupāda writes, "In Kali-yuga, a drunken, half-naked woman embracing a drunken man is a very common sight, especially in the Western countries, and restraining oneself after seeing such things is difficult. Nevertheless, if by the grace of Kṛṣṇa a person adheres to the regulative principles and chants the Hare Kṛṣṇa *mantra,* Kṛṣṇa will certainly protect him" (*Bhāg.* 6.1.60, purport).

We cannot expect to follow Prabhupāda's advice in a vacuum. Unless we have Kṛṣṇa conscious friends to talk with and a society of devotees to live in, we might conclude, "It's impossible to avoid hearing talks of sex, money, and atheists. What am I supposed to do, live alone in a cave?" No, and this is precisely one of the reasons Śrīla Prabhupāda founded the International Society for Krishna Consciousness—to give everyone an opportunity to hear *kṛṣṇa-kathā* in the society of devotees. The benefits of such a practice are numerous, as Lord Kapila states in the *Bhāgavatam* (3.25.25):

satāṁ prasaṅgān mama vīrya-saṁvido
bhavanti hṛt-karṇa-rasāyanā kathāḥ
taj-joṣaṇād āśv apavarga-vartmani
śraddhā ratir bhaktir anukramiṣyati

"The spiritually powerful message of Godhead can be properly discussed only in a society of devotees, and it is greatly pleasing to hear in that association. If one hears from devotees, the way of transcendental experience quickly opens to him, and gradually he attains firm faith that in due course develops into attraction and devotion."

Our weapons in the campaign against *prajalpa* and mind pollution may include novels, dramas, paintings, films, musical recordings, festivals, formal lectures, seminars, and casual meetings—all centered on Kṛṣṇa. Why should the forces of illusion possess all the weapons, and not the devotees?

Nārada previously said that *bhakti* was easy. It is certainly not easy to avoid all mundane sound vibrations. But under the guidance of the pure devotee we may create a pleasant, easy-to-take atmosphere of *kṛṣṇa-kathā* in the home and with friends—even when driving a car or at work—and this hearing will lead to *viṣṇu-smaraṇam,* or remembrance of the Supreme Personality of Godhead.

SŪTRA 64

अभिमानदम्भादिकं त्याज्यम् ॥६४॥

abhimāna-dambhādikaṁ tyājyam

abhimāna—pride; *dambha*—deceit; *ādikam*—and so on; *tyājyam*—should be given up.

TRANSLATION

One should put aside false pride, hypocrisy, and other vices.

PURPORT

Māyā is so subtle that even if one is able to avoid hearing about sex, money, and atheists, and even if one joins a society of devotees, one may still become a victim of pride and hypocrisy. One may think, "I am a better devotee than the others," and thus prepare oneself for a fall. The remedy for pride is to remember that our good fortune, including our spiritual assets, are all due to the mercy of the Supreme Lord and the spiritual masters.

Nārada has used the word *ādi,* "et cetera," to include other vices, such as the demoniac traits listed in the Sixteenth Chapter of the *Bhagavad-gītā.* All of these should be avoided. One should become aware of specific bad habits and try to eliminate them, and therefore Nārada and the *ācāryas* often give detailed instructions. We can examine each *anartha* and see what we can do to renounce it. When we catch ourselves indulging in unwanted thoughts or acts, we should stop them as soon as possible.

At the same time, a "holistic" approach is also recommended. That is, we should be confident that our sincere prosecution of *bhakti-yoga* will eliminate all unwanted habits and desires. In fact, if we try to eliminate vices one by one, we will fail. But by *bhakti* we can eliminate them wholesale. As stated in the *Śrīmad-Bhāgavatam* (6.1.15),

kecit kevalayā bhaktyā vāsudeva-parāyaṇāḥ
aghaṁ dhunvanti kārtsnyena nīhāram iva bhāskaraḥ

"Only a rare person who has adopted complete, unalloyed devotional service to Kṛṣṇa can uproot the weeds of sinful actions with no possibility that they will revive. He can do this simply by discharging devotional service, just as the sun can immediately dissipate fog by its rays."

Devotional service is beyond both piety and impiety. By chanting Hare Kṛṣṇa, hearing about Lord Kṛṣṇa, and performing other routine services in Kṛṣṇa consciousness, one vanquishes all phases of sinful life and all unwanted habits.

The practical application of this principle is to persevere in *sādhana-bhakti* with faith and determination. This is called *śraddhā,* the conviction that one will achieve all goals by practicing Kṛṣṇa consciousness. Śrīla Rūpa Gosvāmī also recommends *niścaya,* "endeavoring with confidence" (*The Nectar of Instruction,* Text 3). Śrīla Prabhupāda explains in his purport, "In devotional service surrender means that one has to become confident. The devotee thinks, *āvaśya rakṣibe kṛṣṇa:* 'Kṛṣṇa will surely protect me and give me help for the successful execution of devotional service.'" And so the devotee uses both negative and positive approaches: He diligently seeks to eliminate particular unwanted habits, but at the same time he is confident that his engagement in devotional service is like a blazing fire that will burn to ashes all the fuel of sinful activities.

SŪTRA 65

तदर्पिताखिलाचारः सन् कामक्रोधाभिमानादिकं
तस्मिन्नेव करणीयम् ॥६५॥

tad arpitākhilācāraḥ san kāma-krodhābhimānādikaṁ tasminn eva karaṇīyam

tat—to Him; *arpita*—having offered; *akhila*—all; *ācāraḥ*—actions; *san*—being; *kāma*—desire; *krodha*—anger; *abhimāna*—pride; *ādikam*—and so on; *tasmin*—toward Him; *eva*—only; *karaṇīyam*—should be done.

TRANSLATION

Offering all one's activities to the Lord, one should feel desire, anger, and pride only with regard to Him.

PURPORT

Nārada now advises that traits normally considered vices may be dovetailed into favorable devotional service. This does not contradict Nārada's previous statement that pride, anger, and lust should be renounced. A pure devotee is always free of vices, and the practicing *bhakta* tries to be free of them by controlling his senses and mind as far as possible. Therefore Nārada here refers to a transcendental application of anger, pride, and lust in relation to the Supreme Lord.

Liberated devotees often apply so-called vices in devotional service, and we can learn the art from them. Hanumān vented his anger upon Rāvaṇa, the enemy of Lord Rāma. Lord Kṛṣṇa instigated Arjuna to become angry so he would fight the Battle of Kurukṣetra. Even Lord Caitanya became angry with the drunken brothers Jagāi and Mādhāi. These are examples of properly directed anger. We cannot stop anger completely. As Śrīla Prabhupāda writes, "To try to create a vacuum in the mind is artificial. The vacuum will not remain. However, if one always thinks of Kṛṣṇa and how to serve Kṛṣṇa best, one's mind will naturally be controlled" (*The Nectar of Instruction,* Text 1, purport).

Even anger directed at Kṛṣṇa can be part of devotional service. The *gopīs,* for instance, often became angry at Him during lovers' quarrels. Once Śrīmatī Rādhārāṇī was displeased with Kṛṣṇa and ordered Her assistants to stop Him from seeing Her at all costs. The cowherd boys would fight with Kṛṣṇa in the forest, and in the heat of play they would sometimes become angry with Him and tell Him they wouldn't play with Him anymore. Lord Kṛṣṇa very much liked these chidings of love, and He asked forgiveness from His friends.

Kaṁsa's hatred of the Lord, however, was not *bhakti.* Kaṁsa was afraid that Kṛṣṇa would kill him, and so his mind became absorbed in animosity toward the Lord. Prabhupāda writes, "The state of mind of a great devotee is also to be absorbed in Kṛṣṇa, but a devotee thinks of Him favorably, not unfavorably" (*Kṛṣṇa,* p. 26).

We should not imitate the transcendental feelings of the pure devotees, but we may become inspired by hearing of them. We should patiently wait for the day when these feelings will naturally manifest within us. At that time we will not be able to stop them even if we want to. Meanwhile we may practice becoming greedy for chances to spread the word of Kṛṣṇa, proud that Kṛṣṇa is our Lord and that we have such an exalted spiritual master in Śrīla Prabhupāda, and angry at the māyic obstacles that prevent us from attaining *bhakti.* If we learn to dovetail everything for Lord Kṛṣṇa in this way, we will have learned the essential lesson Nārada is imparting in this *sūtra.*

SŪTRA 66

त्रिरूपभंगपूर्वकं नित्यदास्यनित्यकान्ताभजनात्मकं
प्रेम कार्यं प्रेमैव कार्यम् ॥६६॥

tri-rūpa-bhaṅga-pūrvakaṁ nitya-dāsya-nitya-kāntā-bhajanātmakaṁ prema kāryaṁ premaiva kāryam

tri-rūpa—of the three material forms (the qualities of goodness, passion, and ignorance); *bhaṅga*—the breaking; *pūrvakam*—preceded by; *nitya*—perpetual; *dāsya*—servitude; *nitya*—perpetual; *kāntā*—as a lover; *bhajana*—service; *ātmakam*—consisting of; *prema*—pure love; *kāryam*—one should manifest; *prema*—pure love; *eva*—alone; *kāryam*—one should manifest.

TRANSLATION

After breaking through the aforementioned coverings of the three modes of nature, one should act only in pure love of God, remaining perpetually in the mood of a servant serving his master, or a lover serving her beloved.

PURPORT

As described in Sūtra 56, there are three secondary forms of devotional service tinged with the *guṇas* (goodness, passion, and ignorance). These are practiced by *sakāma* devotees, who approach the Supreme Lord when in distress, when seeking wealth, or when seeking knowledge. One should transcend these secondary types of devotion and approach the Supreme Lord only with love. In other words, here Nārada is urging us to come to the spontaneous stage, as in the *rasas* of servitude (*nitya-dāsya*) and conjugal love (*nitya-kāntā-bhajana*). We should not think that we have completed the course of *bhakti* by becoming a religionist in the conventional sense—by attending the temple and making obligatory prayers and donations.

As a spiritual master, Nārada has responsibly taught the lower stages of *bhakti* and encouraged anyone with even a drop of faith. But it is also his responsibility to remind us that the goal is *prema,* and *prema* alone. His method is similar to Lord Kṛṣṇa's in the *Bhagavad-gītā,* where the Lord mercifully encourages all kinds of *karmīs, jñānīs,* and *yogīs,* advising them on how to progressively turn their attention toward Him. But then He concludes, "Abandon all varieties of religion and just surrender unto Me" (Bg. 18.66).

Out of love, without seeking reward, a devoted servant tries to please his master, and a wife her husband. We see the perfection of servitude in the spiritual world, in Kṛṣṇa's servants like Raktaka, Dāruka, and Patrī, and we see the perfection of a wife's devotion in the queens of Dvārakā. In Lord Kṛṣṇa we find the perfect master and the perfect beloved, and so His servants and wives are eternally liberated as *nitya-dāsa* and *nitya-kāntā.* Following in the footsteps of such liberated beings, devotees in this world should strive to practice devotional service on the level of pure love. As stated in the *Caitanya-mañjuṣā: premā pum-artho mahān.* "Love for Kṛṣṇa is the supreme goal of life."

SŪTRA 67

भक्ता एकान्तिनो मुख्याः ॥६७॥

bhaktā ekāntino mukhyāḥ

bhaktāḥ—devotees; *ekāntinaḥ*—exclusive; *mukhyāḥ*—principal.

TRANSLATION

Among the Lord's devotees, the greatest are those who are dedicated to Him solely as His intimate servants.

PURPORT

His Divine Grace A. C. Bhaktivedanta Swami Prabhupāda showed an excellent example of *ekānta-bhakti,* single-minded devotion to the Supreme Lord. Prabhupāda showed this in many ways. For example, his commentary on Śrī Kṛṣṇa's book, *Bhagavad-gītā,* does not even slightly deviate from Kṛṣṇa's true intent. Impersonalism taints the vast majority of *Bhagavad-gītā* commentaries, but Śrīla Prabhupāda's purports in *Bhagavad-gītā As It Is* lead the reader directly to the lotus feet of Kṛṣṇa. This is true of all of Prabhupāda's books—*Śrīmad-Bhāgavatam, Caitanya-caritāmṛta,* and so on. His translation of the Sanskrit or Bengali is always accurate from a scholarly point of view, but at the same time he writes as a pure devotee: "Surrender to Kṛṣṇa."

In all of Śrīla Prabhupāda's spontaneous conversations, he was single-mindedly Kṛṣṇa conscious. When he spoke of Kṛṣṇa, he seemed to be talking about his dearmost friend, not merely repeating something he had read. Sometimes his *kṛṣṇa-kathā* took the form of convincing an atheist scientist that there is a supreme controller, sometimes he related the pastimes of Kṛṣṇa to his disciples, and sometimes he assured devotees that Kṛṣṇa is in our hearts and will give us the intelligence to execute a difficult service. Śrīla Prabhupāda maintained this single-mindedness even while undergoing the rigors of constant travel and while living in the biggest cities of the world. Wherever he was, Prabhupāda was on a mission for Kṛṣṇa.

Being single-pointed in devotional service does not mean shutting out reality. Exclusivity *can* become sectarian if one focuses on relative truths or dedicates oneself to an ordinary person. But when the object of appreciation is the Supreme Personality of Godhead, one attains the broadest vision, the vision of a *mahātmā.*

The devotee who is fixed on Kṛṣṇa has actually attained to the complete truth. That the Lord is the complete truth is stated in the Invocation to the *Īśopaniṣad: oṁ pūrṇam adaḥ pūrṇam idam.* "The Personality of Godhead is perfect and complete." A devotee glorifies the Lord as the complete Absolute Truth when he utters the famous Vedic aphorism *tat tvam asi,* "You are that." The impersonalist philosophers adore the *tat tvam asi* aphorism because they take it to mean that they are one with the formless Brahman. But the actual meaning of *tat tvam asi* is different. When the devotee says "You are that," he is addressing the Supreme Lord. Śrīla Prabhupāda explains in his purport to *Bhagavad-gītā* 4.9:

> The Vedic version *tat tvam asi* is actually applied in this case. Anyone who understands Lord Kṛṣṇa to be the Supreme, or who says unto the Lord, "You are the same Supreme Brahman, the Personality of Godhead," is certainly liberated instantly, and consequently his entrance into the transcendental association of the Lord is guaranteed.

A pure devotee who sees Kṛṣṇa in everything can maintain one-pointed concentration on the Lord, even while performing a wide variety of services for Him. By contrast, materialistic persons cannot be *ekāntī,* or focused. Because the field of sense gratification tempts the conditioned souls in many directions, and because the mind is very fickle, the hedonist's attention is splayed. As Lord Kṛṣṇa says,

vyavasāyātmikā buddhir ekeha kuru-nandana
bahu-śākhā hy anantāś ca buddhayo 'vyavasāyinām

"Those who are on this path are resolute in purpose, and their aim is one. O beloved child of the Kurus, the intelligence of those who are irresolute is many-branched" (Bg. 2.41).

Śukadeva Gosvāmī describes the materialist in a similar way in the *Śrīmad-Bhāgavatam* (2.1.2):

śrotavyādīni rājendra nṛṇāṁ santi sahasraśaḥ
apaśyatām ātma-tattvaṁ gṛheṣu gṛha-medhinām

"Those persons who are materially engrossed, being blind to the knowledge of ultimate truth, have many subject matters for hearing in human society, O emperor." Absorbed in political work or scientific research or social and economic betterment, the *gṛhamedhīs* put aside the ultimate problems of old age, disease, and death. They do not inquire about self-realization, which would lead them eventually to Kṛṣṇa consciousness. But a person who wants to succeed in *bhakti* must give up the life of bewildering distractions and take up devotional service under the guidance of a spiritual master.

The best way to cultivate single-minded devotion to Kṛṣṇa is to chant the Hare Kṛṣṇa *mantra.* This practice is what the scriptures and *ācāryas* recommend as the main limb of devotional service for the Age of Kali. By this one simple act—chanting and hearing the holy name—we serve Lord Kṛṣṇa the way He likes best. Haridāsa Ṭhākura set the example by making the chanting of *hari-nāma* his exclusive service. Serious Gauḍīya Vaiṣṇavas follow in his footsteps by chanting daily at least sixteen rounds of Hare Kṛṣṇa on beads. As stated in the *Caitanya-caritāmṛta* (*Antya* 3.268), "The holy name of Kṛṣṇa is so attractive that anyone who chants it—including all living entities, moving and unmoving, and even Lord Kṛṣṇa Himself—becomes imbued with love of Kṛṣṇa. This is the effect of chanting the Hare Kṛṣṇa *mantra.*"

In the beginning stages, the restless mind balks at the single-minded devotion required to chant Hare Kṛṣṇa for long stretches. The holy name is actually the sweetest nectar, but until we reach the spontaneous stage of devotion, one has to outsmart the mischievous mind. The mind is called *cañcala,* or unfaithful, but it can become the devotee's best friend. When one chants Hare Kṛṣṇa and performs other duties with concentration and devotion, the mind clears and the devotee realizes his true interest. Then the devotee becomes attracted to serving the holy names in the *ekāntina* spirit, which Nārada Muni recommends here as the best.

SŪTRA 68

कण्ठावरोधरोमाश्रुभिः परस्परं लपमानाः
पावयन्ति कुलानि पृथिवीं च ॥६८॥

kaṇṭhāvarodha-romāśrubhiḥ parasparaṁ lapamānāḥ pāvayanti kulāni pṛthivīṁ ca

kaṇṭha—of the throat; *avarodha*—with blockage; *roma*—with bodily hair (standing erect); *aśrubhiḥ*—and with tears; *parasparam*—among one another; *lapamānāḥ*—conversing; *pāvayanti*—they purify; *kulāni*—their communities; *pṛthivīm*—the earth; *ca*—and.

TRANSLATION

Conversing among one another with throats choked, hair standing on end, and tears flowing, the Lord's intimate servants purify their own followers and the whole world.

PURPORT

One may ask, "Does Nārada expect *me* to also become a great devotee and experience such ecstasy?" The answer is yes, the ecstasy of devotional service is open to all. But a humble devotee may think himself unfit to experience the advanced stages of Kṛṣṇa consciousness for many lifetimes. We may respond best to a *sūtra* like this by trying to appreciate, at least slightly, the wonderful influence of the great souls who have come to this earth. This will inspire us to seek the association of the servants of the servants of such great souls, to assist them in their mission, and to receive shelter from them against the world of *māyā.*

The symptoms of ecstasy should not be imitated, but it is not wrong to aspire to experience them. In *The Nectar of Devotion,* Rūpa Gosvāmī encourages us to develop a spontaneous attachment for serving the

Lord without any desire for profit. Śrīla Prabhupāda writes,

> In other words, one should learn how to cry for the Lord. One should learn this small technique, and one should be very eager and actually cry to become engaged in some particular type of service. This is called *laulyam,* and such tears are the price for the highest perfection. [*The Nectar of Devotion,* p. 84]

The absence of warm or spontaneous feelings for the Lord may indicate that we are still committing one or more of the ten offenses against the holy name, or that we are indulging in some of the vices mentioned in the *Nārada-bhakti-sūtra.* As Lord Caitanya, taking the role of the neophyte, laments in His *Śikṣāṣṭaka* (2), "I am so unfortunate that I commit offenses while chanting the holy name, and therefore I do not achieve attachment for chanting."

Although the bodily transformations symptomatic of ecstatic love of God (*bhāva*) are sometimes exhibited by great souls, pretenders may imitate them. Real *bhāva,* however, is manifested by steady symptoms:

> *Bhāva* is definitely displayed in the matter of cessation of material desires (*kṣānti*), utilization of every moment in the transcendental loving service of the Lord (*avyartha-kālatvam*), eagerness for glorifying the Lord constantly (*nāma-gāne sadā ruciḥ*), attraction for living in the land of the Lord (*prītis tad-vasati-sthale*), complete detachment from material happiness (*viraktiḥ*), and pridelessness (*māna-śūnyatā*). One who has developed all these transcendental qualities is really possessed of the *bhāva* stage, as distinguished from the stonehearted imitator or mundane devotee. [*Bhāg.* 2.3.24, purport]

The influence of pure devotees of the Lord is very great. Their conversations are entirely Kṛṣṇa conscious, and that is why they purify everyone who hears them, and even the place they inhabit. When bona fide devotees perform *kṛṣṇa-kīrtana* or discuss topics concerning Kṛṣṇa, the Lord is personally present:

> The topics of Lord Kṛṣṇa are so auspicious that they purify the speaker, the hearer, and the inquirer. They are compared to the Ganges waters, which flow from the toe of Lord Kṛṣṇa. Wherever the

> Ganges waters go, they purify the land and the person who bathes in them. Similarly, *kṛṣṇa-kathā,* or the topics of Kṛṣṇa, are so pure that wherever they are spoken the place, the hearer, the inquirer, the speaker, and all concerned become purified. [*Bhāg.* 2.1.1, purport]

The practical effect of a devotee's influence is that people take up spiritual life and abandon their sinful habits. Without devotional reform in society, humanity will degrade to a barbaric species. Prabhupāda writes, "Men face each other in enmity just like cats and dogs snarling. *Śrī Īśopaniṣad* cannot give advice to the cats and dogs, but it delivers the message of Godhead to man through the bona fide *ācāryas,* or holy teachers" (*Īśopaniṣad* 1, purport).

At least on an individual basis every sane person should save himself by coming forward to render service and to hear from Vaiṣṇavas of the caliber Nārada describes in this *sūtra.* If one is under the protection of a pure devotee and sincerely renders service to him in *bhakti-yoga,* one will be able to counteract all sinful reactions, including the accumulated sinful *karma* of the whole world population. Nārada praises the influence of devotees, but Lord Kṛṣṇa praises the influence of Nārada:

> If someone is able, by chance, to see face to face a great saintly person like Nārada, who is always serene and merciful to everyone, then immediately that conditioned soul becomes liberated. This is exactly like being situated in the full light of the sun; there cannot be any visionary impediment. [*Kṛṣṇa,* p. 97]

SŪTRA 69

तीर्थीकुर्वन्ति तीर्थानि सुकर्मीकुर्वन्ति कर्माणि
सच्छास्त्रीकुर्वन्ति शास्त्राणि ॥६९॥

tīrthī-kurvanti tīrthāni su-karmī-kurvanti karmāṇi sac-chāstrī-kurvanti śāstrāṇi

tīrthī—into holy places; *kurvanti*—they make; *tīrthāni*—the holy places; *su-karmī*—into auspicious works; *kurvanti*—they make; *karmāṇi*—works; *sat*—pure; *śāstrī*—into scriptures; *kurvanti*—they make; *śāstrāṇi*—the scriptures.

TRANSLATION

Their association makes holy places holy, works auspicious, and the scriptures authoritative.

PURPORT

A *tīrtha* is a place made sacred because the Supreme Lord performed His pastimes there. For example, Vṛndāvana is sacred because Śrī Kṛṣṇa spent His youth there, Navadvīpa because Śrī Caitanya Mahāprabhu began His *saṅkīrtana* movement there. Places like Dhruva-ghāṭa or Naimiṣāraṇya, where *mahā-janas* performed devotional service, are also *tīrthas.* Devotees like to reside in *tīrthas* and perform their *bhajana* there, and pilgrims seeking purification go to bathe in the sacred rivers flowing through the sacred sites. But the *tīrthas* become burdened by the sins of visiting pilgrims, who sometimes commit new sins even while traveling on pilgrimage. In all the religions of the world, commercialism tends to spring up and pollute the famous shrines. Because of this, the Gauḍīya Vaiṣṇava *ācārya* Narottama dāsa Ṭhākura stated that in the Kali-yuga going on pilgrimage creates bewilderment. Śrīla Prabhupāda writes:

> In India it is still a practice that many advanced transcendentalists give up their family lives and go to Vṛndāvana to live there alone and completely engage in hearing and chanting the holy pastimes of the Lord. This system is recommended in the *Śrīmad-Bhāgavatam,* and the six Gosvāmīs of Vṛndāvana followed it, but at the present moment many *karmīs* and pseudo devotees have overcrowded the holy place of Vṛndāvana just to imitate this process recommended by Śukadeva Gosvāmī. [*Kṛṣṇa,* p. 881]

To purify the *tīrthas* of the influence of the nondevotees, saints occasionally visit them. In fact, it is the presence of the saints that actually makes the places holy. If one visits a *tīrtha* and only does some shopping and takes a ritual bath there, without inquiring from saintly persons, his visit is useless.

When the sage Vidura went to the palace of the Kurus in Hastināpura, Yudhiṣṭhira Mahārāja praised him with the same words Nārada uses here: *tīrthī-kurvanti tīrthānī.* Śrīla Prabhupāda writes,

> By their actions the pure devotees of the Lord can render any place into a place of pilgrimage, and the holy places are worth the name only on their account. Such pure devotees are able to rectify the polluted atmosphere of any place, and what to speak of a holy place rendered unholy by the questionable actions of interested persons who try to adopt a professional life at the cost of the reputation of the holy place. [*Bhāg.* 1.13.10, purport]

In a similar passage, the sage Bhagīratha praised the river Ganges and the saints who bathe in her waters: "When such pure devotees bathe in your water, the sinful reactions accumulated from other people will certainly be counteracted, for such devotees always keep in the core of their hearts the Supreme Personality of Godhead, who can vanquish all sinful reactions" (*Bhāg.* 9.9.6).

If the saints are so influential just by their presence, then we can just imagine how much their acts are worshipable and worth following. Most people's actions result in reactions (*karma*), but the acts of great souls convert *karma* into *bhakti*. Whoever serves a pure devotee gains a permanent spiritual asset, even if he does so unknowingly (*ajñāta-sukṛti*). Although we cannot expect to equal the deeds of pure devotees, we should not shy away from trying to emulate them. As Śrīla Prabhupāda used to say, "Do as I am doing."

Nārada states that the best devotees add spiritual authority even to the scriptures. A striking example of this is Śrīla Prabhupāda's fulfillment of a prediction of Lord Caitanya's recorded in the *Caitanya-bhāgavata:*

pṛthivīte āche yata nagarādi-grāma
sarvatra pracāra haibe mora nāma

"In every town and village of the world, My name [the holy name of Kṛṣṇa] will be preached." This statement used to puzzle Vaiṣṇava scholars; some said it was to be taken allegorically. How could *mlecchas* in Western countries take up the worship of Lord Kṛṣṇa and Lord Caitanya and chant Hare Kṛṣṇa in their towns and cities? But Śrīla Prabhupāda proved the skeptics wrong: On his spiritual master's order and by Lord Caitanya's grace, he created the Hare Kṛṣṇa movement, which quickly spread until newspapers and commentators proclaimed: "Kṛṣṇa Chant Startles London," and "'Hare Kṛṣṇa' has become a household word."

Śrīla Prabhupāda's preaching of the *Bhagavad-gītā* provides another example of how the pure devotees give authority to the scriptures. For more than two hundred years before Śrīla Prabhupāda came to the West with *Bhagavad-gītā As It Is,* the *Bhagavad-gītā* had been known in Western countries as "the sacred gospel of the Hindus." And yet no one had become a devotee of Lord Kṛṣṇa from reading *Bhagavad-gītā,* although Lord Kṛṣṇa teaches surrender to Him as the goal of the *Gītā.* But through his realized translations and purports Śrīla Prabhupāda brought life to the text of *Bhagavad-gītā,* and now thousands of non-Hindus throughout the world are recognizing Lord Kṛṣṇa as the Supreme Personality of Godhead and becoming His sincere devotees.

Nārada will now explain why saintly persons are so auspicious and influential.

SŪTRA 70

तन्मयाः ॥७०॥

tan-mayāḥ

tat—with Him; *mayāḥ*—filled.

TRANSLATION

The intimate servants of the Supreme Lord are fully absorbed in loving Him.

PURPORT

Nārada's definitions give us portraits of complete dedication, of love, and of oneness of interest between the Supreme Lord and His devotee. When we read a superb *sūtra* such as number 49 or 67 we may think, "Now he has given the last word on *bhakti:* nothing more can be said as briefly and as well." But then Nārada delights us with even more precise aphorisms on *bhakti-yoga.*

This *sūtra* is quite similar to number 41: "The Lord and His pure devotees are nondifferent." In the *Gurv-aṣṭaka,* Śrīla Viśvanātha Cakravartī Ṭhākura states, "The spiritual master is to be honored as much as the Supreme Lord because he is the most confidential servitor of the Lord. This is acknowledged in all revealed scriptures and followed by all authorities." Although a qualified student of *bhakti* knows that the Vaiṣṇava is not God Himself, the disciple experiences Kṛṣṇa's direct presence in the form of His dedicated servant. And the disciple is fully satisfied in serving the Supreme Lord by serving His pure devotee, who is the transparent medium to Kṛṣṇa.

When Sanātana Gosvāmī met Lord Caitanya, the Lord told him, "Lord Kṛṣṇa has saved you from life's deepest hell." Sanātana replied, "I do not know who Kṛṣṇa is. As far as I am concerned, I have been released from prison only by Your mercy" (Cc. *Madhya* 20.64). The disciple's gratitude toward the Vaiṣṇava is also expressed in Bhaktivinoda Ṭhākura's song *Ohe! vaiṣṇava ṭhākura:* "Kṛṣṇa is yours. You're able to give Him to me, for such is your power. I am indeed wretched and simply run after you, crying, 'Kṛṣṇa! Kṛṣṇa!'"

This is why the place where great devotees reside is a *tīrtha* and why Nārada says that they purify established holy places and give authority to the scriptures—because they are *tan-mayāḥ,* "filled with Him."

SŪTRA 71

मोदन्ते पितरो नृत्यन्ति देवताः सनाथा चेयं भूर्भवति ॥७१॥

modante pitaro nṛtyanti devatāḥ sa-nāthā ceyaṁ bhūr bhavati

modante—become joyful; *pitaraḥ*—forefathers; *nṛtyanti*—dance; *devatāḥ*—demigods; *sa-nāthā*—having good masters; *ca*—and; *iyam*—this; *bhūḥ*—earth; *bhavati*—becomes.

TRANSLATION

Thus the pure devotees' forefathers become joyful, the demigods dance, and the world feels protected by good masters.

PURPORT

A great devotee is so dear to the Supreme Lord that his family members receive the Lord's blessings even though they may not appreciate their devotee relative. When Lord Nṛsiṁhadeva rescued His dearmost *bhakta,* Prahlāda, from his demonic father, Prahlāda

Mahārāja asked that his father be excused and not punished in the next life for his heinous crimes. Lord Nṛsiṁhadeva replied, "My dear Prahlāda, most pure, O great saintly person, your father has been purified, along with twenty-one forefathers in your family. Because you were born in this family, the entire dynasty has been purified. Whenever and wherever there are peaceful, equipoised devotees who are well behaved and decorated with all good qualities, that place and the dynasties there, even if condemned, are purified" (*Bhāg.* 7.10.18–19).

Lord Caitanya also gave special mercy to His devotees' relatives. Amogha, the son-in-law of Sārvabhauma Bhaṭṭācārya, blasphemed Lord Caitanya and had to suffer cholera. But Lord Caitanya spared him and said, "You are the object of My affection because you are the son-in-law of Sārvabhauma Bhaṭṭācārya. Everyone in Sārvabhauma's house is very dear to Me, including his maids and servants and even his dog. And what to speak of his relatives?" (Cc. *Madhya* 15.283–4). A pure devotee identifies more with the family of all living entities than with his bodily relatives, and yet whoever is even remotely connected with a pure devotee, even a distant relative, receives benefit. The influence of the devotee is that great.

Next Nārada says *nṛtyanti devatāḥ,* "The demigods dance when they see a pure devotee appear." The *devas* are staunch devotees of Lord Viṣṇu, and they hate to see the demons gain control. Sometimes the demons capture the demigods' palaces, as during the rule of Hiraṇyakaśipu. But the pure devotee Prahlāda caused the appearance of Lord Nṛsiṁhadeva, who destroyed Hiraṇyakaśipu. Hiraṇyakaśipu was "like a fever of meningitis in the head of the three worlds." When he was killed by Lord Nṛsiṁhadeva, the demigods prayed, "When this demon was condemned by devotees because they were disgusted with him, then he was killed by You" (*Bhāg.* 7.8.53). Thus the pure devotee's work is so significant that it affects the whole universe and creates a shift in favor of godliness. The demigods' joy at the appearance of a Vaiṣṇava proves that the *devas* are also Vaiṣṇavas. They are more pleased with a pure devotee who renders service unto the Supreme Lord than they are with their own worshipers who seek material boons from them.

Finally Nārada states that with the appearance of a pure devotee, the earth gets a savior. Mother Earth is abused in Kali-yuga in many ways. When Kali-yuga began, Mahārāja Parīkṣit found a *śūdra* beating the earth personified, who appeared in the form of a cow. Nowadays the earth is drilled recklessly for oil, deforested, blown up, polluted by chemicals, stripped of fertile topsoil, and filled up with cheaters and liars who create an intolerable burden.

The earth is not a dead mass to be exploited by the human species; rather, she is a living entity meant to be protected. When the earth is protected, she gives ample space and a peaceful and prosperous residence for all living entities. But when human beings plunder the earth, she seeks protection from a magnanimous devotee. Though a devotee may appear to work as a humble mendicant without much power, higher beings and truly learned souls know that a savior has appeared.

The devotee is especially a savior for human beings, most of whom would surely fall down into lower species in their next lives without the devotee's efforts to reform them. According to time, place, and person, every pure-devotee savior teaches the same message: "Do not rot in this material world; follow the word of God and be saved." The world still worships saviors such as Jesus Christ, Lord Buddha, and Lord Caitanya. Many other pure devotees continue to appear, as the son of God or as *śakty-āveśa avatāras,* to save the human race. Considering the far-reaching auspicious effects of a pure devotee's presence, which are mostly beyond normal comprehension, we can appreciate better why Śrīla Prabhupāda said, "If only one man becomes a pure devotee of the Lord, we shall consider our attempt a success."

SŪTRA 72

नास्ति तेषु जातिविद्यारूपकुलधनक्रियादिभेदः ॥७२॥

nāsti teṣu jāti-vidyā-rūpa-kula-dhana-kriyādi-bhedaḥ

na asti—there is not; *teṣu*—in them; *jāti*—of class; *vidyā*—education; *rūpa*—beauty; *kula*—family; *dhana*—wealth; *kriyā*—occupation; *ādi*—and so on; *bhedaḥ*—difference.

TRANSLATION

There are no distinctions among such pure devotees in terms of social class, education, bodily beauty, family status, wealth, occupation, and so on.

PURPORT

Śrī Kṛṣṇa, the Supreme Personality of Godhead, does not discriminate among devotees based on their birth, wealth, and so on, so why should we? Kṛṣṇa says, "O son of Pṛthā, those who take shelter in Me, though they be of lower birth—women, *vaiśyas* [merchants], and *śūdras* [workers]—attain the supreme destination" (Bg. 9.32). And according to the *Padma Purāṇa,* "Anyone who thinks of the Deity of Viṣṇu as merely stone or the *guru* as an ordinary man, or who thinks a Vaiṣṇava belongs to a particular family or country, is a resident of hell."

In his *Upadeśāmṛta* (6), Rūpa Gosvāmī has also warns us not to take a material view of devotees: "Being situated in his original Kṛṣṇa conscious position, a pure devotee does not identify with the body. Such a devotee should not be seen from a materialistic point of view. Indeed, one should overlook a devotee's having a body born in a low family, a body with a bad complexion, a deformed body, or a diseased or infirm body. According to ordinary vision, such imperfections may seem prominent in the body of a pure devotee, but despite such seeming defects, the body of a pure devotee cannot be polluted. It is exactly like the waters of the Ganges, which sometimes during the rainy season are full of bubbles, foam, and mud. The Ganges waters do not become polluted. Those who are advanced in spiritual understanding will bathe in the Ganges without considering the condition of the water."

Śrīla Prabhupāda states that one should not think, "Oh, here is an American *gosvāmī,*" and on that basis discriminate against him. On the other hand, Westerners who have come to Kṛṣṇa consciousness by Prabhupāda's grace should not be puffed up and think themselves better than Indian *brāhmaṇas.* The *śāstras* state, *kalau śūdra-sambhavaḥ:* "In the Age of Kali, everyone is born a *śūdra.*" We are elevated by the process of Kṛṣṇa consciousness, but we have nothing to be proud of on our own account: it is all due to the mercy of the Lord and His pure devotee. Śrīla Haridāsa Ṭhākura set the example: even after he became the most elevated transcendentalist, he did not assert himself as a superior person but wished to be regarded as lowborn. In the name of becoming a transcendentalist, one should not become captured again by false pride.

Only one who is ignorant of the transforming power of *bhakti* discriminates against devotees on the basis of material designations. Prabhupāda writes, "One should therefore avoid observing a pure devotee externally, but should try to see the internal features and understand how he is engaged in the transcendental loving service of the Lord" (*The Nectar of Instruction,* Text 6, purport).

In her prayers to Lord Kapila, Devahūti affirmed that the Lord's holy names possess the transcendental power to transform anyone: "Oh, how glorious are they whose tongues are chanting Your holy name! Even if born in families of dog-eaters, such persons are worshipable" (*Bhāg.* 3.33.7).

SŪTRA 73

यतस्तदीयाः ॥७३॥

yatas tadīyāḥ

yataḥ—because; *tadīyāḥ*—His.

TRANSLATION

Pure devotees are not distinguished by externals like social class, for they belong to the Lord.

PURPORT

Here Nārada explains why one should avoid caste-conscious prejudice toward devotees of Kṛṣṇa: because devotees are all one class—they are all His own. And because they belong to the Supreme Lord (*tadīyāḥ*), the devotees are worshipable:

ārādhanānāṁ sarveṣāṁ viṣṇor ārādhanaṁ param
tasmāt parataraṁ devi tadīyānāṁ samarcanam

"Of all types of worship, worship of Lord Viṣṇu is best, and better than the worship of Lord Viṣṇu is the worship of His devotee, the Vaiṣṇava" (*Padma Purāṇa*).

Tadīya means "in relation to Him." The devotees are intimately related to the Lord because they are under the shelter of His internal energy. Thus they always accompany Him and serve Him as His carrier Garuḍa, His couch Ananta Śeṣa, His cows, His *gopas* and *gopīs,* and so on.

In a general sense, *all* living entities are part and parcel of Kṛṣṇa—

"My eternal fragmental parts," Kṛṣṇa says—and that is another reason why one should not judge someone higher or lower by material standards. But although all *jīvas* are dear to Lord Kṛṣṇa, He is dear only to His devotees, and therefore they receive His special attention. As He says in the *Bhagavad-gītā* (9.29),

samo 'haṁ sarva-bhūteṣu na me dveṣyo 'sti na priyaḥ
ye bhajanti tu māṁ bhaktyā mayi te teṣu cāpy aham

"I envy no one, nor am I partial to anyone. I am equal to all. But whoever renders service unto Me in devotion is a friend—is in Me—and I am also a friend to him."

During a conversation with Sanātana Gosvāmī and Haridāsa Ṭhākura in Jagannātha Purī, Lord Caitanya once elaborately explained the same truth expressed in this *sūtra*. Sanātana had contracted a skin disease that produced oozing sores. Out of humility he considered his body useless for devotional service, and he decided to commit suicide under the wheel of Lord Jagannātha's chariot. But Lord Caitanya read his mind and forbade him to do so, telling him that he had already surrendered his body to the Lord for service. Lord Caitanya used to embrace Sanātana, and this made Sanātana feel mortified because his oozing sores touched the Lord's body. And so Sanātana decided to leave Jagannātha Purī. But Lord Caitanya explained that He was not offended by Sanātana's body; rather, He felt great bliss while embracing Sanātana because He saw his body as transcendental. Śrī Caitanya Mahāprabhu quoted the *Bhagavad-gītā* (5.18):

vidyā-vinaya-sampanne brāhmaṇe gavi hastini
śuni caiva śva-pāke ca paṇḍitāḥ sama-darśinaḥ

"The humble sages, by virtue of true knowledge, see with equal vision a learned and gentle *brāhmaṇa,* a cow, an elephant, a dog, and a dog-eater [outcaste]."

On hearing this quote, Haridāsa said, "What You have spoken deals with external formalities." Lord Caitanya then revealed His inner thoughts regarding His love for His devotees:

> My dear Haridāsa and Sanātana, I think of you as My little boys, to be maintained by Me. The maintainer never takes seriously any faults of the maintained. . . .When a child passes stool and urine that touch the body of the mother, the mother never hates the child. On the contrary, she takes much pleasure in cleaning him. The stool and urine of the child appear like sandalwood pulp to the mother. Similarly, when the foul moisture oozing from the sores of Sanātana touches My body, I have no hatred for him. [Cc. *Antya* 4.184–7]

Lord Caitanya then further explained the glories of devotional service and how it transforms a devotee's body into spiritual existence.

In conclusion, the body of a pure devotee is never material. Even if it appears so, Kṛṣṇa still accepts the devotee as dear and embraces him as His own. By the Lord's mercy, the devotee is spiritualized, and in his transcendental body he renders service to the Lord's lotus feet.

CHAPTER 5

Attaining Perfection

SŪTRA 74

वादो नावलम्ब्यः ॥७४॥

vādo nāvalambyaḥ

vādaḥ—debate; *na*—not; *avalambyaḥ*—to be resorted to.

TRANSLATION

One should not indulge in argumentative debate.

PURPORT

Nārada discourages the egotistic wrangling spirit. One who is proud of his debating skills and eager to defeat others will lose his humility, which, as Nārada says in Sūtra 27, is essential for pleasing Kṛṣṇa. The existence of God is not something to be proven or disproven merely by a battle of logical wits. The spiritual reality cannot be understood by material logic or the speculations of the material mind. As the *Vedānta-sūtra* (2.1.11) declares, *tarkāpratiṣṭhānāt:* "Logical reasoning is inconclusive."

However, when a Kṛṣṇa conscious preacher defends the Lord or the Vaiṣṇavas against blasphemy, that should not be taken as vain controversy. The devotee doesn't argue on his own account, but on Kṛṣṇa's. Also, a devotee's preaching is not based on mental speculation, which is always imperfect, but on the perfect process of receiving knowledge from the *śāstra* and the *ācāryas.* As it is said, "Mistakes, illusion, cheating, and defective perception do not occur in the sayings of the authoritative sages" (Cc. *Ādi* 2.86). Also, the Vaiṣṇava *ācāryas* have all argued against Māyāvāda interpretations. This kind of argumentation is not to be avoided but is rather one of the duties of the *madhyama-bhakta,* or preacher. Kṛṣṇadāsa Kavirāja states, "A sincere student should not neglect the discussion of such conclusions [concerning the philosophy of Kṛṣṇa consciousness], considering them controversial, for such discussion strengthens the mind. Thus one's mind becomes attached to Kṛṣṇa" (Cc. *Ādi* 2.117).

But sometimes a preacher will avoid a fight if he sees that the challenger simply wants to argue for the sake of argument. Rūpa Gosvāmī once declined to debate a rascal who came to defeat him, but then Rūpa's nephew, Jīva Gosvāmī, took up the challenge. So a devotee may or may not choose to meet the challenges of the atheists and voidists, depending on the circumstances, but in any case he knows that debate and challenge do not lead to a true understanding of God.

Certainly the devotee himself has no challenging spirit when he approaches the scriptures or the *ācāryas.* He accepts them axiomatically, beyond argument. The best method for solving one's personal doubts is to inquire submissively from advanced Vaiṣṇavas, who will always be able to answer in terms of *śāstra* and reason.

SŪTRA 75

बाहुल्यावकाशत्वादनियतत्वाच्च ॥७५॥

bāhulyāvakāśatvād aniyatatvāc ca

bāhulya—for excessiveness; *avakāśatvāt*—because of involving opportunities; *aniyatatvāt*—because of not being decisive; *ca*—and.

TRANSLATION

Such argumentation leads to excessive entanglements and is never decisive.

PURPORT

In the *Mahābhārata,* Yudhiṣṭhira Mahārāja describes the defect of argumentation as follows: *tarko 'pratiṣṭhaḥ śrutayo vibihinnā nāsāv ṛṣir yasya mataṁ na bhinnam.* "Dry arguments are inconclusive. A great personality whose opinion does not differ from others is not considered a great sage. Simply by studying the *Vedas,* which are variegated, one cannot come to the right path by which religious principles are understood" (*Mahābhārata, Vana-parva* 313.117).

If you base your philosophical conclusions on logical arguments, a superior logician will eventually defeat you. This is the method of Western philosophers, and India also has its *munis*. A *muni* is not considered distinguished unless he defeats the arguments of previous thinkers. But then another *muni* comes and finds flaws in the arguments of the current champion and claims to replace him with "the latest philosophy." Those who study argumentation come to the conclusion that there is no final truth. This is skepticism, the fruit of mental speculation.

A *bhakta* should not take part in the tedious, inconclusive contests of logicians. The Vedic truths have been thoroughly researched since time beyond memory and are established conclusively. The *ācāryas* who guide the destiny of Vedic culture, such as Madhva, Rāmānuja, and Lord Caitanya, did not invent the Vedic *siddhānta* (conclusion), though they all presented it according to time, place, and recipients.

King Yudhiṣṭhira continues: *dharmasya tattvaṁ nihitaṁ guhāyāṁ mahā-jano yena gataḥ sa panthāḥ.* "The solid truth of religious principles is hidden in the heart of an unadulterated self-realized person. Consequently, as the *śāstras* confirm, one should accept whatever progressive path the *mahā-janas* advocate."

The *bhakti* method of receiving truth is by *paramparā,* or disciplic succession. It is confirmed by a checks-and-balances system of hearing from *guru, śāstra,* and *sādhu.* On the other hand, one who rejects the *paramparā* system and persists in hearing argumentation will never understand the Absolute Truth. As Lord Kṛṣṇa states, *bhaktyā mām abhijānāti:* "One can understand Me only by devotional service" (Bg. 18.55).

When Lord Caitanya first came to Jagannātha Purī, a dispute arose between His followers and Sārvabhauma Bhaṭṭācārya, who was at that time a mundane logician. The Bhaṭṭācārya and his students refused to accept that Lord Caitanya was the Supreme Personality of Godhead, although Gopīnātha Ācārya presented much evidence from Vedic scriptures. Finally the disciples of the Bhaṭṭācārya said, "We derive knowledge of the Absolute Truth by logical hypothesis." Gopīnātha Ācārya replied, "One cannot attain real knowledge of the Supreme Personality of Godhead by such logical hypothesis and argument" (Cc. *Madhya* 6.81). Gopīnātha Ācārya further stated that only that person who has received the mercy of the Lord by rendering Him devotional service can understand Him. Logical hypothesis is not the way, but rather *śabda-brahma,* hearing from authorized sources. Lord Brahmā made the same point in his prayers to Lord Kṛṣṇa in Chapter Fourteen of the Tenth Canto of *Śrīmad-Bhāgavatam:*

athāpi te deva padāmbuja-dvaya-
prasāda-leśānugṛhīta eva hi
jānāti tattvaṁ bhagavan-mahimno
na cānya eko 'pi ciraṁ vicinvan

"My Lord, one who is favored by even a slight trace of the mercy of Your lotus feet can understand the greatness of Your personality. But those who speculate in order to understand the Supreme Personality of Godhead are unable to know You, even though they continue to study the *Vedas* for many years" (*Bhāg.* 10.14.29).

Vain controversy may also include gossip and rumor (*prajalpa*). Nārada previously stated that a *bhakta* shouldn't hear from people who speak of women, wealth, and atheists (Sūtra 63). Even members of a religious movement have to be careful in their talks, or they too may become another association of harsh and idle talkers like the nondevotees. One has to distinguish between responsible dialogue on important issues and talk that leads nowhere. If we enter into controversial topics, we should do so with restraint, sincerely seeking the Vaiṣṇava *siddhānta* according to *guru, śāstra,* and *sādhu.* The *śāstras* are not to be researched merely as so much ammunition for our own opinions. When we enter debate with an egoistic zest to defeat the opposition, we miss the point and end up fighting with the Vaiṣṇavas. In the prayer known as the *Haṁsa-gūhya,* offered by Dakṣa to Lord Viṣṇu, Dakṣa concluded that the method of logical dispute is actually a product of illusion:

> I offer my respectful obeisances unto the Supreme Personality of Godhead, who is full of unlimited qualities and whose different potencies bring about agreement and disagreement between disputants. Thus the illusory energy again and again covers the self-realization of both disputants. [*Bhāg.* 6.4.31]

SŪTRA 76

भक्तिशास्त्राणि मननीयानि तद्बोधककर्माणि करणीयानि ॥७६॥

bhakti-śāstrāṇi mananīyāni tad-bodhaka-karmāṇi karaṇīyāni

bhakti—of devotional service; *śāstrāṇi*—the scriptures; *mananīyāni*—should be respected; *tat*—by them; *bodhaka*—made known; *karmāṇi*—prescribed activities; *karaṇīyāni*—should be executed.

TRANSLATION

One should respect the revealed scriptures of devotional service and discharge the duties they prescribe.

PURPORT

The most important *bhakti-śāstras* have been translated with *paramparā* purports by His Divine Grace A. C. Bhaktivedanta Swami Prabhupāda. Śrīla Prabhupāda writes, "In our Kṛṣṇa consciousness movement we have therefore limited our study of Vedic literature to *Bhagavad-gītā, Śrīmad-Bhāgavatam, Caitanya-caritāmṛta,* and *Bhakti-rasāmṛta-sindhu.* These four works are sufficient for preaching purposes. They are adequate for the understanding of the philosophy and the spreading of missionary activities all over the world" (Cc. *Madhya* 22.118, purport).

The *Vedas* are vast, comprising millions of Sanskrit *ślokas.* And while the conclusion of all branches of Vedic literature is to render devotional service to the Supreme Personality of Godhead, some parts of the Vedic literature are addressed to materialistic religionists and therefore teach a gradual process of elevation. The sages at Naimiṣāraṇya, therefore, asked Sūta Gosvāmī to teach them the essence of the *Vedas.* In Kali-yuga most people do not have the time, energy, or interest to go through all the *Vedas,* nor is it advisable to try. The essence, selected by Sūta Gosvāmī, is *Śrīmad-Bhāgavatam,* which teaches *bhakti-yoga* as the supreme *dharma* and rejects all "cheating religion." To bring transcendental light into the age of darkness, Śrīla Vyāsadeva, the compiler of all the *Vedas,* gave the world the *Śrīmad-Bhāgavatam* as his mature contribution:

anarthopaśamaṁ sākṣād bhakti-yogam adhokṣaje
lokasyājānato vidvāṁś cakre sātvata-saṁhitām

"The material miseries of the living entity, which are superfluous to him, can be directly mitigated by the linking process of devotional service. But the mass of people do not know this, and therefore the learned Vyāsadeva compiled this Vedic literature, which is in relation to the Supreme Truth" (*Bhāg.* 1.7.6).

Bhakti-śāstras include contemporary works written in pursuance of the conclusions of *Śrīmad-Bhāgavatam, Bhagavad-gītā,* and so on. The writing of commentaries and other *bhakti* literary works can continue for the edification of people in every age and create a movement away from mundane and speculative books.

Nārada states that a person should not only read *bhakti-śāstras* but also live by their instructions. The serious student should render service in terms of what he has heard from the spiritual master and the *bhakti-śāstras.* Śrīla Prabhupāda writes, "Without hearing such literatures, one cannot make actual progress. And without hearing and following the instructions, the show of devotional service becomes worthless and therefore a sort of disturbance on the path of devotional service. Therefore, devotional service is established on the principles of *śruti, smṛti, purāṇa,* and *pañcarātra* authorities. The make-show of devotional service should at once be rejected" (*Bhāg.* 1.2.12, purport).

SŪTRA 77

सुखदु:खेच्छालाभादित्यक्ते काले
प्रतीक्षमाणे क्षणार्धमपि व्यर्थं न नेयम् ॥७७॥

sukha-duḥkhecchā-lābhādi-tyakte kāle pratīkṣamāṇe kṣaṇārdham api vyarthaṁ na neyam

sukha—happiness; *duḥkha*—unhappiness; *icchā*—hankering; *lābha*—profiteering; *ādi*—and so on; *tyakte*—having given up; *kāle*—the time; *pratīkṣamāṇe*—being waited for; *kṣaṇa*—of a moment; *ardham*—one half; *api*—even; *vyartham*—vainly; *na neyam*—should not be wasted.

TRANSLATION

Patiently enduring till the time when one can put aside material happiness, distress, desire, and false gain, one should not waste even a fraction of a second.

PURPORT

Human birth is rare and one's life span brief. Why is human life so precious? Because we can use it for self-realization and get free of birth and death. But, as implied by this *sūtra*, much of our human lifetime is consumed in the struggle for existence. While instructing his young schoolmates on the urgency of Kṛṣṇa consciousness, Prahlāda Mahārāja made a calculation of how human life is wasted:

> Every human being has a maximum duration of life of one hundred years, but for one who cannot control his senses, half of those years are completely lost because at night he sleeps twelve hours, being covered by ignorance. Therefore such a person has a lifetime of only fifty years.
>
> In the tender age of childhood, when everyone is bewildered, one passes ten years. Similarly in boyhood, engaged in sporting and playing, one passes another ten years. In this way twenty years are wasted. Similarly, in old age, when one is an invalid, unable to perform even material activities, one passes another twenty years wastefully.
>
> One whose mind and senses are uncontrolled becomes increasingly attached to family because of insatiable lusty desires and very strong illusion. In such a madman's life, the remaining years are also wasted because even during those years he cannot engage himself in devotional service. [*Bhāg.* 7.6.6–8]

Whenever we misspend time, it is an irretrievable loss. As Cāṇakya Paṇḍita states, all the gold in a rich man's possession cannot buy back a single moment of time.

A devotee uses his time well, and this is one of the symptoms of his advancement. Śrīla Prabhupāda writes, "He is always anxious to utilize his time in the devotional service of the Lord. He does not like to be idle. He wants service always, twenty-four hours a day without deviation" (*The Nectar of Devotion,* p. 138).

We cannot wait until after we complete our many duties before starting to remember Kṛṣṇa. If we give *bhakti* such a low priority, our practice will never be more than a formality, a hurried prayer stolen from our time for "real" business or a perfunctory visit to the temple once a week. Rather, as Nārada has observed, "One achieves *bhakti* by hearing and chanting about the Supreme Lord's special qualities, even while engaged in the ordinary activities of life in this world" (*Nārada-bhakti-sūtra* 37). Let us remember Lord Kṛṣṇa's advice in *Bhagavad-gītā* (8.7): "Remember Me and fight."

The voice of delusion says, "When I'm older, I'll be less occupied with the struggle for existence. *Then* I'll take to Kṛṣṇa consciousness." But we may die before old age ever comes, or we may be too feeble at that time. As King Kulaśekhara prays (*Mukunda-māla-stotra* 40),

kṛṣṇa tvadīya-pada-paṅkaja-pañjarāntam
adyaiva me viśatu mānasa-rāja-haṁsaḥ
prāṇa-prayāṇa-samaye kapha-vāta-pittaiḥ
kaṇṭhāvarodhana-vidhau smaraṇaṁ kutas te

"O Lord, at this moment let the royal swan of my mind enter the network of the stems of the lotus flower of Your feet. How will it be possible for me to remember You at the time of death, when my throat will be choked up with mucus, bile, and air?"

Nārada advises that one should "patiently endure." This is advice for the devotee. He should fully engage himself in Kṛṣṇa consciousness with the goal of going back to Godhead, and in the meantime he should tolerate the dualities of life. As Lord Kṛṣṇa advises Arjuna, "O son of Kuntī, the nonpermanent appearance of happiness and distress, and their disappearance in due course, are like the appearance and disappearance of winter and summer seasons. They arise from sense perception, O scion of Bharata, and one must learn to tolerate them without being disturbed" (Bg. 2.14). "Patiently endure" does not mean that one should stoically put up with life's dualities and not fully engage in Kṛṣṇa consciousness! The devotee spends all his days and moments wholeheartedly engaged in devotional service, but still he has to contend with material upheavals. So in the face of these inevitable changes, he should patiently endure and go on chanting Hare Kṛṣṇa.

SŪTRA 78

अहिंसासत्यशौचदयास्तिक्यादिचारित्र्याणि परिपालनीयानि ॥७८॥

ahiṁsā-satya-śauca-dayāstikyādi-cāritryāṇi paripālanīyāni

ahiṁsā—of nonviolence; *satya*—truthfulness; *śauca*—cleanliness;

dayā—compassion; *āstikya*—faith; *ādi*—and so on; *cāritryāṇi*—the characteristics; *paripālanīyāni*—should be cultivated.

TRANSLATION

One should cultivate such good qualities as nonviolence, truthfulness, cleanliness, compassion, and faith.

PURPORT

Throughout the *Bhakti-sūtras,* Nārada has taught the best, the ultimate. He has never given mediocre definitions of *bhakti,* but from his own realizations and from other Vaiṣṇavas he has taught *parā bhakti.* Similarly, Śrīla Prabhupāda would always give definitions containing the fullest Kṛṣṇa conscious substance.

The present verse, therefore, must be understood in the context of what has gone before. Far from cultivating the listed virtues for themselves, the aspiring devotee should understand that all virtues will remain within the framework of the material modes until they are dovetailed in Kṛṣṇa consciousness. The good man is the paragon of the *sāttvika* mode, but even he cannot attain liberation if he fails to surrender to the Supreme Personality of Godhead. As Lord Kṛṣṇa states, "Those situated in that mode [*sattva-guṇa*] become conditioned by a sense of happiness and knowledge" (Bg. 14.6).

Defining *ahiṁsā,* Śrīla Prabhupāda took it to its ultimate conclusion for the life of a devotee:

> Nonviolence is generally taken to mean not killing or destroying the body, but actually nonviolence means not to put others into distress. People in general are trapped by ignorance in the material concept of life, and they perpetually suffer material pangs. So unless one elevates people to spiritual knowledge, one is practicing violence. One should try his best to distribute real knowledge to the people, so that they may become enlightened and leave this material entanglement. That is nonviolence. [Bg. 13.12, purport]

Śrīla Prabhupāda preached tirelessly against violence to animals, especially to the cow. Whenever he met a religionist or educated person, Śrīla Prabhupāda would test him on this point. He never conceded that it was permissible to kill God's creatures "because they have no soul," or for whatever reason the meat-eaters invented. To the followers of Lord Buddha Śrīla Prabhupāda challenged, "We are glad that people are taking interest in the nonviolent movement of Lord Buddha. But will they take the matter very seriously and close the animal slaughterhouses altogether? *If not, there is no meaning to the* ahiṁsā *cult*" (*Bhāg.* 1.3.25, purport; italics in original).

Lord Kṛṣṇa lists *satya,* "truthfulness," as one of the divine qualities. But truthfulness depends on recognizing the Absolute Truth to be the Supreme Personality of Godhead. Otherwise, no matter how strenuously one practices honesty, it remains relative and not fully pleasing to the Supreme Lord. But when a person recognizes that the Supreme Personality of Godhead is the supreme embodiment of truth and thus dedicates his life to following the truth and distributing that truth, then he can begin to be an honest person.

Cleanliness refers to both inner and outer states. Both are important, but internal purity is more important. Lord Caitanya declared that the congregational chanting of the holy names is the best process for cleaning the mind. All material concepts—such as identifying the self as the body, seeing dualities in the world, and hankering for sense gratification—are "dirty things" in the heart. The *bhakta* is always busy cleaning and polishing, freeing himself from the accumulation of dust, by the practice of chanting Hare Kṛṣṇa, Hare Kṛṣṇa, Kṛṣṇa Kṛṣṇa, Hare Hare/ Hare Rāma, Hare Rāma, Rāma Rāma, Hare Hare.

As for *dayā,* there can be no better kindness than to attain pure Kṛṣṇa consciousness yourself and to share it with others.

The word *āstikya,* "faith," implies that we should not interpret the words of scripture but take it "as it is." When Kṛṣṇa says in *Bhagavad-gītā* "Surrender to Me," one should not think himself wiser than Kṛṣṇa and claim that it is not to the person Kṛṣṇa whom we have to surrender but to the spirit within Kṛṣṇa. "Faith" also means to practice devotional service without motivation and without interruption.

In discussing a similar list of virtues in the *Bhagavad-gītā* (13.8–12), Śrīla Prabhupāda writes, "The process of knowledge terminates in unalloyed devotional service to the Lord. So if one does not approach, or is not able to approach, the transcendental service of the Lord, then the other nineteen items have no particular value. But if a person takes to devotional service in full Kṛṣṇa consciousness, the other nineteen items automatically develop within him."

By listing prominent virtues and using the word *ādi,* indicating that there are many others, Nārada reminds us that *bhakti* has to be situated on a foundation of good behavior. A *bhakta* cannot be a coarse fool or rascal. Śrīla Prabhupāda was once asked by a TV interviewer, "How would I be able to tell a devotee of Kṛṣṇa?" Prabhupāda replied, "He would be a perfect gentleman."

SŪTRA 79

सर्वदा सर्वभावेन निश्चिन्तैर्भगवानेव भजनीयः ॥७९॥

sarvadā sarva-bhāvena niścintair bhagavān eva bhajanīyaḥ

sarvadā—always; *sarva-bhāvena*—with all one's feeling; *niścintaiḥ*—by those who are free from doubt; *bhagavān*—the Supreme Lord; *eva*—indeed; *bhajanīyaḥ*—should be worshiped.

TRANSLATION

Those who are free of doubts should constantly worship the Supreme Lord with all their hearts.

PURPORT

In his purport to Sūtra 12, Śrīla Prabhupāda writes, "The *Nārada-bhakti-sūtra* is a summary of the *Bhagavad-gītā* and the *Śrīmad-Bhāgavatam.*" Here again we see the truth of that statement, since this *sūtra* is very similar to Lord Kṛṣṇa's confidential statements in the *Bhagavad-gītā*. For example, at the end of Chapter Fifteen He says,

yo mām evaṁ asammūḍho jānāti puruṣottamam
sa sarva-vid bhajati māṁ sarva-bhāvena bhārata

iti guhyatamaṁ śāstram idam uktaṁ mayānagha
etad buddhvā buddhimān syāt kṛta-kṛtyaś ca bhārata

"Whoever knows Me as the Supreme Personality of Godhead, without doubting, is the knower of everything. He therefore engages himself in full devotional service to Me, O scion of Bharata. This is the most confidential part of the Vedic scriptures, O sinless one, and it is disclosed now by Me. Whoever understands this will become wise, and his endeavors will know perfection" (Bg. 15.19–20). And again in the Eighteenth Chapter:

sarva-guhyatamaṁ bhūyaḥ śṛṇu me paramaṁ vacaḥ
iṣṭo 'si me dṛḍham iti tato vakṣyāmi te hitam

man-manā bhava mad-bhakto mad-yājī māṁ namaskuru
mām evaiṣyasi satyaṁ te pratijāne priyo 'si me

"Because you are My very dear friend, I am speaking to you My supreme instruction, the most confidential knowledge of all. Hear this from Me, for it is for your benefit. Always think of Me, become My devotee, worship Me, and offer your homage unto Me. Thus you will come to Me without fail. I promise you this because you are My very dear friend" (Bg. 18.64–65).

There is no difference between Lord Kṛṣṇa's instruction to "think of Me always" and Nārada's instruction to "always think of Bhagavān Kṛṣṇa." And indeed, any follower of Nārada's in disciplic succession can repeat his words: "The Supreme Personality of Godhead alone should always be worshiped wholeheartedly." But our words must be uttered with the conviction born from a life dedicated to the practices Nārada has given in the *Bhakti-sūtras.*

Our words and acts in devotional service cannot be mechanical. To qualify as *bhakti,* they must be done with loving feelings. As Lord Kṛṣṇa says, "If one offers Me with love and devotion a leaf, a flower, a fruit, or water, I will accept it" (Bg. 9.26). And again, "To those who are constantly devoted to serving Me with love, I give the understanding by which they can come to Me" (Bg. 10.10).

The wholehearted, exclusive devotion to Kṛṣṇa Nārada recommends is echoed in Bhīṣma's definition of love: "Love means reposing one's affection completely upon one person, withdrawing all affinities for any other person" (*The Nectar of Devotion,* p. 147). This stage was attained by all great devotees, such as Prahlāda, Uddhava, Nārada, and the residents of Vṛndāvana.

We must remember that constant, ecstatic absorption in Lord Kṛṣṇa is the goal of *bhakti,* and that *bhakti* includes the approach to that goal. In the Twelfth Chapter of the *Bhagavad-gītā,* Lord Kṛṣṇa recommends the topmost stage, spontaneous love, but He also encourages us by saying that undertaking the practices of *bhakti-yoga* will bring one to the ultimate stage:

mayy eva mana ādhatsva mayi buddhiṁ niveśaya
nivasiṣyasi mayy eva ata ūrdhvaṁ na saṁśayaḥ

atha cittaṁ samādhātuṁ na śaknoṣi mayi sthiram
abhyāsa-yogena tato mām icchāptuṁ dhanañjaya

"Just fix your mind upon Me, the Supreme Personality of Godhead, and engage all your intelligence in Me. Thus you will live in Me always, without a doubt. My dear Arjuna, O winner of wealth, if you cannot fix your mind upon Me without deviation, then follow the regulative principles of *bhakti-yoga.* In this way develop a desire to attain Me" (Bg. 12.8–9).

Hearing from *mahā-janas* who are in the spontaneous stage of *bhakti* is itself one of the most important services of the practicing devotee. Even Lakṣmaṇā, one of Lord Kṛṣṇa's wives, confided that her attraction to the Lord had been evoked by hearing the words of Nārada: "My dear queen, many times I heard the great sage Nārada glorifying the pastimes of Lord Kṛṣṇa. I became attracted to the lotus feet of Kṛṣṇa when I heard Nārada say that the goddess of fortune, Lakṣmī, was also attracted to His lotus feet" (*Kṛṣṇa,* p. 708).

Let us always keep Nārada and his representatives as our worshipable preceptors. They will lead us to Lord Kṛṣṇa.

SŪTRA 80

स कीर्त्यमानः शिघ्रमेवाविर्भवत्यनुभावयति भक्तान् ॥८०॥

sa kīrtyamānaḥ śīghram evāvirbhavaty anubhāvayati bhaktān

saḥ—He; *kīrtyamānaḥ*—being glorified; *śīghram*—quickly; *eva*—indeed; *āvirbhavati*—appears; *anubhāvayati*—gives realization; *bhaktān*—to the devotees.

TRANSLATION

When He is glorified, the Lord swiftly reveals Himself to His devotees and allows them to know Him as He is.

PURPORT

The *Śrīmad-Bhāgavatam* describes how Nārada attained direct perception of Lord Kṛṣṇa. After Nārada heard about Kṛṣṇa from sages who were visiting his house, he continued living with his mother, since he was only a five-year-old boy. But his mother suddenly died, and Nārada took to wandering. Once, as he sat under a banyan tree and began to meditate upon the Supersoul, the Lord appeared to him. Nārada relates, "As soon as I began to meditate upon the lotus feet of the Personality of Godhead with my mind transformed in transcendental love, tears rolled down my eyes and without delay the Personality of Godhead, Śrī Kṛṣṇa, appeared on the lotus of my heart" (*Bhāg.* 1.6.16).

After this initial *darśana*, the Supreme Lord withdrew Himself in His personal form but spoke to Nārada: "O virtuous one, you have only once seen My person, and this is just to increase your desire for Me, because the more you hanker for Me, the more you will be freed from all material desires" (*Bhāg.* 1.6.22). The Supreme Lord further told Nārada that he would eventually "become My associate in the transcendental world after giving up the present deplorable material worlds."

And so Nārada's life is a personal testimony to his own instruction given in this *sūtra*. Nārada went on to become one of the twelve authorities on Kṛṣṇa consciousness known as *mahā-janas*, and he is the spiritual master of such stalwarts as Prahlāda, Dhruva, and Vyāsadeva.

Nārada once came to Vyāsadeva when Vyāsa was feeling despondent, even after having compiled most of the Vedic scriptures. Nārada quickly diagnosed his disciple's depression and spoke to him:

> You have not actually broadcast the sublime and spotless glories of the Personality of Godhead. That philosophy which does not satisfy the transcendental senses of the Lord is considered worthless. Please, therefore, describe the transcendental pastimes of the Supreme Personality of Godhead, Kṛṣṇa, more vividly. [*Bhāg.* 1.5.8, 21]

Vyāsa took Nārada's instructions to heart and began composing the *Śrīmad-Bhāgavatam,* which is filled with the glories of Lord Kṛṣṇa in His many incarnations, as well as narrations of the Lord's pure devotees. Vyāsadeva later expressed his profound gratitude by glorifying Śrī Nāradadeva in various verses of the *Śrīmad-Bhāgavatam:*

aho devarṣir dhanyo 'yaṁ yat kīrtiṁ śārṅga-dhanvanaḥ
gāyan mādyann idaṁ tantryā ramayaty āturaṁ jagat

"All glory and success to Śrīla Nārada Muni because he glorifies the activities of the Personality of Godhead, and in so doing he himself takes pleasure and also enlightens all the distressed souls of the universe" (*Bhāg.* 1.6.38).

SŪTRA 81

त्रिसत्यस्य भक्तिरेव गरीयसी भक्तिरेव गरीयसी ॥८१॥

tri-satyasya bhaktir eva garīyasī bhaktir eva garīyasī

tri—in three ways (by his mind, body, and words); *satyasya*—for one who is truthful; *bhaktiḥ*—devotional service; *eva*—alone; *garīyasī*—most dear; *bhaktiḥ*—devotional service; *eva*—alone; *garīyasī*—most dear.

TRANSLATION

Devotional service is the most precious possession of a person who honestly uses his mind, body, and words.

PURPORT

The word *tri-satya* may refer to the three ways of expressing truth—with one's thoughts, actions, and words. Then again, *tri-satya* may be taken to indicate that *bhakti* is the best way of realizing the truth in all three phases of time—namely, past, present, and future. Lord Kapila told His mother, Devahūti, "I shall now explain unto you the ancient *yoga* system, which I explained formerly to the great sages. It is serviceable and practical in every way" (*Bhāg.* 3.25.14). In his purport Prabhupāda writes, "When we have a superexcellent process already present in the Vedic scriptures, there is no need to concoct a new system to mislead the innocent public. At present it has become a fashion to reject the standard system and present something bogus in the name of a newly invented process of *yoga*" (*Bhāg.* 3.25.14, purport). *Bhakti* is ancient wisdom, an immediate practical program, and the vision of the future. It is *tri-kāla-jñāna,* knowledge of past, present, and future.

As the best use of body, speech, and mind, *bhakti* is the best happiness, the best action, and the best meditation. When Lord Caitanya asked Rāmānanda Rāya to explain the very best thing, Rāmānanda Rāya described *bhakti* in many ways:

> The Lord inquired, "Of all types of education, which is the most important?" Rāmānanda Rāya replied, "There is no education that is important other than the transcendental devotional service of Kṛṣṇa."
>
> Śrī Caitanya Mahāprabhu then inquired, "Out of all liberated persons, who should be accepted as the greatest?" Rāmānanda replied, "He who has love for Kṛṣṇa has attained the topmost liberation."
>
> Śrī Caitanya Mahaprabhu asked, "Out of all topics people listen to, which is the best for living entities?" Rāmānanda Rāya replied, "Hearing about the loving affairs between Rādhā and Kṛṣṇa is most pleasing to the ear." [Cc. *Madhya* 8.245, 249, 255]

In this *sūtra* Nārada says the same thing as Rāmānanda Rāya did, but in condensed form: *Bhakti* is the best in every category. Why should we doubt it? And why should we dilute *bhakti* with other truths, as if *bhakti* is in need of help? *Bhakti* itself confers all knowledge and renunciation. It offers the most courageous action, as well as the best art, science, and recreation. Most important of all, *only bhakti* is pleasing to the Supreme Personality of Godhead. As Lord Kṛṣṇa says, "One can understand Me as I am, as the Supreme Personality of Godhead, only by devotional service. And when one is in full consciousness of Me by such devotion, he can enter into the kingdom of God" (Bg. 18.55). Even if we think that we may be able to accomplish something just as well by a non-*bhakti* method, our effort would still fail to please the Lord, and thus we would not find self-satisfaction.

Bhakti is best, and *bhakti* means devotional service to the Supreme Lord, Śrī Kṛṣṇa. Once Nārada visited Lord Kṛṣṇa in Vṛndāvana and praised His unique position:

> My Lord, let me offer my respectful obeisances unto Your lotus feet. . . . Your unlimited potency cannot even be measured by anyone. My dear Lord, You are the supreme controller. You are under Your own internal potency, and it is simply vain to think that You are dependent on any of Your creations. . . . Your advent on the surface of the earth in Your original form of eternal blissful knowledge is Your own pastime. You are not dependent on anything but Yourself; therefore I offer my respectful obeisances unto Your lotus feet. [*Kṛṣṇa,* p. 303]

Let us keep Nārada's spirited words in our hearts so that we may practice *bhakti-yoga* without doubt. And let us proclaim the glories of Kṛṣṇa joyfully, as Nārada does. Nārada is a space traveler, and wherever he goes he sings the Lord's glories to the accompaniment of his *vīṇā:*

nārada muni bājāya vīṇā
rādhikā-ramaṇa nāme

"Playing his *vīṇā,* Nārada Muni chants the names of Lord Rādhikā-ramaṇa." As followers of Nārada Muni, we may also select a "*vīṇā,*" or method of *bhajana,* and use it to please the Lord. Playing our *vīṇā* like Nārada, we may tell everyone we meet, "*Bhakti* is the best path, *bhakti* is the best!"

SŪTRA 82

गुणमाहात्म्यासक्तिरूपासक्तिपूजासक्तिस्मरणासक्तिदास्यासक्ति-
वात्सल्यासक्तिकान्तासक्त्यात्मनिवेदनासक्ति-
तन्मयासक्तिपरमविरहासक्तिरूपैकधाप्येकादशधा भवति ॥८२॥

guṇa-māhātmyāsakti-rūpāsakti-pūjāsakti-smaraṇāsakti-dāsyāsakti-vātsalyāsakti-kāntāsakty-ātma-nivedanāsakti-tan-mayāsakti-parama-virahāsakti-rūpaikadhāpy ekādaśadhā bhavati

guṇa—of the (Lord's) qualities; *māhātmya*—to the greatness; *āsakti*—attachment; *rūpa*—to His beauty; *āsakti*—attachment; *pūjā*—to worship; *āsakti*—attachment; *smaraṇa*—to remembrance; *āsakti*—attachment; *dāsya*—to service; *āsakti*—attachment; *vātsalya*—to parental affinity; *āsakti*—attachment; *kāntā*—as a conjugal lover; *āsakti*—attachment; *ātma*—of one's self; *nivedana*—to the offering; *āsakti*—attachment; *tat-maya*—to being full of thought of Him; *āsakti*—attachment; *parama*—supreme; *viraha*—to separation; *āsakti*—attachment; *rūpā*—having as its forms; *ekadhā*—onefold; *api*—although; *ekādaśakhā*—elevenfold; *bhavati*—becomes.

TRANSLATION

Although devotional service is one, it becomes manifested in eleven

forms of attachment: attachment to the Lord's glorious qualities, to His beauty, to worshiping Him, to remembering Him, to serving Him, to caring for Him as a parent, to dealing with Him as a lover, to surrendering one's whole self to Him, to being absorbed in thought of Him, and to experiencing separation from Him. This last is the supreme attachment.

PURPORT

Nārada has taught that *bhakti* is the best of all processes for realizing truth, and he has described the rules and regulations leading to perfection. He has told us that we have to experience *bhakti* for ourselves, and that it is the highest bliss. Now he indicates the liberality of *bhakti* by listing the various ways one may render devotional service.

There has been nothing to suggest that Nārada is presenting a theoretical treatise. Thus we should not conclude our reading of the *Nārada-bhakti-sūtra* without deciding how *we* shall render practical service to Kṛṣṇa. Once a college student came to visit Śrīla Prabhupāda and told him that he had already read the *Bhagavad-gītā*. Śrīla Prabhupāda asked, "So, what is your conclusion?" The student admitted that he had not reached any particular conclusion after his study of the *Gītā*. Prabhupāda explained that the conclusion of the *Bhagavad-gītā* is that Lord Kṛṣṇa is the Supreme Personality of Godhead and that one should give up all other processes of religion and serve Him. An intelligent reader of the *Bhagavad-gītā* should know this and take up devotional service. Similarly, here at the end of the *Bhakti-sūtras* Nārada is telling us how we may serve the Supreme Lord.

Of course, the *rasas* with Kṛṣṇa are for the liberated devotees and cannot be taken up arbitrarily. Our service to Kṛṣṇa should be guided by our spiritual master. He will help us to serve according to our psychophysical nature, in a way that is most effective for our purification. But from the beginning we can at least know that Lord Kṛṣṇa is served by His liberated associates in many ways and that our own perfection will be to discover how we are meant to serve Him eternally to our heart's content.

A devotee appreciates the many services the Lord's devotees engage in, and he studies how to become perfect in his particular relationship with the Lord. Nārada's eleven ways of *bhakti* appear to be a combination of the nine process of *bhakti* taught by Prahlāda Mahārāja and the five main *rasas* with Lord Kṛṣṇa described by Rūpa Gosvāmī in his *Bhakti-rasāmṛta-sindhu.* Examples of devotees who achieved perfection by practicing one of the nine processes of *bhakti* are as follows:

(1) Mahārāja Parīkṣit became perfect by hearing about Kṛṣṇa; (2) Śukadeva Gosvāmī became perfect by speaking the glories of the Lord; (3) Prahlāda Mahārāja became perfect by remembering the Lord; (4) Lakṣmīdevī became perfect by serving the lotus feet of the Lord; (5) Mahārāja Pṛthu became perfect by worshiping the Lord; (6) Akrūra became perfect by offering prayers to the Lord; (7) Hanumān became perfect by serving the Lord; (8) Arjuna became perfect by befriending the Lord; and (9) Bali Mahārāja became perfect by offering everything to the Lord.

As for the five *rasas,* they are: (1) adoration of the Lord (*śānta*), (2) servitude (*dāsya*), (3) friendship (*sakhya*), (4) parental love (*vātsalya*), and (5) conjugal love (*mādhurya*). Prominent examples of devotees in each of these *rasas* are as follows: the four Kumāras in *śānta-rasa;* Hanumān and Kṛṣṇa's various servants in Dvārakā and Mathurā in *dāsya-rasa;* Śrīdāmā, Sudāmā, and Stoka-kṛṣṇa in *sākhya-rasa;* Kṛṣṇa's parents in *vātsalya-rasa;* and the *gopīs* of Vṛndāvana and the queens in Dvārakā in *mādhurya-rasa.*

All liberated devotees are situated in absolute transcendence, and one devotee does not hanker for the perfection of another. But the Vaiṣṇava *ācāryas* have analyzed the *rasas* to show that there is a progression in affection—and a diminishing in feelings of awe and reverence toward the Lord—from *dāsya-rasa* up to *mādhurya-rasa.* All the qualities of the other *rasas* are fully contained in conjugal love. As for love in separation, which Nārada mentions as the eleventh and highest stage of attachment, that was especially demonstrated by the *gopīs* of Vṛndāvana, and also by Lord Caitanya. Lord Caitanya's demonstration of *viraha,* or transcendental anguish in separation from Kṛṣṇa, is the highest of all possible expressions of love of God.

Although there is a progression in intimacy in the *rasas* from *dāsya-rasa* to *mādhurya-rasa,* all are based on the ecstasy of *service* to the Lord. Kṛṣṇadāsa Kavirāja writes, "Love for Kṛṣṇa has this one unique effect: it imbues superiors, equals, and inferiors with the spirit of service to Lord Kṛṣṇa" (Cc. *Ādi* 6.53). Kṛṣṇa's friends in Vṛndāvana feel pure fraternal affection for Him, yet they too worship His lotus feet in a spirit of servitude. Kṛṣṇa's mother and father sometimes chastise the Lord, thinking that He is their little son, and yet they always think of themselves as His servants. Kṛṣṇa's father, Nanda Mahārāja, once said to Uddhava, "May our minds be attached to the lotus feet of your Lord Kṛṣṇa, may our tongues chant His holy names, and may our bodies lie prostrate before Him" (Cc. *Ādi* 6.60). Even the *gopīs* of Vṛndāvana regard themselves as Kṛṣṇa's maidservants. Śrīmatī Rādhārāṇī prays, "O My Lord, . . . reveal Yourself to Your maidservant, who is very much aggrieved by Your absence" (*Bhāg.* 10.33.9). Being a servant of the Supreme Lord is so auspicious and blissful that even Lord Kṛṣṇa Himself descended as Lord Caitanya to accept the emotions and form of His own servant. Therefore all devotees can best cultivate their loving relationship with Lord Kṛṣṇa by becoming the servant of other Vaiṣṇava devotees. If we fix ourselves in steadfast and spontaneous loving service to the Lord's devotees, Kṛṣṇa will reveal Himself to us and indicate new, intimate ways in which we may serve Him.

SŪTRA 83

इत्येवं वदन्ति जनजल्पनिर्भया एकमताः
कुमारव्यासशुकशाण्डिल्यगर्गविष्णुकौण्डिल्य-
शेषोद्धवारुणिबलिहनूमद्विभीषणादयो भक्त्याचार्याः ॥८३॥

ity evaṁ vadanti jana-jalpa-nirbhayā eka-matāḥ kumāra-vyāsa-śuka-śāṇḍilya-garga-viṣṇu-kauṇḍilya-śeṣoddhavāruṇi-bali-hanūmad-vibhīṣaṇādayo bhakty-ācāryāḥ

iti—thus; *evam*—in this way; *vadanti*—they speak; *jana*—of ordinary people; *jalpa*—of the gossip; *nirbhayāḥ*—unafraid; *eka*—of one; *matāḥ*—opinion; *kumāra-vyāsa-śuka-śāṇḍilya-garga-viṣṇu-kauṇḍilya-śeṣa-uddhava-aruṇi-bali-hanūmat-vibhīṣaṇa-ādayaḥ*—the Kumāras, Vyāsa, Śuka, Śāṇḍilya, Garga, Viṣṇu, Kauṇḍilya, Śeṣa, Uddhava, Aruṇi, Bali, Hanumān, Vibhīṣaṇa, and others; *bhakti*—of devotional service; *ācāryāḥ*—the founding authorities.

TRANSLATION

Thus say the founding authorities of devotional service: the

Kumāras, Vyāsa, Śuka, Śāṇḍilya, Garga, Viṣṇu, Kauṇḍilya, Śeṣa, Uddhava, Aruṇi, Bali, Hanumān, Vibhīṣaṇa, and others—speaking without fear of worldly gossip and sharing among themselves one and the same opinion.

PURPORT

Nārada previously gave definitions of *bhakti* according to sages like Vyāsa and Garga, and now he gives a longer list. He also adds that there are many other authorities who could also be cited. In this way, although Nārada's word is sufficient, he increases the authority of his conclusion that *bhakti* is the best of all paths.

While praising Lord Kṛṣṇa as the Supreme Brahman and the God of gods, Arjuna also referred to great sages in order to support his statement:

paraṁ brahma paraṁ dhāma pavitraṁ paramaṁ bhavān
puruṣaṁ śāśvataṁ divyam ādi-devam ajaṁ vibhum

āhus tvām ṛṣayaḥ sarve devarṣir nāradas tathā
asito devalo vyāsaḥ svayaṁ caiva bravīṣi me

"You are the Supreme Personality of Godhead, the ultimate abode, the purest, the Absolute Truth. You are the eternal, transcendental, original person, the unborn, the greatest. All the great sages such as Nārada, Asita, Devala, and Vyāsa confirm this truth about You, and now You Yourself are declaring it to me" (Bg. 10.12–13).

Śrīla Prabhupāda writes, "It is not that because Kṛṣṇa is Arjuna's intimate friend Arjuna is flattering Him by calling Him the Supreme Personality of Godhead, the Absolute Truth. Whatever Arjuna says in these two verses is confirmed by Vedic truth" (Bg. 10.12–13, purport). When Yamarāja wanted to impress upon his messengers, the Yamadūtas, that Lord Viṣṇu is the supreme authority and that *bhakti* is the supreme path, he also quoted an impressive list of names. These teachers are known as the twelve *mahā-janas,* or authorities in Kṛṣṇa consciousness:

svayambhūr nāradaḥ śambhuḥ kaumāraḥ kapilo manuḥ
prahlādo janako bhīṣmo balir vaiyāsakir vayam

dvādaśaite vijānīmo dharmaṁ bhāgavataṁ bhaṭāḥ
guhyaṁ viśuddhaṁ durbodhaṁ yaṁ jñātvāmṛtam aśnute

"Lord Brahmā, Bhagavān Nārada, Lord Śiva, the four Kumāras, Lord Kapila [the son of Devahūti], Svāyambhuva Manu, Prahlāda Mahārāja, Janaka Mahārāja, Grandfather Bhīṣma, Bali Mahārāja, Śukadeva Gosvāmī, and I myself know the real religious principle. My dear servants, this transcendental religious principle, which is known as *bhāgavata-dharma,* or surrender unto the Supreme Lord and love for Him, is uncontaminated by the material modes of nature. It is very confidential and difficult for ordinary human beings to understand, but if by chance a person fortunately understands it, he is immediately liberated, and thus he returns home, back to Godhead" (*Bhāg.* 6.3.20–21).

In his purport, Śrīla Prabhupāda stresses not only the importance of the individual sages but the fact that they are representatives of Vaiṣṇava *sampradāyas:*

> There are four lines of disciplic succession: one from Lord Brahmā, one from Lord Śiva, one from Lakṣmī, the goddess of fortune, and one from the Kumāras. The disciplic succession from Lord Brahmā is called the Brahmā-sampradāya, the succession from Lord Śiva (Śambhu) is called the Rudra-sampradāya, the one from the goddess of fortune, Lakṣmījī, is called the Śrī-sampradāya, and the one from the Kumāras is called the Kumāra-sampradāya. One must take shelter of one of these four *sampradāyas* in order to understand the most confidential religious system. In the *Padma Purāṇa* it is said, *sampradāya-vihīnā ye mantrās te niṣphalā matāḥ:* "If a person does not follow the four recognized disciplic successions, his *mantra* or initiation is useless." [*Bhāg.* 6.3.20–21, purport]

Nārada states that the *ācāryas* of the Absolute Truth were not afraid of criticism. In bygone ages fools criticized pure devotees and even the Supreme Lord Himself. Once the powerful progenitor Dakṣa cursed Nārada because he had convinced Dakṣa's sons to reject marriage and remain celibate. Dakṣa called Nārada a sinful rascal posing as a devotee. Nārada tolerated Dakṣa's curse without retaliation, but he continued his preaching.

In his purports, Śrīla Prabhupāda compares the criticism Nārada received to the criticism he himself received from his disciples' parents. Their accusation was the same as Dakṣa's—that the spiritual master has unreasonably caused young boys (and girls) to give up the normal life of sense gratification and take to extreme forms of renunciation and devotion to God. The criticism of the Kṛṣṇa consciousness movement has taken organized shape as part of the "anticult movement," but Śrīla Prabhupāda assured his followers not to be afraid of attacks:

> We have no business creating enemies, but the process is such that nondevotees will always be inimical toward us. Nevertheless, as stated in the *śāstras,* a devotee should be both tolerant and merciful. Devotees engaged in preaching should be prepared to be accused by ignorant persons, and yet they must be very merciful to the fallen, conditioned souls. If one can execute his duty in the disciplic succession of Nārada Muni, his service will surely be recognized. . . . Preaching can be a difficult, thankless task, but a preacher must follow the orders of the Supreme Lord and be unafraid of materialistic persons. [*Bhāg.* 6.5.39, purport]

Critics deride the Hare Kṛṣṇa movement as a concocted new cult. But just as the *Nārada-bhakti-sūtra* is supported by venerable authorities and *mahā-janas,* so the Kṛṣṇa consciousness movement, created by His Divine Grace A. C. Bhaktivedanta Swami Prabhupāda, is also authoritative. In fact, the same authorities Nārada has cited also back up the Kṛṣṇa consciousness movement. Śrīla Prabhupāda comes in the disciplic line of the Brahma-Madhva-Gauḍīya-sampradāya, a line that includes Brahmā, Nārada, Vyāsadeva, Madhva, and Lord Caitanya. In the *praṇāma-mantra* Śrīla Prabhupāda's followers chant, the phrase *gaura-vāṇī-pracāriṇe* means that Śrīla Prabhupāda teaches the message of Lord Caitanya. The *saṅkīrtana* movement, the congregational chanting of Hare Kṛṣṇa, was begun by Lord Caitanya Himself, and so the Kṛṣṇa consciousness movement now spreading around the world is not a new religion but a continuation of the original *sampradāya.* As Śrīla Prabhupāda says, "Actually the original father of this movement is Lord Kṛṣṇa Himself, since it was started a very long time ago but is coming down to human society by disciplic succession" (*Bhagavad-gītā As It Is,* preface).

SŪTRA 84

य इदं नारदप्रोक्तं शिवानुशासनं विश्वसिति
श्रद्धते स भक्तिमान् भवति स प्रेष्ठं लभते प्रेष्ठं लभते इति ॥८४॥

ya idaṁ nārada-proktaṁ śivānuśāsanaṁ viśvasiti śraddhate sa bhaktimān bhavati sa preṣṭhaṁ labhate sa preṣṭhaṁ labhata iti

yaḥ—one who; *idam*—this; *nārada-proktam*—spoken by Nārada; *śiva*—auspicious; *anuśāsanam*—instruction; *viśvasiti*—trusts; *śraddhate*—is convinced by; *saḥ*—he; *bhakti-mān*—endowed with devotion; *bhavati*—becomes; *saḥ*—he; *preṣṭham*—the most dear (Supreme Lord); *labhate*—attains; *saḥ*—he; *preṣṭham*—the most dear; *labhate*—attains; *iti*—thus.

TRANSLATION

Anyone who trusts these instructions spoken by Nārada and is convinced by them will be blessed with devotion and attain the most dear Lord. Yes, he will attain the most dear Lord.

PURPORT

Nārada ends the *Bhakti-sūtras* by stating that one has to hear them with faith. Inquiries and even doubts may be placed before the *guru*, just as Arjuna expressed his doubts before Lord Kṛṣṇa. But an attitude of disbelief will prevent us from understanding. As Lord Kṛṣṇa states,

aśraddadhānāḥ puruṣā dharmasyāsya paran-tapa
aprāpya māṁ nivartante mṛtyu-saṁsāra-vartmani

"Those who are not faithful in this devotional service cannot attain Me, O conqueror of enemies. Therefore they return to the path of birth and death in this material world" (Bg. 9.3). And as stated in the *Śvetāśvatara Upaniṣad* (6.23),

yasya deve parā bhaktir yathā deve tathā gurau
tasyaite kathitā hy arthāḥ prakāśante mahātmanaḥ

"Unto those great souls who have implicit faith in both the Lord and the spiritual master, all the imports of the *Vedas* are automatically revealed."

This final *sūtra* declares that if a person hears the *Nārada-bhakti-sūtra* with faith, then Nārada blesses him with devotion to the Supreme Personality of Godhead. This means that Nārada Muni is present and acting through the teachings of the *sūtras*. The same potent blessing Nārada has given to many persons enabling them to become staunch *bhaktas* are available even now through his *vāṇī*, or teachings. As the *Skanda Purāṇa* states, "My dear Nārada, of all the saintly persons, you are so great and glorious that simply by your good wishes a lowborn hunter also has become a great, elevated devotee of Lord Kṛṣṇa" (*The Nectar of Devotion*, p. 137).

Let us gratefully receive this benediction and repeatedly hear the *Nārada-bhakti-sūtra* for our transcendental pleasure and benefit. Nārada wishes to bless us that we shall attain the *parāṁ gatim*, the ultimate goal of life, the most cherished desire. But we must ask ourselves, "What do I desire?" If we desire to attain *kṛṣṇa-bhakti* and if we lead our life in accordance with the teachings of Kṛṣṇa consciousness, then Nārada promises we will attain the ultimate in this life and the next: we will render devotional service to Lord Kṛṣṇa, the supreme beloved. As Rūpa Gosvāmī states in his *Bhakti-rasāmṛta-sindhu*, the goal of *bhakti* is very rarely attained. The Supreme Lord doesn't grant devotion as easily as He grants liberation, because when He gives devotion one gets an opportunity to serve Him directly. Śukadeva Gosvāmī tells Mahārāja Parīkṣit, "Those engaged in getting the Lord's favor attain liberation from the Lord very easily, but He does not very easily give the opportunity to render direct service unto Him" (*Bhāg.* 5.6.18).

Nārada assures us twice, so there should be no doubt about it: although *bhakti* is very rare and hard to attain, with the blessings of Nārada and his representatives we will attain the supreme beloved, we will attain the supreme beloved.

—Completed on Unmīlanī Mahā-dvādaśī, November 24, 1989, in Jagannātha Purī, as desired by His Divine Grace A. C. Bhaktivedanta Swami Prabhupāda

Appendixes

His Divine Grace
A. C. Bhaktivedanta Swami Prabhupāda

His Divine Grace A. C. Bhaktivedanta Swami Prabhupāda appeared in this world in 1896 in Calcutta, India. He first met his spiritual master, Śrīla Bhaktisiddhānta Sarasvatī Gosvāmī, in Calcutta in 1922. Bhaktisiddhānta Sarasvatī, a prominent religious scholar and the founder of sixty-four Gauḍīya Maṭhas (Vedic institutes) in India, liked this educated young man and convinced him to dedicate his life to teaching Vedic knowledge. Śrīla Prabhupāda became his student and, in 1933, his formally initiated disciple.

At their first meeting Śrīla Bhaktisiddhānta Sarasvatī requested Śrīla Prabhupāda to broadcast Vedic knowledge in English. In the years that followed, Śrīla Prabhupāda wrote a commentary on the *Bhagavad-gītā,* assisted the Gauḍīya Maṭha in its work, and, in 1944, started *Back to Godhead,* an English fortnightly magazine. Single-handedly, Śrīla Prabhupāda edited it, typed the manuscripts, checked the proofs, and even distributed the individual copies. The magazine is now being continued by his disciples in the West.

In 1950 Śrīla Prabhupāda retired from married life, adopting the *vānaprastha* (retired) order to devote more time to his studies and

writing. He traveled to the holy city of Vṛndāvana, where he lived in humble circumstances in the historic temple of Rādhā-Dāmodara. There he engaged for several years in deep study and writing. He accepted the renounced order of life (*sannyāsa*) in 1959. At Rādhā-Dāmodara, Śrīla Prabhupāda began work on his life's masterpiece: a multivolume commentated translation of the 18,000-verse *Śrīmad-Bhagavatam* (*Bhāgavata Purāṇa*). He also wrote *Easy Journey to Other Planets.*

After publishing three volumes of the *Bhāgavatam,* Śrīla Prabhupāda came to the United States, in September 1965, to fulfill the mission of his spiritual master. Subsequently, His Divine Grace wrote more than fifty volumes of authoritative commentated translations and summary studies of the philosophical and religious classics of India.

When he first arrived by freighter in New York City, Śrīla Prabhupāda was practically penniless. Only after almost a year of great difficulty did he establish the International Society for Krishna Consciousness, in July of 1966. Before he passed away on November 14, 1977, he had guided the Society and seen it grow to a worldwide confederation of more than one hundred *āśramas,* schools, temples, and farm communities.

In 1972 His Divine Grace introduced the Vedic system of primary and secondary education in the West by founding the *gurukula* school in Dallas, Texas. Since then his disciples have established similar schools throughout the United States and the rest of the world.

Śrīla Prabhupāda also inspired the construction of several large international cultural centers in India. The center at Śrīdhāma Māyāpur is the site for a planned spiritual city, an ambitious project for which construction will extend over many years to come. In Vṛndāvana are the magnificent Kṛṣṇa-Balarāma Temple and International Guesthouse, *gurukula* school, and Śrīla Prabhupāda Memorial and Museum. There is also a major cultural and educational center in Bombay. Major centers are planned in Delhi and in a dozen other important locations on the Indian subcontinent.

Śrīla Prabhupāda's most significant contribution, however, is his books. Highly respected by scholars for their authority, depth, and clarity, they are used as textbooks in numerous college courses. His writings have been translated into over fifty languages. The Bhaktivedanta Book Trust, established in 1972 to publish the works of His Divine Grace, has thus become the world's largest publisher of books in the field of Indian religion and philosophy.

In just twelve years, despite his advanced age, Śrīla Prabhupāda circled the globe fourteen times on lecture tours that took him to six continents. Yet this vigorous schedule did not slow his prolific literary output. His writings constitute a veritable library of Vedic philosophy, religion, literature, and culture.

References

The purports of *Nārada-bhakti-sūtra* are all confirmed by standard Vedic authorities. The following authentic scriptures are cited in this volume. For specific page references, consult the general index.

Ādi Purāṇa

Bhagavad-gītā

Bhakti-rasāmṛta-sindhu

Brahma-saṁhitā

Bṛhan-nāradīya Purāṇa

Caitanya-bhāgavata

Caitanya-candrodaya-nāṭaka

Caitanya-caritāmṛta

Caitanya-mañjuṣā

Hari-bhakti-sudhodaya

Hari-bhakti-vilāsa

Īśopaniṣad

Kātyāyana-saṁhitā

Kṛṣṇa, the Supreme Personality of Godhead

Lalita-mādhava

Mahābhārata

Mukunda-māla-stotra

Nārada-bhakti-sūtra

Nārada Pañcarātra

Nectar of Devotion, The

Padma Purāṇa

Path of Perfection, The

Ṛg Veda

Śikṣāṣṭaka

Skanda Purāṇa

Śrīmad-Bhāgavatam

Śvetāśvatara Upaniṣad

Teachings of Lord Caitanya

Upadeśāmṛta

Vedānta-sūtra

Vidagdha-mādhava

Sanskrit Pronunciation Guide

The system of transliteration used in this book conforms to a system that scholars have accepted to indicate the pronunciation of each sound in the Sanskrit language.

The short vowel **a** is pronounced like the **u** in b**u**t, long **ā** like the **a** in f**a**r. Short **i** is pronounced as in p**i**n, long **ī** as in p**i**que, short **u** as in p**u**ll, and long **ū** as in r**u**le. The vowel **ṛ** is pronounced like the **ri** in **ri**m, **e** like the **ey** in th**ey**, **o** like the **o** in g**o**, **ai** like the **ai** in **ai**sle, and **au** like the **ow** in h**ow**. The *anusvāra* (**ṁ**) is pronounced like the **n** in the French word *bo***n**, and *visarga* (**ḥ**) is pronounced as a final **h** sound. At the end of a couplet, **aḥ** is pronounced **aha**, and **iḥ** is pronounced **ihi**.

The guttural consonants—**k, kh, g, gh,** and **ṅ**—are pronounced from the throat in much the same manner as in English. **K** is pronounced as in **k**ite, **kh** as in Ec**kh**art, **g** as in **g**ive, **gh** as in di**g h**ard, and **ṅ** as in si**ng.**

The palatal consonants—**c, ch, j, jh,** and **ñ**—are pronounced with the tongue touching the firm ridge behind the teeth. **C** is pronounced as in **ch**air, **ch** as in staun**ch-h**eart, **j** as in **j**oy, **jh** as in he**dgeh**og, and **ñ** as in ca**ny**on.

The cerebral consonants—**ṭ, ṭh, ḍ, ḍh,** and **ṇ**—are pronounced with the tip of the tongue turned up and drawn back against the dome of the palate. **Ṭ** is pronounced as in **t**ub, **ṭh** as in ligh**t-h**eart, **ḍ** as in **d**ove, **ḍh** as in re**d-h**ot, and **ṇ** as in **n**ut. The dental consonants—**t, th, d, dh,** and **n**—are pronounced in the same manner as the cerebrals, but with the forepart of the tongue against the teeth.

The labial consonants—**p, ph, b, bh,** and **m**—are pronounced with the lips. **P** is pronounced as in **p**ine, **ph** as in u**ph**ill, **b** as in **b**ird, **bh** as in ru**b-h**ard, and **m** as in **m**other.

The semivowels—**y, r, l,** and **v**—are pronounced as in **y**es, **r**un, **l**ight, and **v**ine respectively. The sibilants—**ś, ṣ,** and **s**—are pronounced, respectively, as in the German word **s***prechen* and the English words **sh**ine and **s**un. The letter **h** is pronounced as in **h**ome.

Index

Boldface page numbers indicate verses of the *Nārada-bhakti-sūtra.*